RELOCATED MEMORIES

Irish Studies
James MacKillop, *Series Editor*

Select titles in Irish Studies

Compassionate Stranger: Asenath Nicholson and the Great Irish Famine
Maureen O'Rourke Murphy

Israelites in Erin: Exodus, Revolution, and the Irish Revival
Abby Bender

Joyce/Shakespeare
Laura Pelaschiar, ed.

Political Acts: Women in Northern Irish Theatre, 1921–2012
Fiona Coffey

Postcolonial Overtures: The Politics of Sound in Contemporary Northern Irish Poetry
Julia C. Obert

Seamus Heaney as Aesthetic Thinker: A Study of the Prose
Eugene O'Brien

Standish O'Grady's Cuculain: A Critical Edition
Gregory Castle and Patrick Bixby, eds.

The Snake's Pass: A Critical Edition
Bram Stoker; Lisabeth C. Buchelt, ed.

RELOCATED MEMORIES

The Great Famine in Irish and Diaspora Fiction, 1846–1870

Marguérite Corporaal

SU

Syracuse University Press

Syracuse, New York 13244-5290

First Edition 2017

17 18 19 20 21 22 6 5 4 3 2 1

∞ The paper used in this publication meets the minimum requirements of the American National Standard for Information Sciences—Permanence of Paper for Printed Library Materials, ANSI Z39.48-1992.

For a listing of books published and distributed by Syracuse University Press, visit www.SyracuseUniversityPress.syr.edu.

ISBN: 978-0-8156-3498-0 (hardcover)
978-0-8156-3513-0 (paperback)
978-0-8156-5398-1 (e-book)

Library of Congress Cataloging-in-Publication Data

Available from the publisher upon request.

Manufactured in the United States of America

Contents

Illustrations

Acknowledgments

THIS STUDY is the result of research carried out in the context of my ERC Starting Grant project Relocated Remembrance: The Great Famine in Irish (Diaspora) Fiction, 1847–1921 (GA 262898). I am very grateful to the European Research Council for the funding that I received, which made it possible to consolidate a research team and to examine vast resources of underexplored Famine fiction in profound detail.

This book would not have been realized without the support of various colleagues over the years. I would like to thank several colleagues from Radboud University: Christopher Cusack, Lindsay Janssen, and Ruud van den Beuken for the successful and pleasurable teamwork and their feedback on parts of the manuscript and Liedeke Plate, Anneke Smelik, and Lotte Jensen for stimulating discussions as part of the research groups Performances of Memory and Europe and (Trans)national Identities at the Institute for Historical, Literary, and Cultural Studies.

Several Famine scholars, from various disciplines, have been very helpful during the progress of my research project and the process of completing this study. I cannot possibly do justice to all of them, but want to single out a few with whom I have had the pleasure to publish articles, organize conferences, and collaborate in my International Network of Irish Famine Studies over the past years. Oona Frawley, Peter Gray, Margaret Kelleher, Jason King, Emily Mark-FitzGerald, Chris Morash, David Lloyd, David Nally, Andrew Newby, and Ciarán Reilly, it has been a great pleasure to meet on so many occasions over the past few years and to exchange and test out ideas and findings.

Many thanks are also due to Syracuse University Press, in particular Deborah Manion, for the excellent cooperation on this book and for giving guidance throughout the process. I would also like to express my gratitude to the archives and museums (National Folklore Archive, University College Dublin; Ireland's Great Hunger Museum, Quinnipiac University, Hamden, CT; and Victoria and Albert Museum, London) and publishers that have given permission to reproduce images as well as extracts of previously published work. I have given acknowledgment to them in relevant endnotes and in the captions.

Last but not least, there are three persons in particular who deserve praise for bearing up with a hardworking partner and mother: Albert, Imogen, and Deirdre, thanks for all your patience and for providing so many moments of happiness during the writing process.

RELOCATED MEMORIES

Introduction

In William Gorman Wills's three-decker *The Love That Kills* (1867), a novel set during Ireland's Great Famine, the main protagonist, William Clayton, and his friend Dr. Molar elaborately discuss how the human mind processes recollection. Seeking oblivion from his failed attempt to persuade Ellen Rae into marrying him, Clayton wonders by what causes "certain recollections" can become "suddenly erased" from the mind, as "old men, by some law of the brain, forget what grieved them yesterday, and yet may be storehouses of knowledge and anecdote."[1] While Clayton's inquiries are mainly concerned with the dynamics of individual remembrance, recent research in the humanities has particularly addressed the interaction between amnesia and recollection in performances of collective memory. Rooted in the premise that memory is inherently fluid, is transportable,[2] and "changes with each actualization, continually and dynamically,"[3] over the past two decades scholars have particularly trained their focus on the transferability of memory across generations, across cultural communities, and across genres.

The growing awareness that memories are transformed in each act of recall by the present concerns and future agendas of those communities who do the remembering[4] has encouraged scholars such as Marianne Hirsch and Alison Landsberg to make distinctions between the ways in which a fateful event is reconfigured by those individuals who directly experienced this past and later generations who can have only indirect access to it in the form of "postmemory" or "prosthetic memory."[5] The generally accepted notion that migrants have "transnational affiliations," and participate in transnational spaces "shared by both immigrants and natives," has sparked an awareness of the existence of communal memories that transcend national borders.[6] Aleida Assmann and Sebastian Conrad have therefore argued in favor of a transnational approach in examining memory dynamics, as "migrants carry their heritage, memories and traumas with them," which "are transferred and brought into new social constellations and political contexts."[7]

More recently, Lucy Bond and Jessica Rapson have sought to define the notion of transcultural memory as "the travelling of memory *within* and *between* national, ethnic and religious collectives," thereby applying a broader scope to memory transfer that moves beyond the context of emigration. This idea of traveling memory is also espoused by Astrid Erll in her contribution to the collection *Transcultural Memory* (2014), which challenges the tendency to tie memory to "clear-cut territories and social formations," since it circulates "*across* . . . and also *beyond* cultures." While memory studies today are characterized by a transgenerational and transnational turn, current scholarship also examines the forms in which memory is transferred and by which it is shaped. Astrid Erll and Ann Rigney, for example, contend that literature not only plays a prominent role in producing cultural memory, but also functions as a carrier of memory that transmits the past to later generations as well as a medium that "makes remembrance observable" by showing "how memory works for individuals and groups."[8]

These three trends in memory studies have given a great impetus to the field, providing useful tools and terms for future research as well as suggesting new parameters that stimulate a cross-disciplinary dialogue with interrelated areas such as diaspora and migration studies. Furthermore, these new approaches broaden the horizon of memory research: Kendall Phillips and Mitchell Reyes have pleaded for an interactive study of regional, national, and transnational levels of cultural recollection and the ways in which transnational movements de- and reterritorialize local and national sites of memory, for instance. However, while scholars such as Daniel Levy and Natan Sznaider have asked how one should configure forms of memory that transcend national and ethnic boundaries, so far very few studies have examined the ways in which the recollection of a certain past transforms and progresses when it is relocated over time and space.[9]

If cultural memory can cross the boundaries of time and generation, how then does it evolve in later acts of recall? What patterns can we discern in the transmutation of memory with the passing of time? Similar questions can be raised with regard to the transmission of memory over space. How do recollections change when they are transported to other geographical and cultural spaces—for example, through migration? Can we speak of a specific diasporic development of the cultural memories that are connected to the former homeland? The present study aims to address these crucial, underexplored questions, attempting to investigate developments in the temporal and spatial transference of the memory of one of Ireland's most harrowing episodes, the Great Famine (1845–50), in fiction. As a period of mass starvation—caused by a wide-scale potato disease and resulting in the mass eviction of impoverished tenants and in some cases even the bankruptcy of the Anglo-Irish aristocracy; tense relationships between the country and its ruler, England; and an excessive outpouring of emigrants—the Great Famine left its imprint on Ireland's cultural legacies at home and in diaspora.

As novelist Emily Lawless wrote in *Ireland* (1885), the history of her native country was "beset with such distracting problems, bristling with such thorny controversies," that many eras could be viewed as formative for the country's memory. In fact, in recent years scholarly interest in Irish memory has grown exponentially, motivated by recollections of the Troubles and institutional abuse and, more recently, by the Decade of Centenaries. Guy Beiner's award-winning *Remembering the Year of the French* (2007) traces the reverberations of the 1798 rebellion in folk memory and oral history, David Lloyd's *Irish Times: Temporalities of Modernity* (2008) analyzes the role of trauma in the construction of an Irish modernity, Graham Dawson's *Making Peace with the Past* (2008) and Cillian McGrattan's *Memory, Politics and Identity* (2012) discuss the cultural and political ramifications of traumatic memory during Northern Ireland's Troubles as well as the subsequent peace process, and Emilie Pine explores the "Irish cultural obsession with the past" as well as Ireland's "tendencies of anti-nostalgia" in *The Politics of Irish Memory* (2010).[10] In 2012 Pine established a thriving Irish Memory Studies Network, hosted by University College Dublin, and Oona Frawley's four-volume series *Memory Ireland* (2011–14) has significantly advanced the discussion of Irish memories in relation to postcolonialism, trauma, and history. Moreover, recent projects bear witness to the pivotal role that academics specializing in Irish memory play in the translation and dissemination of Ireland's past to the general public. Some examples are the collaboration between the Institute for Irish-British Studies (University College Dublin) and the Ulster Museum in hosting a conference to complement the exhibition *Art of the Troubles* (2014), the contributions by historians Mary Daly and Emmett O'Connor to the six-part documentary series *Citizens' Lockout, 1913–2013* that was broadcast on RTÉ Radio 1, and the participation of scholars such as Luke Gibbons and Fearghal McGarry in documentaries shown at the *1916 Rising* exhibition, at the GPO Witness History Visitor Centre in Dublin.

Investigating Underexplored Issues: The Great Irish Famine

While the many historical events recently taken up by Irish studies scholars and social institutions—ranging from the 1798 United Irishmen Rebellion to the 1916 Easter Rising—qualify as what Jan Assmann call "fateful events of the past, whose memory is maintained through cultural formation (texts, rites, monuments) and institutional communication (recitation, practice, observance)," this monograph specifically considers the Great Famine as a "figure of memory" in the earliest fiction written on the subject. The reasons for doing so are manifold. First of all, Great Famine legacies constitute a most interesting case study for investigating the temporal dynamics of memory transmission in general because of their longue durée. As early as 1846, D. J. Corrigan predicted that the Famine would leave a genetic and especially psychological mark, not only on the "generation that had thus suffered," but also on "generations to come." Several decades after the traumatic era, writers such as former member of Parliament (MP) Alexander Sullivan and Emily Lawless not only emphasized the event's fundamental effect on Irish society, but also suggested that the memory of the Famine was vivid. In 1877 Sullivan describes the Famine as "one of the most important events in Irish history for more than two hundred years," and Lawless in 1885 speaks of "men and women, still alive, who remember the famine" and who "look back across it as we all look back across some personal grief, some catastrophe, which has shattered our lives and made havoc of everything we cared for."[11]

Famine recollection was not restricted to those persons who lived through the event but was also performed by many successive generations, well into the present day: the 150th anniversary of the Famine was marked by what Emily Mark-FitzGerald has aptly termed a "memory boom" that involved commemorative activities,[12] such as Cathal Póirtéir's radio series *Famine Echoes*, broadcast in 1995, but also the erection of monuments, such as the *Western New York Irish Famine Memorial* (1995); John Behan's "Coffin Ship," the *National Famine Memorial* in Murrisk, County Mayo (1997); and Rowan Gillespie's *Famine* on Dublin's Custom House Quay (1997). The Famine past had a cultural significance well beyond its sesquicentennial and into the twenty-first century: commemorative sites were created in Liverpool (2000), at New York's Battery Park in the form of Brian Tolle's *Irish Hunger Memorial* (2002), in Philadelphia (2003), and in Providence, Rhode Island (2007).[13] Since 2009 annual international Famine commemoration days have been held in Ireland and in North America, and the National Famine Museum at Strokestown Park, County Roscommon, organized a project to bring descendants from Famine emigrants to the Irish estate as part of the nationwide Gathering during the summer of 2013. Furthermore, the Famine past continues to play a crucial role in discourses on Europe's current economic crisis: in December 2013, finance minister Michael Noonan stated upon the successful completion of the bailout that Ireland's financial crash was "the greatest crisis that this country has experienced since the famine."[14] This strong transgenerational valence of the Famine past makes its memories an exemplary case study to realize one of the major objectives of this work: an investigation of the dynamics of cultural remembrance over time.

Second, legacies of the Great Famine are essentially transnational and thereby help us to examine how memory evolves following spatial relocation. Although the strongest reverberations of Famine miseries were experienced regionally, the effects of the Great Famine must be analyzed on different spatial levels that range from the local to the transnational,[15] especially as the Famine years and their immediate aftermath witnessed a thitherto unrivaled outflux of population. Fleeing the threats of starvation and the limited opportunities for sustenance in their mother country, between 1845 and 1855 2.1 million Irish men and women settled in North (the United States and Canada) and South Americas (Argentina, Brazil) as well as Australia.[16] Bringing the painful memories of the Great Famine with them to their new homelands, the migrants of the so-called Famine generation literally transported memories of the event to new territories, where they were kept alive as "prosthetic memory" by future generations, well into the twenty-first century.[17] For instance, in 1998 the city of Melbourne created a memorial site to commemorate the arrival of the first cohort of Famine orphan girls in 1848, and in 1999 Gaelic Park in the city of Chicago dedicated a monument to the Famine victims, designed by Father Anthony Brankin. In 2012 Ireland's Great Hunger Museum at Quinnipiac University, Connecticut, opened its doors in order to display nineteenth-century as well as contemporary artworks that remember the Great Famine. Its exhibition spaces testify to the relevance of the Famine past for today's artists and its enduring significance in the countries that received Famine emigrants.

Third, the focus of this study on early Famine fiction, written between 1846 and 1870, is motivated by the urge to reassess the persistent, erroneous assumption that the first decades after the food crisis were marked by a pervasive silence on the catastrophe. Especially from the mid-1990s, scholars in Irish studies have for the first time directed their attention to the presence of the Famine in nineteenth-century literature, thereby contesting Terry Eagleton's widely repeated claim that Famine memory is notoriously absent from the

Irish literary canon.[18] Christopher Morash edited a pioneering anthology of Famine poetry, *The Hungry Voice* (1989), and in *Writing the Irish Famine* (1995) discussed representations of the Great Famine in fiction by such authors as William Carleton and Anthony Trollope. Margaret Kelleher's *The Feminization of Famine* (1997) examines various Famine writings by, among others, Asenath Nicholson, Annie Keary, and Margaret Brew, while Melissa Fegan's *Literature and the Irish Famine, 1845–1919* (2002) records and briefly analyzes an important range of texts that are invested with Famine remembrance. These publications signify important strides in charting the hitherto overlooked role of Famine memory in key works of Irish literature. Nevertheless, they have not succeeded in rooting out the traumatic paradigm in Irish Famine research that has persistently identified the Famine with silence, as will be discussed shortly.[19]

At the same time, these studies fail to consider the corpus of nineteenth- and early-twentieth-century Famine fiction extensively let alone exhaustively, for they particularly limit their scope to Famine fiction written in the homeland and the more established, canonized authors. The present monograph, however, aims to analyze the full spectrum of Famine novels and short stories that recall the Great Famine and were published during the period 1846–70, on the basis of an extensive investigation of catalogs of nineteenth-century fiction like S. J. M. Brown's *Ireland in Fiction* (1919) and Rolf Loeber and Magda Loeber's *Guide to Irish Fiction* (2006), as well as painstaking research in copyright libraries and archives in Ireland, the United Kingdom, Canada, and the United States. The book explores a large unexamined body of Famine fiction written in Ireland and its British and North American diaspora, part of which was published in the form of serialized novels or short stories in periodicals that catered either to audiences who identified with an Irish ethnicity or to broader readerships. It covers canonical texts as well as popular fiction that was commercially very successful and influential in its own age, but has now largely been forgotten: for example, Mary Anne Sadlier's Famine narrative *New Lights; or, Life in Galway* went through five editions between 1853 and 1903, and novels such as Miss Mason's *Kate Gearey; or, Irish Life in London* and Alice Nolan's *The Byrnes of Glengoulah* were serialized in the popular press.[20] As such, this study aspires to bring significant expressions of Famine recollection in fiction back to the attention of scholars and provide a wider vista of literary Famine memories than research has hitherto sustained.[21]

Relocated Famine Recollections: Mapping New Territories

Why does this study limit itself to Famine fiction written during the final years of the calamity and the two following decades? First of all, this examination of the earliest Famine novels and stories will increase our understanding of the ways in which narratives negotiate recent excruciating events. According to Jeffrey Alexander, "Cultural trauma occurs when members of a collectivity feel they have been subjected to a horrendous event that leaves indelible marks upon their group consciousness, marking their memories forever and changing their future identity in fundamental and irrevocable ways." Famine scholars have debated intensively whether the Great Famine and its legacies should be interpreted as such a cultural collective trauma. Kevin Whelan states that "Ireland was culturally traumatised in the immediate post-Famine period," which in his view was manifested in a cultural silence on the Great Famine.[22] Emily Mark-FitzGerald, Joseph Lennon, and Joseph Valente have recently warned against a too uncritical espousal of trauma theory and its vocabulary of silence and repression in research of the Great Famine and its memories, for doing so blinds our vision to the often very explicit ways in which memories of the Great Irish Famine were addressed and strategically utilized in politics, historiography, and art, in both the past and the present.[23] At the same time, scholars such as Margaret Kelleher and Oona Frawley have demonstrated the useful ways in which concepts from trauma studies can account for the displacements in and generic instability of Famine writings.[24]

The present study acknowledges that the Great Famine was often experienced as a traumatic era that affected many layers of society:[25]

the event was often believed too distressing to address explicitly, as becomes evident from, for instance, Alexander Sullivan's observation that even as late as 1877, he is uncertain "whether the time has even yet arrived" to write a balanced account of the painful years.[26] As will be demonstrated, many works of fiction central to this study, moreover, represent the Great Famine as unrepresentable in several respects. At the same time, despite the freshness of Famine-related horrors, these narratives are far from reticent about the afflictions suffered during the Great Famine. Rather, they employ specific narrative and generic techniques to circumvent certain agonizing details. Scrutiny of these earliest examples of Famine fiction will therefore generate novel insights into the textual mediation of trauma that go beyond common assumptions of silence. Furthermore, this book will argue that in these earliest narratives, Famine memory should not just be read in light of trauma, as it is often consciously used as a strategic tool to redress current political affairs, such as the position of the tenantry in post-Famine Ireland, nationalism and Anglo-Irish relations, and as part of identity politics.

Second, research into literary Famine recollections of this particular period makes it possible to compare expressions of lived memory with expressions of prosthetic memory. While for most authors from this period the Famine was an event that they had experienced themselves, there were also writers who were living outside Ireland at the time of the fateful tragedy and therefore could have only indirect, mediated memories. For instance, Mary Anne Sadlier emigrated to Canada in 1844, the year before the Great Famine.[27] She must therefore have relied on news about the miseries in Ireland through correspondence with relatives and friends, on the accounts of immigrants who had escaped from their Famine-stricken homeland, and, most likely, on newspaper accounts of the dire circumstances in Ireland in her endeavors to reconstruct the experiences of Famine in her novels. Similarly, the preface to Elizabeth Hely Walshe's novel *Golden Hills: A Tale of the Irish Famine* (1865) suggests that her memory of the Famine is prosthetic, stating that the main sources of information for the writer were "the personal experiences of men who lived in the midst of the troubles of those years. . . . Narratives of peril and deliverance far more exciting than anything written in the following pages, have been brought to the knowledge of the writer by those who were the chief actors in them."[28] An issue that will therefore be central to the following analysis of Famine recollection is which distinctions can be witnessed when we compare lived memory with prosthetic memory. Do cultural recollections that are rooted in lived experience develop along different lines than transmitted prosthetic memories?

Third, focusing on Famine memory in fiction from this specific time frame enables an exploration of cultural memory that emanates from a period that was associated with temporal rupture. Today, scholars generally acknowledge that the Famine was an important "watershed in many areas of Irish life—demographics, economics, society, culture."[29] Although in John O'Rourke's view "the English people, and many in Ireland, long adhered to the opinion, that there was much exaggeration in the Irish newspapers regarding both the Blight and the Famine,"[30] on the basis of the available records many Famine historians estimate that approximately one million people lost their lives during the Great Famine.[31] Due to the high mortality rates and extensive emigration, Ireland's population dropped from 8.1 million people in 1841 to 6.5 million in 1851,[32] a circumstance that, according to Luke Gibbons, caused Ireland "to undergo the shock of modernity" in the form of social and cultural "disintegration and fragmentation."[33] Losses were particularly heavy among the Catholic, Gaelic-speaking rural lower classes,[34] so that particular folklore and language traditions were on the wane.[35] Moreover, the Famine led to the "forced economic modernization" of the countryside:[36] the proven unreliability of the potato as a crop for sustenance and outdated farming practices were denounced in favor of agricultural reform, such as "modern and scientific appliances" to transform bogs into arable land.[37] Land that had previously been used for agriculture was converted into pasture, because grazing cattle proved more profitable to the landed class than accommodating a tenantry that was unable to pay the rent.[38]

As a result of these drastic social transformations, the Famine was also memorialized as a radical break with previous eras. Alexander

Sullivan in 1877 states that "it is impossible for any one who knew the country" previous to the Famine, "and who has thoughtfully studied it since, to avoid the conclusion that so much has been destroyed, or so greatly changed that the Ireland of old time will be seen no more." Likewise, Emily Lawless saw the Famine as a "black stream, all but entirely blotting out and effacing the past," since "whole phases of life, whole types of character, whole modes of existence and ways of thought passed away then and have never been renewed. The entire fabric of the country was torn to pieces, and has never reformed itself upon the same lines again."[39] Because the Famine was experienced as a disruption between two different phases in Irish history, this study will concern itself not only with the ways in which recollections of the Great Famine develop over time, but also with the question of to what extent a sense of temporal disruption marks early Famine memory in fiction, especially as post-Famine Ireland was gradually advancing to a state of modernity. Moreover, as "social change and upheaval" often give rise to nostalgia, that is, the mobilization of an idealized, stable epoch whereby "conflicts are elided and social solidarity promoted," this examination of temporal transformations in Famine recollection will address to what extent the rupture represented by the Famine is shifted to the background in favor of memories of romanticized earlier pasts.[40]

The period between the Great Famine and the Landlord and Tenant Act of 1870 was politically and economically turbulent. Key figures in Young Ireland who had been exiled from their country after the failed 1848 rebellion and had settled in North America, such as John Mitchel, became important spokesmen propagating the idea of an independent Ireland, and in so doing expressed resentment over the London government's policies during the Famine years.[41] For example, in *The Last Conquest of Ireland (Perhaps)* (1861), Mitchel proclaimed that during the Great Famine, a "million and a half of men, women and children, were carefully, prudently, and peacefully slain by the English government," which deliberately neglected circumstances on the sister island.[42] The establishment of the Fenian Brotherhood in the United States and the affiliated Irish Republican

Brotherhood in Ireland, both in 1858, gave a strong impetus to nationalist sentiments,[43] but hope for Irish independence received a blow after the abortive uprising of 1867.[44]

While the Famine was followed by a brief period of relative prosperity, the 1860s and 1870s were marked by ongoing tensions between tenants and landlords that were reminiscent of conditions during the Famine. As, for example, a series of sketches republished from the *Illustrated London News* of 1870 suggests, in the "spring of 1870" the farming population in the Kildare countryside was still weighed down by "the wholesale eviction of forty-two families, numbering 152 individuals in all," and extreme poverty, as "a more starving, ragged, ill-housed community than the occupants of the wretched mud-cabins that lined one side of one of the principal streets in Kildare, was hardly possible to conceive." Around the same time, "the Relief Committee" in County Sligo supplied starving women with meal. Furthermore, threats of recurring famines were paramount: the article "Another Potato Famine: Emigration to New Brunswick Should Be Encouraged," printed in the New Brunswick paper the *Morning Freeman* on October 19, 1861, reports that "a deficient harvest" and "utter failure" of the potato crops have increased the threat of another famine, calling for timely relief measures so that "the scenes of '47 and '48" may not repeat themselves. Similarly, "The Famine in Ireland," published in the *Pilot* in 1862, warns that "once more is that terrible scourge, famine, stalking through the length and breadth of poor, dear, old Ireland."[45] This study will therefore also investigate in what ways these narratives employ and modify Famine memory as an instrument to engage with contemporary issues. In what ways does the Famine past become politicized? How is its representation informed by current affairs and conditions in subsequent decades? The mediation of Great Famine memories in this early fiction sheds interesting light on its function in the contexts of imperialism and anticolonial sentiments.

Finally, the focus of this study on the period 1846–70 also facilitates an examination of the early stages of memory transference across national borders. Although Breda Gray has convincingly argued that "emigration occupies a contradictory position in Irish cultural memory as something to be forgotten and remembered depending on socio-political context," its experience is inextricably bound up with Famine memory.[46] Whereas prior to the Famine, multitudes of Irish, especially from the Northern province of Ulster, had departed to countries such as England, Canada, and the United States,[47] emigration levels reached their peak during and in the immediate aftermath of the Famine. The massive exodus of Irish during and after the Great Famine implies that the cultural remembrance of the event as lived experience was transported to geographical areas outside Ireland. By investigating developments in diaspora Famine recollection in fiction during the period 1847–70, this monograph intends to outline evolutions in a memory that is relocated to the host societies of migrant communities. This transported memory progresses from the lived memory of the Famine generation of immigrants to forms of prosthetic remembrance by either pre-Famine Irish migrant communities or the descendants of Famine immigrants born in the new homelands.

Famine Memories beyond Borders: Transnational Perspectives

The corpus of Famine fiction that will be explored in this book includes fiction written in Ireland as well as in the three most prominent diaspora areas where Famine immigrants settled, namely, Britain, the Canadas, and the United States. Many Irish emigrants of the poorest class, who were obviously affected most by destitution, could not afford the passage across the Atlantic and therefore settled in English cities such as Liverpool, Manchester, and London.[48] As a result, England, Scotland, and Wales counted 727,000 Irish-born citizens in the 1851 census, an increase of 608,000 in comparison to the 1841 population survey.[49] Most Irish Famine immigrants, however, moved to North America. As the *Illustrated London News* wrote on July 6, 1850, "The Irish emigration flows with full force upon the United States," where, according to rough estimates, between 1846 and 1855 1,442,000 Irish men and women landed.[50] During the same period, approximately 300,000 Irish immigrants set up new homes in British and French Canadian territories,[51] especially in New Brunswick, Upper Canada, Quebec City, and Montreal.[52] As Nicholas Flood Davin famously observes in *The Irishman in Canada* (1877), in 1848 alone Irish immigration to the United States "exceeded that from all other sources," as "98,061 persons of Irish birth passed into the Union," while, owing to their great influx in the 1840s and 1850s, the Irish constituted the largest ethnic group in Montreal, Huntingdon, and Quebec.[53]

The reception of Irish Famine immigrants in these three host countries differed in various respects: In Britain and the United States, the Irish newcomers met with great opposition in their quest for employment and social acceptance, because the Roman Catholic creed of the majority of Famine immigrants was seen as a threat to the British and Anglo-American Protestant communities. In British urban environments, such as Liverpool, there was fierce competition over labor, and violent clashes occurred between Orangeists and Irish Catholic newcomers.[54] Vehement mobbing of Irish emigrants was not uncommon in America, either, where the Nativist or Know-Nothing Party proclaimed a violent hostility to the Irish immigrant tide entering the United States, accusing the predominantly Catholic immigrants of encroaching upon the fundamental rights and principles of the American-born population.[55] As a pamphlet written for readers of the *Patriot* suggested, the arrival of so many Roman Catholic Irish emigrants made American citizens feel "tampered with in our religion . . . injured in our labor . . . assailed in our freedom of speech."[56]

By contrast, the Famine immigrants who came to the Canadas would often settle in areas such as Quebec, where the Catholics already outnumbered Protestants, and they were regarded as an ethnic group that had contributed significantly to the infrastructures of Canadian society as settlers of the frontier.[57] Nonetheless, tensions between the newly arrived Irish Catholics and Protestants, including Irish Orangeists who supported loyalty to the British Crown and professed a fierce anti-Catholicism,[58] were also common in British North America, in particular in New Brunswick and Ontario.[59] Catholic processions in Toronto were attacked by Protestants, for example, in 1864 and in 1875, a big outbreak of violence known as the Jubilee Riots.[60]

The influence of Orangeism in Canada disconcerted Canadian politician and Irish emigrant Thomas D'Arcy McGee, who saw this movement as a serious threat to Irish Canadian Catholics.[61] In all three host societies, moreover, the Irish who had fled the Famine were often confined to accommodation in the poorest urban segregated ghettoes, which constituted "little Irelands,"[62] while they suffered from negative racial stereotyping in the press.[63]

The problematic integration in their new countries of settlement appears to have instigated a sense of ethnic separatism among Irish Famine migrant communities, especially on the North American continent. "Two Sides of a Question," an essay published in the Boston-based *O'Neill's Irish Pictorial* on March 5, 1859, states that while the Irish in America "melted and mingled down with the people and became willing to be absorbed in the national element," they have been encouraged to adhere to "any distinct traits of national character . . . owing to the bigotry and intolerance in the native born . . . who instead of receiving them with a true Republican welcome, throw every obstacle in their way; who, instead of inspiring confidence in the stranger, receive them with suspicion." A speech delivered at the dinner of the St. Patrick's Society, Toronto, on March 17, 1860, by William Halley suggests that Irish Famine emigrants to the Canadas strongly clung to a sense of identity that they associated with their native soil: Halley points to the enduring love of country, soil, and kind among these emigrants of the Famine generation that "at once invokes history and tradition" and "penetrates the misty realms of the past."[64]

The physical and social exclusion and alienation experienced by Irish Famine immigrants in various diaspora contexts sparked a tendency to envisage what Benedict Anderson calls "imagined communities" of Irish in exile. Irish British, Irish American, and Irish Canadian migrants of the Famine generation established their own cultural-religious institutions, such as churches, schools, hospitals, and newspapers, which were rooted in specific values that they associated with Irishness, such as Catholicism.[65] This point is, for example, demonstrated by the preface to Father Hugh Quigley's novel *The Cross and the Shamrock* (1853), which identifies the "faithful Irish-American Catholic citizens of the whole Union" with "their steady loyalty to the virtues symbolized by the 'Cross and the Shamrock'—on account of their attachment to the land of St. Patrick, and to the religion of her patriot princes and martyrs."[66]

Considering these close ties with the culture and religion of the motherland that were fostered by Irish Famine migrant communities in Britain and North America, the question arises whether the manifestations of Famine recollection in these three major diasporas were affected by the politics of ethnic segregation within most Irish migrant communities. Bearing in mind Andreas Huyssen's warning that a diasporic community's "tenuous and often threatened status within the majority culture . . . may make a given diaspora appear more homogeneous than it is in reality," can we nevertheless speak of a specific diasporic memory of a traumatic event in the country of origin that is marked by particular traits, turns, and transitions?[67] Taking into account Stuart Hall's insight that "cultural identity . . . is a matter of 'becoming' as well as of 'being,'" in what ways are changes in the social status of the migrant community translated into shifts in the cultural memory that is related to the former homeland?[68]

These issues will be considered in my analyses of the corpus of early Famine novels and short stories. Registering similarities and differences between recollections of Ireland's Great Famine in fiction written in both the homeland and the three major diasporas, this study explores in what respects we can discern overlaps or cross-fertilizations between Famine memory performed in Ireland, Britain, Canada, and the United States. In what ways do memory traditions of the Famine in these territories speak back to one another? To what extent do specific developments of Famine recollection in diaspora territories result in reconfigurations of memories of this fateful event in the homeland? In seeking to provide answers to these questions, I will refer back to Michael Rothberg's seminal work *Multidirectional Memory*, which argues for a conception of the public sphere "as a malleable discursive space in which groups do not simply articulate established positions but actually come into being through their dialogical interactions with others." According to Rothberg, we should move beyond the idea of "competitive memory" taking place in "a pregiven, limited space in which already-established groups engage in a life-and-death struggle," to account for the complexity of "dynamic transfers that take place between diverse places and times during the act of remembrance" and are manifested in translations of one "figure of memory" into the images and discourses of another remembrance.[69] Building upon Rothberg's valuable insights, the current study will map the ways in which Famine recollections in Irish diaspora fiction intersected with other memory traditions circulating in the host communities.

Adopting such a comparative, transcultural approach toward early Famine fiction written on both sides of the Atlantic appears legitimate in view of the fact that quite a few Famine narratives written in Ireland were also distributed to North American audiences, in the form of either specific reissues for English or transatlantic literary markets or publication in installments in periodicals catering to Irish immigrant readerships. Thus, Mrs. Hoare's collection of stories *Shamrock Leaves* (1851) was published in one edition for the Irish (J. M'Glashan) and one for the English market (Patrick and Oakey), and Richard Baptist O'Brien's *Ailey Moore: A Tale of the Times* (1856) was issued in London (Charles Dolman) as well as Baltimore (J. Murphy). Allen H. Clington's Famine novel *Frank O'Donnell* (1861), which had initially been published in Dublin by James Duffy in 1859 (as *The Old House at Home: The Adventures of Frank O'Donnell*), was serialized in the *Pilot* from January until July 1863. Ten years later, the text was reissued under the title *The O'Donnells of Glen Cottage* for American and Canadian markets by D. and J. Sadlier. Charles Joseph Kickham's narrative of the Great Hunger *Sally Cavanagh; or, The Untenanted Graves* (1869) was first serialized in the *Hibernian* in 1864 and subsequently in the *Irish-American* from March 1866 onward; the narrative was then issued in book form in Dublin by W. B. Kelly in 1869 and serialized in the *Pilot* in the late summer and autumn of the same year.

Conversely, Mary Anne Sadlier's *The Blakes and Flanagans* was originally published by D. and J. Sadlier in New York in 1855, but also by P. J. Kennedy in Montreal and James Duffy in Dublin in the same year. The transnational literary networks through which these works of Famine fiction reached several audiences across national borders reveal the fluidity and transportability of Famine memory in early fiction. The fact that these early works of Famine fiction often "traveled" through various communities in time and space calls for an awareness of the complex interactions between homeland and diaspora recollections of the Great Famine. Memories of the Famine in fiction did not always exclusively belong to a specific community of writers and readers, a point that is also underlined by the phenomenon that writers without any direct ethnic ties to Ireland themselves, such as Anna Dorsey, also wrote Famine fiction specifically directed at Irish North Americans.[70]

Investigating the reenactment of the Famine past in this transcultural corpus of fictional narratives, this study will direct itself to a third and final main concern: Which generic aspects of these works of fiction play a central role in the transmission of Famine remembrance? And what can we possibly conclude about the function of Famine fiction in the transference of memory on the basis of these findings? While past and present research has successfully mapped the reconfigurations of the Famine in historiography and the press, the generically distinct ways in which fiction has shaped Famine memories deserve further attention, especially in view of the popularity of novels and short stories among a heterogeneous group of readers. Therefore, in the following six chapters, I will pay specific attention to elements of narrative fiction that are traditionally believed to be significant vehicles of memory: focalization, narrative voice, and emplotment.

These chapters will focus on three major themes that are associated with the Great Hunger in cultural memories—victims of starvation, the landscape, and emigration—and will discuss the ways in which early Famine novels and stories relocate the recollections of deprivation, loss, and displacement that are inextricably linked to the crisis. Chapters 1–3 examine the ways in which these narratives of the Great Famine remember starvation and its many victims. Chapter 1 investigates the narrative strategies employed in this fiction to displace excruciating details of starvation, as well as the ways in which these texts relocate images and experiences of famine through narrative time and space. Chapter 2 will explore the (re)configuration of spectacles of starvation in these novels and short stories, revealing how the emaciated bodies of Famine victims are represented and (re)contextualized, in settings ranging from the cottier's cabin to the courtroom. Irish literature is known for a well-established Gothic tradition, and chapter 3 will investigate the ways in which Gothic conventions such as thresholds, the sublime, and haunting are used to give expression to the dehumanization of the famishing as well as the burden of Famine memory.

Chapters 4–5 deal with the pivotal role that landscapes play in early recollections of the Great Famine in fiction. Chapter 4 analyzes the politicization of blighted fields in various novels and stories and shows how especially in texts written in and for the North American diaspora, images of wastelands are often relocated from the narrative center in favor of contrasting pastoral images that suggest either a hopeful post-Famine future in Ireland or an alternative bower of bliss in diaspora. Chapter 5 considers the textual *lieux de mémoire*, the backdrops and settings of the narrative that play a crucial role in the recollection of the Famine performed in these novels and short stories, such as ruins, monuments, and graves. These sites are represented either as rooted in Irish soil or as relocatable carriers of memory. Michel Foucault's influential theory will be employed to demonstrate that these sites often function as heterotopia, "in which all the real arrangements, all the other real arrangements that can be found within society, are at one and the same time represented, challenged, and overturned," and as such they become vehicles for anti-imperial critique.[71]

Finally, chapter 6 will review the recollections of Famine emigration in these writings and will specifically elaborate upon the transatlantic passage in these texts. Steerage conditions on board the ships taking the Irish to the United States and Canada were notoriously dire: on average, up to 30 percent of all passengers perished at sea, owing to the unhealthy atmosphere belowdecks, which often resulted in epidemic disease.[72] Chapter 6 will investigate how the coffin ship functions as a heterotopic narrative space of "multidirectional memory" that helps negotiate the Famine past and vent political criticism. Additionally, this chapter will discuss relocation in terms of the recurrent figure of the remigrant who returns to an Ireland scarred by death and loss.

The six chapters will demonstrate that the earliest recollections of the Great Famine in fiction are marked by liminality. The term "liminality" can be interpreted in various ways: as the transitional stage or rite of passage between two phases or as that which exists at a physical or moral boundary. As chapter 1 makes clear, early Famine novels and short stories relocate the harrowing past textually by narrative shifts that negotiate its representability. As such, Famine memory in fiction is characterized by narrative liminality: at once narrated and suppressed, simultaneously tangible and elusive, the Famine past in these novels and short stories appears to be in a "transitional phase of becoming, a state of flux between two different states of being."[73] Chapter 3 will make clear that the Famine past is also represented as liminal through its identification with haunting and spectrality. In *Liminality and the Modern: Living through the In-between* (2014), Bjorn Thomassen defines liminality as "moments or periods of transition during which the normal limits to thought, self-understanding and behaviour are relaxed, opening the way to novelty and imagination, construction and destruction."[74] As will be illustrated in chapters 2 and 3, Famine fiction written in the immediate aftermath of the sustenance crisis reconfigures the period of mass starvation as an episode that pushes the boundaries of normality and acceptability in a more negative sense, letting readers experience a world at and "beyond the threshold."[75]

Chapters 3–6 will furthermore explore the liminal spaces that are central to the recollection of the Famine in these works of fiction. As normal limits of human condition relax, the home and land are reimagined either as unsettling spaces that contest common understandings or as transitions to brighter postcolonial futures. In diaspora Famine fiction, liminal spaces at the geographical margins of the New World express the cultural liminality of the Famine generation of emigrants and their quest for new identities that are suspended between "home" and host society. Early Famine fiction is therefore concerned with physical and symbolical boundaries that curb, can be shifted, and can be crossed. This study aims to push the frontiers of the discipline of memory research in its comprehensive examination of transgenerational and transnational memory, and it will transcend the boundaries of the flourishing interdisciplinary field of Irish Famine studies. The following analyses will reconsider existing paradigms and parameters of Great Famine research, in particular the notion of traumatic silence and the idea that Famine memory is infused with only Irish pasts.

1 | Displacing the Famine

"Sketches in the West of Ireland," a series of engravings made by Cork-born artist James Mahoney for the *Illustrated London News* that were accompanied by "descriptive notes" that "he was enabled to collect," are among the earliest representations of the Famine that problematized the ways in which the horrors of the event could be conveyed.[1]

Boy and Girl at Cahera (fig. 1), an image published as part of the second installment on February 20, 1847, depicts two malnourished siblings: the cold and hungry boy looks out of the picture defiantly, returning the gaze of the spectator. His squatting sister, meanwhile, fruitlessly scans the barren fields for a morsel to eat. This well-known and often reprinted sketch presents the harrowing conditions in Ireland as a liminal experience in several respects. First of all, the deprivation of the two infants places them at the margins of civilization, a condition at the borders of existence that is underscored by the bleakness of the surrounding landscape, which bears no sign of habitation.

Second, as Niamh O'Sullivan points out, Mahoney uses the style of the vignette, a "densely centred composition, with indeterminate peripheries," to thereby invite viewers to imagine things beyond the scope of the picture that may be unrepresentable. This sense of dehumanization that cannot be visualized but is left to readers' imagination is enhanced by Mahoney's remark in the written report: "Not far from the spot where I made this sketch . . . and less than fifty perches from the high road, is another of the many sepulchres above ground, where six dead bodies had lain for twelve days, without the least chance of interment, owing to their being so far from the town."[2]

1. James Mahoney, *Boy and Girl at Cahera*, *Illustrated London News*, February 20, 1847. Engraving. Courtesy of Ireland's Great Hunger Museum, Quinnipiac University, Hamden, CT.

While in Mahoney's report, then, the horrors of famine are confronted visually, some particularly harrowing aspects are deliberately removed from focus.

As the following discussion will illustrate, Mahoney's sketch is symptomatic of the ways in which early works of fiction remember the Great Famine. Rather than shrouding the harrowing details of the Great Famine in silence, these novels and short stories at times address them openly and at others shift them from the affective center of the narrative, thereby bearing witness to a liminality of remembrance. As an example of what Astrid Erll describes as the "poetic and narrative strategies" that play a crucial role in the affective impact of memories that are performed in a narrative, early Famine fiction written in Ireland and its British and North American diaspora sometimes places spectacles of starvation at a comfortable distance from the central consciousness of the narrative.[3] These novels and stories do so by the use of narrative voice, focalization, and generic conventions. As a result, the Famine is not always remembered explicitly in these texts. Rather, the event and its memories are rendered through narrative traces that enable the recovery of this past as well as the alleviation of its painful aspects.

Scholars in trauma studies have argued that painful pasts often resist narrative integration, both in the individual's consciousness and in cultural expressions.[4] This chapter intends to present a more complicated picture, in that the negotiation of a painful past does not merely involve a displacement of memories from the narrative voice or plot, for these experiences may actually be expressed indirectly through a specific narrative script. The discussion aims to take stock of the various complex ways in which these early works of fiction relocate the acutest aspects of the Famine past, arguing that the experience of famine is displaced diegetically and temporally as well as spatially. As will be demonstrated, one can speak of a transnational repertoire of such strategies: Irish and Irish North American Famine fiction employs similar techniques to negotiate the most excruciating aspects of Famine memory. However, we can also speak of very distinct ways in which North American Famine novels and stories reconfigure the Famine past: narratives written for Irish readerships tend to emphasize the bleak aftereffects of the Famine, whereas North American Famine narratives tend to imagine a post-Famine Ireland from which all scars of the trying years have disappeared. As will be explained, this different perspective on the Famine past in fiction written for Irish Canadian and Irish American audiences can be attributed to the conditions of the North American Famine diaspora.

Famine Memory and Narrative Experientiality

The cover image, an engraving by Hullmandel and Walton, entitled *Famine in Ireland* (1850), depicts the interior of a cabin inhabited by a starving family. The parents lie on beds of straw, "sick with famine," and the famishing children are forced to look after themselves. While the image directly exposes its viewers to Famine-related suffering, the accompanying text suggests that "the more revolting features are omitted." The print reveals the conflicting registers that underlie early recollections of the Famine past and can also be witnessed in early Famine fiction. On the one hand, the painful memories are addressed; on the other, there is the tendency to steer way from too harrowing details.

Traumatic histories are often identified with unrepresentability, the failure to embed the past into a narrative.[5] Early Famine fiction indeed expresses a sense of unspeakability: the horrors of starvation and death are often diegetically evaded, in that the narrative voice consciously distances itself from the severest distress. *A Tale of the Irish Famine in 1846 and 1847* (1847) by "Ireland" gives an account of the sufferings of the main protagonist, Honour McCarthy, who has to deal with the trials of blight and starvation single-handedly, because her husband is in America. The extradiegetic narrator sometimes displaces him- or herself from the extreme misery that Honour McCarthy has to endure, stating that he or she "will not dwell upon all the sights of horror" that the mother and her famished children meet on the road once they have been forced to give up their cottage. Later on in the story, when Honour and most of her children have succumbed to famine and Honour's husband has returned too late to save them, the narrator exclaims that McCarthy's "bitter anguish" and "deep disappointment" are "the most painful part of my sad narrative and I must hasten over it." At the same time, this narrative by "Ireland" does not spare the sensibilities of its readers, for it conveys the dire effects of starvation in detail. The narrator does not gloss over the fact that Dennis's only surviving son, Mike, has become "sightless and speechless" owing to malnutrition, and, earlier on, a minute account is given of the "half mutilated" bodies of Famine victims that had been "dragged by ferocious dogs from beneath the earth where they had been so recently and so hastily buried."[6] Identifying the memories of very recent painful experiences with silence therefore oversimplifies the liminal status of Famine horrors in this narrative, because they are both acutely present and absent.

It makes more sense to think in terms of what Monika Fludernik has called the "experientiality" of a literary text: the ways in which narrative aspects direct the reader's "perception" of that which is narrated. Narrative voice, focalization—the manner in which a story is narrated and the character through whose eyes the events are rendered—and what Rick Altman has called the "following patterns," that is, the characters and actions that are followed in the narrative, together constitute the consciousness of a text and greatly determine its affective impact. A close look at *A Tale of the Irish Famine in 1846 and 1847* reveals that the extradiegetic narrator distances him- or herself from a painful episode when it concerns one of the main characters who serve as subjects of focalization or who are central to the "following patterns" in the narrative and with whom readers are therefore likely to empathize: Honour and Dennis McCarthy. By contrast, the "frightful fragments" of corpses are a series of loose tangents in the narrative, mere descriptions of scenery, and are emotionally unconnected from the main characters.[7]

Similar instances of diegetic evasion on the part of the narrator can be found in the stories collected in *Shamrock Leaves* (1851), by Mary Ann Hoare (née Pratt), who witnessed the horrors of the Famine in Ireland firsthand during her early years of marriage to solicitor William Barry Hoare.[8] Here the narrative voice likewise circumvents the extreme suffering of the main characters who are central to the "following patterns," placing painful details outside the scope of experience that it communicates. In "The Black Potatoes," the narrator communicates the trauma of the Famine to an audience that may not have any lived memories of the fateful event, for she dedicates her volume of tales to readers outside Ireland, hoping they may not "utterly despise these few wild 'Shamrock Leaves,'" that is, stories, "gathered with a loving hand from the famine-stricken fields of my native country." Nevertheless, too agonizing observations in connection to the main protagonist, the widowed Jude Mahoney, who faces the trials of poverty, homelessness, and starvation and eventually dies of famine, are expelled from the diegetic center. For example, when the first-person narrator reaches the stage that should present the miserable ramble of Jude and her children by the roadside, he or she remarks, "It would be tedious and harrowing to the feelings to accompany this poor family through their wanderings for the next month." Further on, the narrator also consciously leaves out painful experiences by refusing to dwell on Jude's grief upon the loss of her infants: "I will not try to paint the mother's anguish; nor what she felt when, on that day week, another child was taken."[9]

In another story from the volume, "A Sketch of Famine," the extradiegetic narrator shifts away from touching upon the lonesome struggle of the homeless, perishing widow Sullivan and her hunger-stricken children: "We will not follow the miserable family through their wanderings during the bitter season of midwinter. Before the end of January the two younger children were dead, and their mother, as she dug their graves, had scarcely power to weep."[10] The first-person narrator's involvement of the reader through the use of the personal pronoun "we" suggests an intimate transmission of memory. This intimacy, however, is simultaneously undermined by this tendency to withhold memories that are too agonizing to transmit.

In these early Famine narratives, which render the perspective of Famine victims as subjects of focalization, narrative acceleration is also used as a strategy to displace painful experiences from the textual center.[11] This narrative acceleration is often achieved through a plotline that involves the physical journey of the subjects of focalization and signifies a rupture with narrative time. Such an acceleration is, for example, the case in "Ellen Harrington," a story published in the collection *The Lacemakers* (1865), by the Irish-born Susanna Meredith, years after her settlement in England. The narrative is probably inspired by the author's own observation of Famine atrocities and the miseries confronted by her father, the governor of County Cork Gaol, who during the Famine had "organized . . . a co-operative company to keep down the price of bread, and a soup kitchen for . . . relief, and had started an asylum for the pauper blind."[12] The story describes the arrival of a vessel bringing food to the Famine-stricken population of a West Coast village in June 1848. Its beginning, which relates to the Great Famine, is focalized through Captain Hartley, who carries supplies on board to relieve the starving in a coastal village and finds that they are by no means sufficient for the mob that brutally seizes the cargo and eats "the uncooked substances with ravenousness."[13] The first section of the story renders the outsider perspective of Hartley, who is initiated into the plight of the community by Reverend Longwood and Dr. Neligan. This perspective makes the story accessible to non-Irish readers who may be unfamiliar with Ireland's Famine past.

At the same time, Hartley's role as a traveler between England and Ireland ensures that these unbearable pains are distanced from the central consciousness of the story, whenever the narrative veers toward the horrors of destitution and death with which the villagers have to cope. Hartley's two excursions into Famine-afflicted Ireland are followed by his journeys back to England and his subsequent returns with new freights of food. During these intervals, some of the most dire events occur: the reverend's wife falls prey to the contagious disease that had previously afflicted her husband, and, subsequently, Mr. Longwood also contracts fever. As the text presents the course of action from Hartley's perspective, the details of the dying couple's suffering in his absence are not provided: Hartley hears a brief report of the "circumstances of privation" that led to Mrs. Longwood's death when *The Breeze* has sailed back to the village harbor.

Furthermore, the narrative only briefly touches upon the fact that Mr. Longwood's brother had arrived just in time to "close the wearied eyes of the martyred minister," as Hartley learns when he comes back after a fortnight. Hartley's journeys thus signify a fast-forward movement in narrative time, which results in a compression of harrowing Famine memories. At the same time, the fact that Hartley's travels to the community are repeatedly overshadowed by accounts of loss suggests a narrative expression of trauma processing. As Dominick LaCapra explains, in the reenactment of a past, the traumatic experience "hauntingly returns," and Hartley's moments of revisiting the community are marked by a repetition of Famine-related loss.[14]

In "The Black Potatoes," instances of narrative evasion on the part of the narrator are similarly framed by a template of traveling. The narrator refrains from commenting on the "tedious and harrowing" hardships faced by Jude Mahoney and her infants when necessities have forced them to leave their cabin and take to the road: "They travelled, as the poor little ones' failing strength would admit, over a distance of many miles." The narrator's subsequent refusal to dwell upon the mother's anguish when her children die is followed by a shift to the final stages of the story, which describe how Jude's wanderings bring her "back to her former abode," where she and her "two remaining children" seek shelter from the cold winds "beneath its desolate roof."[15] Thus, a plotline of departure and return that effects narrative acceleration is attended by a circumvention of the miseries of Famine-related suffering.

Likewise, William Carleton's "Owen M'Carthy; or, The Landlord and Tenant," a story published in *Alley Sheridan, and Other Stories* (1857) that depicts how the once prosperous farmer Owen is beaten down by the blight and "the united visitations of disease and scarcity," employs a template of departure and return. Presumably set during a time of famine in the 1820s, the story nevertheless resonates with the more recent sustenance crisis, for the frequent allusions to "disease" in the crops are reminiscent of the notorious potato blight of the mid-1840s. While the text elaborates upon the physical degeneration of Owen and his wife, who have become "gaunt skeletons" as a result of their poverty, the suffering of their little daughter, Alley, who starves to death, is displaced from narrative "experientiality." Although the story briefly describes how Alley's luxurious locks remain "bright and fair," even when her "colours" are "gone" and her "little hands are wasted away too" by lack of nourishment, her eventual death is not directly narrated. The "following pattern" in the narrative centers on Owen and his journey to Dublin in order to ask his absentee landlord for an extension of payment. Alley's dreadful collapse takes place during Owen's absence, and as the story describes his fruitless mission in the city, Alley's sad decline is not narrated in detail. Rather, Owen—and, by extension, the reader—learns afterward that the little girl is dead and buried and that he has "neither house nor home" after the brutal eviction of the rest of his relatives while he was away.[16]

The story, then, does not steer away from the pain of loss endured by many rural families during the age of famine, but agonizing details of starvation that are directly connected to the subject of focalization and his family are relegated to the margins of narrative consciousness. This narrative displacement is generated by the template of traveling, which directs the focus away from the miseries suffered by a famishing child. The use of the same narrative template in these three Famine stories underlines the point made by, among others, Christopher Morash and David Lloyd, that Famine narratives tend to resort to "painfully similar scenes and . . . rhetoric," but calls for reconsideration of the widely assumed notion that "the literature of the famine . . . exists as a series of tangents," that is, loose images in the text that are not fully integrated, because they are not intertwined with plot structure.[17] Rather, as the above analyses make clear, Famine memory in fiction written in its aftermath constitutes a liminal, shadowy presence that is embedded in frequently used narrative schemes that at once repress and express its most gruesome features.

Diegetic Displacement: Narrative Structure and Genre

In its presentation of Famine suffering, Mahoney's "Sketches in the West of Ireland" makes use of fragments from reports and diaries that are embedded in the overall narrative. Thus, the article cites the diary of Dr. Donovan to give an impression of the degree of deprivation in the countryside: "In this horrible den, in the midst of a mass of human putrefaction, six individuals, males and females, labouring under most malignant fever, were huddled together, as closely as were the dead in the graves around."[18] While quoting reports, letters, and eyewitness accounts was common in newspaper coverage of the Great Famine, in Mahoney's sketches the inclusion of Dr. Donovan's diary as a framework narrative inserts additional textual layers between the horrifying spectacle of starving bodies that are described on the intradiegetic level of the text, the extradiegetic narrator, and reading audiences.

Famine fiction from especially the 1850s diegetically displaces the horrors of hunger in a similar fashion, by incorporating framed narrative structures that create further distance between narrative "experientiality" and the excruciating memories. This displacement is, for instance, the case in the novel *Poor Paddy's Cabin; or, Slavery in Ireland* (1854) by "An Irishman."[19] Part of the horrors of death and decline caused by the Famine are narrated through the embedded report of a scripture reader to whom the rector's wife refers as proof that adults and children alike succumbed to starvation. The account, which is presented in the form of diary entries dating from March 1847, explicitly describes the intense suffering that the Protestant evangelist encounters in the cabins of the poor: "little famished-looking" orphans who sit on the ground of a cabin floor amid their recently deceased parents and the sorrows of a recently confined woman whose infant lies "dead near her in the bed; it had been lying there dead three days; her old mother was there and two starving children."[20] Because these images of brutal deprivation are presented as a narrative within the greater narrative, and because the scripture reader is a rather anonymous character, an extra layer of remoteness is established between the narrated horrors and the consciousness that the narrative produces.

Charles Lever's *The Martins of Cro' Martin* (1856)—a novel "tinged by the sadness of his own experiences when ministering to the suffering of cholera patients in Clare"—also puts up a screen between traumatic Famine memory and "experientiality" through the use of a framework narrative.[21] When Famine breaks out, Mary Martin—a pure-hearted young woman who will spare neither effort nor expense to alleviate the tenants' sufferings—is charged with the management of the estate of her uncle and aunt, who are absentee landowners. In her despair at facing the crisis of mass starvation, and without having extra means to offer relief, Mary writes a letter to convince her uncle Richard Martin and his indifferent spouse, Dorothea, that she requires further financial assistance. The novel incorporates Mary's letter, which offers further details about the tenants' suffering, thus presenting the calamities of hunger and disease as text within text: "But, worse than all these, typhus is amongst us, and cholera, they say, coming. I might stretch out this dreary catalogue, but here is enough, more than enough, to awaken your sympathies and arouse you to action. There is a blight on the land; the people are starving—dying."[22]

On the one hand, this passage brings the memories of Famine close to home because the narrator and focalizer is one of the major sympathetic characters. On the other, the framed structure positions the dreadful experiences at a further stretch from the textual consciousness. This sense of remoteness from the famishing peasantry that the narrative thus evokes has an additional function: it emphasizes the indifference of the absentee Martins to the lot of their tenantry, for they have metaphorically "left the ship in a storm."[23]

Early Famine fiction also employs narrative allusion to avoid bringing the trauma of starvation too close, and, intriguingly, this strategy features most prominently in diaspora texts that chart the experiences of Irish immigrants. *Bickerton; or, The Immigrant's Daughter* (1855) is a novel by Charles Canon, the son of Catholic immigrants to New York, who compiled school readers for Catholic publisher Edward Dunigan.[24] In the narrative, it remains unclear why Manus O'Hanlon and his wife, Moya, have left their beloved motherland, apart from the fact that it has come to represent "a ruined home" and an "Island of Sorrow."[25] These remarks could be interpreted as references to a Famine-stricken motherland from which many Irish feel forced to flee.

Kate Gearey; or, Irish Life in London, serialized in the *Rambler* from February until October 1852, and written by a Miss Mason who, according to the preface, witnessed Irish immigrant settlement in London, also illustrates how Famine memories can be transmitted through textual allusion.[26] The novel is set in 1849, when young immigrant Kate arrives from Ireland in London to seek employment. The plot thus begins during one of the later years of the Famine, and the idea is evoked that in the preceding years Kate's family suffered great losses owing to starvation and deprivation: "In her fifteenth year, the child grew old in the world's cares; the pig died first, then the cow, then her gentle pious mother."[27] This description is, however, just a hint at Famine-related suffering, and the rest of the novel bypasses the recent event and its miseries entirely. Although this relegation of the Famine to a mere allusion in the text may be attributed to its focus on the conditions of Irish immigrants in the British capital, it remains interesting given that Kate's traumatic past is presented in such a veiled manner.

The same can be said of Mary Anne Sadlier's *The Blakes and Flanagans* (1855), which centers on the lives of Catholic Irish families in the American diaspora. In this novel, the Famine past looms in the background in the form of a brief inference: Tim Flanagan remarks that in America at least, "fine specimens" of the "murphies," that is, potatoes, may be had, "considering that they didn't grow in Ireland." The Famine also functions as a mnemonic subtext that looms in the background in *Tim Doolan* (1869), a novel published in London by author William Anderson Cawthorne, who called himself "Canada West" and who implies in the preface that the Irish migrant experiences in the New World have come "under his own observation."[28] As in *Kate Gearey* and *The Blakes and Flanagans*, the core of the narrative is constituted by the protagonist's experiences of settlement in North America. Famine memories are conjured up by a humorous anecdote related by Tim about a corpse hidden in a potato bag.

Back in Ireland, Tim met his acquaintance Con Sweeny on the market, who told him that he had to "lave those pratees" that he carried with him in a bag "at a gentleman's house." When Tim unexpectedly sees Con enter the doctor's house with the suspiciously large potato bag, it proves to contain the body of a dead man that Con dug up from the grave to sell to a doctor: "He had a corpus in one o' the bags, an' he wanted me out o' the way ontill he could get it out o' the car into the house."[29] Although the incorporated anecdote can be read as a tall tale that spices up the narrative, Tim's digression associates the potato crop—or, rather, a bag without potatoes—with death. As such, the novel appears to insinuate a less lighthearted past in which lack of potatoes resulted in mass mortality.

Early Famine fiction written in the North American diaspora employs additional strategies of narrative displacement. Many American and Canadian Famine narratives move painful Famine recollections to a narrative subplot. This shift happens, for instance, in *Tim Doolan*. The narrative contains a subplot in which Noonan, whom Tim meets on board the emigrant vessel, relates how his family was affected by unemployment and extreme want when "it was a bad saisin for crops"—a remark that implies that he talks about the Famine era.[30] In Mary Anne Sadlier's novel *Elinor Preston; or, Scenes at Home and Abroad*, written and issued after the author's settlement in America upon her marriage to publisher James Sadlier,[31] memories of the Great Hunger are likewise consigned to the margins of the narrative. The painful Famine past is addressed in the life account of a minor character, Margaret Gilmartin, one of the young women on board the coffin ship to Boston. Readers learn that when Margaret's father had departed to America in order to financially support his family back in Ireland when "the dismal year of the famine came on," Norah Gilmartin and her little daughter were "reduced to beggary and starvation." At last, Norah and young Margaret "were forced to go into the poorhouse in order to escape starvation." There, however, "the food was hardly sufficient, either in quantity or quality, to keep body and soul together," so that eventually the mother falls prey to disease and dies. Margaret's story of bereavement in the Famine era runs parallel to Elinor Preston's tale of personal loss. Her family has to give up its family home during the "years of commercial depression—that dismal lull which followed the extinction of the great Repeal movement, and ushered in the Famine," and subsequently her closest relatives die.[32] Although the Famine period is briefly mentioned here, the novel does not connect Elinor's deep grief at finding herself alone in the world with the Great

Hunger. Rather, it is the context of subnarratives like that of Margaret's misfortune that suggests such an interrelation. Generally, the novel appears to dissociate Elinor's deprivations from the Famine past.

Furthermore, Famine fiction written by or for the Irish North American diaspora before 1870 is notably different from homeland Famine fiction in its use of a melodramatic plot twist. Fiction written in Ireland often fully exposes the afflictions of Famine-related mortality and ends with the main characters' death and the disintegration of family life. As we saw, *A Tale of the Famine in 1846 and 1847* by "Ireland" (1847) and "The Black Potatoes" by Mrs. Hoare (1851) follow rather similar narrative templates. The two mothers central to the story—Honour McCarthy and Jude Mahoney, respectively—are forced to live by the roadside and suffer the starvation of their children before they succumb to hunger and disease themselves at the conclusion of the narratives.

Moreover, in both cases, the sense of tragedy is enhanced by the fact that help from the New World is untimely.[33] In "The Black Potatoes," Jude's brother-in-law James, who had made his fortune in America, returns too late to offer his support to Jude. The widow collapses with hunger and dies, presenting a heartbreaking spectacle and an "awful scene." In *A Tale of the Irish Famine in 1846 and 1847*, McCarthy speeds back from America to Ireland upon hearing about the Famine miseries, hoping to take his family "to his adopted country . . . where he had made every provision for Honour's comfort." However, to his "bitter anguish" and "deep disappointment," he arrives too late to save his wife and most of his infants. As in "The Black Potatoes," Ireland fails to offer a future home: McCarthy and his only surviving son, Mike, leave for America together. The narrative suggests that they will find little consolation there, for Dennis has changed from "a powerful, upright man, in the prime of his life," into a person "bent, and withered, and grey haired."[34]

This recurring schematic narrative template of personal loss and an irredeemable Ireland does not feature in early examples of North American Famine fiction, often written by and for Irish immigrants of the Famine generation. By contrast, these North American Famine narratives frequently push the agonizing recollections of the Famine to the narrative margins by introducing a rather forced happy conclusion in the face of impending calamity. Such a conclusion figures, for example, in *Tim Doolan*. When Noonan's family is running out of the last scraps of food and the prospect of starvation looms, his daughter finds a pocketbook full of banknotes. While the contents could relieve the family's distress, the father decides to do what is right and returns the wallet to its rightful owner. He is consequently rewarded by the gentleman, who offers him land and tells him to "pay me whativer yearly rint ye think it is worth, afther affording yerself an' family a comfortable livin', and somethin' to put by for owld age."[35] The use of a narrative template that offers an unexpected twist toward a joyful ending, and is moreover infused with Christian morality, shifts any direct treatment of Famine miseries to the background.

A similar treatment of the Famine can be found in Mary Anne Sadlier's novel *Bessy Conway; or, The Irish Girl in America* (1862). While the plot centers on the adventures of a young Irish immigrant woman in New York, toward the novel's conclusion the narrative focus shifts back to Ireland. As one can read, dismal times have begun for Bessy's father, Denis Conway, and many other tenant farmers all over Ireland, as it is "the terrible year of the Famine." The conditions of Denis Conway's family have reached a pitiful state: "Famine and disease had found their way into that happy household, and misery sat on the threshold"; the family has to sup on "water and nettles, with a handful or so of oatmeal." Nancy Conway has transformed into "a living picture of hunger," while little Ellen, Bessy's once lively sister, is wasting away: "But the terrible fangs of hunger had fastened on her vitals, and disease was wearing her young life away." However, this brief evocation of Famine trials and the imminent eviction of the Conway family is immediately followed by the miraculous reappearance of Bessy from America, who manages to avert her relatives' ejection and starvation just in time. Bessy brings about a complete plot reversal. With the money she earned in the New World, she can pay off the bailiffs and buy nutritious food for her parents and siblings. As a result, the empty table is transformed into a setting for a sumptuous banquet: "And to be sure that was the supper that was well relished. No royal family in Europe was as happy that night as Denis Conway's, for their cup of bliss was made sweeter than nectar by the recollection of sorrow and misery past." Moreover, Ellen's "pinched, parched look" has disappeared as if by magic, "and the ghastly paleness of the sweet features was tinted with a more lifelike hue."[36] As such, the novel conjures up the trauma of Famine to dispel it immediately afterward by a schematic template that provides a romantic turn of events.[37]

The death of the main protagonist's only daughter, Kate, is likewise averted in Robert Curtis's "McCormack's Grudge," which, though written by a county inspector in Ireland, was first serialized in the *Irish-American* in September 1862.[38] Ironically, the fact that the girl is sent to the poorhouse after the family's eviction saves her life, for once there she is sent off to the hospital: "Had the M'Cormacks not been turned out, Kate, without medical aid or warmth, would have pined away and died." It is, moreover, Myles's heroic rescue of the land agent's son Harry from a raging bull, which almost cost him his own life, that forms the onset to further happiness: Myles receives back his land, and at the narrative conclusion he is a prosperous farmer.

The fact that transatlantic Irish fiction of the 1860s manifests such distinctive traits to displace painful memories of the Great Famine creates the impression that one may speak of what Andreas Huyssen calls a specific "diasporic memory" in contexts of migration.[39] The question emerges: How can we account for the frequent relegation of Famine memory to subplots and the stronger presence of melodrama as a tool to picture a redeemed and rejuvenated Ireland in diaspora fiction? After all, the 1860s in Ireland were far from peaceful, and the tensions that had marked the Famine era had far from disappeared: although the 1850s had brought more prosperity, the transition from tillage to livestock on many estates that had already started before the Famine years meant that employment for agricultural laborers diminished and that many Irish looked for alternative opportunities in Britain and North America.[40] Furthermore, while as of 1860 a succession of laws, such as the Landlord and Tenant Law Amendment Act, sought to improve the position of tenantry, rent rates would not be agreed upon by both parties, but be set "by the obligatory acceptance by the tenant of the landlord's terms."[41] In other words, Ireland was far from the Edenic, regenerated post-Famine land that these North American diaspora narratives conceived.

One explanation could lie in the fact that some of these transatlantic Famine narratives constitute examples of "prosthetic memory," because their authors, such as Mary Anne Sadlier, who moved to Montreal in 1844, did not witness Famine horrors themselves. While this may explain the marginal presence of Famine atrocities in her novels *Bessy Conway* and *Elinor Preston*, such a clarification is by no means applicable to all transatlantic Famine narratives. After all, the preface by "Canada West," who intimates that he is familiar with the miseries of Irish transatlantic migration, creates the impression that his text may build upon lived experiences of the Famine era.[42]

A more adequate explanation may lie in the fact that these texts aimed to create "prosthetic memory" for future generations of Irish Americans and Irish Canadians. As many scholars in diaspora studies have argued, the construction of diasporic remembrance is often steeped in an idealization of and nostalgia for the country of origin, in which the home of the past becomes a symbolic space that is defined by its relation to the foreign and alien places of the host country.[43] As Andreas Huyssen claims, diaspora communities, which constitute a minority culture with a "tenuous and often threatened status within the majority culture" and are subject to "stereotyping of otherness combined with . . . exclusionary mechanisms," therefore tend to "create a unified or even mythic memory of the lost homeland." This nostalgia functions as a strategy to cope with present identity crises,[44] especially since memory constitutes such an important fundament in the concretion of a group identity.[45] Moreover, as Susannah Radstone observes, nostalgia is intertwined with "social change and upheaval," in particular a "lost sense of continuity with the past."[46] As such, nostalgia is inherent to the situations of migrant cultures that find themselves physically cut off from the contexts of their cultural pasts.

Huyssen's and Radstone's valuable insights certainly apply to the Irish American and Irish Canadian communities of the Famine exodus. The great geographical distance between Ireland and North America meant that very few Irish immigrants ever returned to their native soil,[47] and the immigrants' sense that they had been forced by circumstances to leave their beloved motherland gave rise to the sustaining myth of Irish Famine migration as forced exile.[48] This idea of the North American exodus as exile became particularly pronounced from 1847 onward,[49] as is testified by the poetry of, among others, Helen Selina, Lady Dufferin: "The Emigrant Ship" (1848), for instance, equates the departing Irish with "poor exiles" who shall never more hear "words of kindly cheer" in "Irish tongue, upon the longing ear!"

While the Irish outflux to North America came to be identified with the decline of cultural heritage and irretrievable loss, the Famine generation in British Canada and America in particular faced stigmatization as a cultural group.[50] George Brown, the editor of the Toronto-based newspaper the *Globe*, wrote on February 1, 1858, that "Irish beggars are to be met everywhere, and they are as ignorant and vicious as they are poor. They are lazy, improvident and unthankful; they fill our poorhouses and our prisons, and are as brutish in their superstition as Hindoos."[51] In the American press, there were many examples of ethnic stereotyping. The cartoon *A Mere Matter of Taste*, printed in *Harper's Weekly* on December 12, 1868, suggested that Irish Americans spent their meager income on whiskey rather than coal. Thomas Nast's caricature *The Usual Irish Way of Doing Things*, published in *Harper's Weekly* on September 2, 1871, depicts a rowdy, drunken Irishman who lights a powder keg.

The opposition that the Irish newcomers faced led Thomas D'Arcy McGee to complain about the fact that Americans cared little for the social position of the immigrants who, in their view, are only "well enough to do the drudgery of cleaning the continent."[52] In a similar vein, the broadside *What Irish Boys Can Do: An Answer to "No Irish Need Apply"* (1864) took issue with the discrimination of Irish immigrants by American employers, who refused to take on those individuals who came from the Emerald Isle and continuously insulted them: "They'll call him green, an Irish bull: it happens every day." The outsider status of Irish emigrants of the Famine generations in British Canada and America may therefore have fueled the cultural construction of an idealized version of Ireland from which all recent trauma of pestilence had to be dissociated.[53]

The Temporal Displacement of Famine Memories

Time is an inherent feature of narrative, in that "the act of storytelling places the narrative 'in' time."[54] In many novels and stories written in the immediate aftermath of the Great Famine, the plot is set during an earlier Irish famine: temporal distancing occurs in that the unbearable memories of recent starvation are displaced to a more distant past. It needs, of course, be noted that previous to the bleak 1840s, Ireland had known a long history of famines. In the summers of 1816 and 1817, for instance, exceptionally cold and humid weather destroyed the crops and led to a small-scale famine.[55] The year 1822 was marked by a famine in the West of Ireland, resulting from abominable weather conditions[56] and, as John Mitchel wrote in 1859, a dramatic fall in prices for agricultural produce,[57] while the 1831–32 famine led to excessive mortality.[58]

Several narratives written in the trail of the Great Hunger set their plots of starvation during one of these earlier nineteenth-century famines. William Carleton's story "Owen M'Carthy; or, The Landlord and Tenant" (1857) appears to take place around the famine of 1816, for the text suggests that "up until the peace of 1814," the eponymous protagonist was able to make a living as a tenant farmer by his "unremitting toil." Carleton's novel *The Black Prophet* also suggests the context of the 1816–17 famine, although the novel implies that Ireland is almost annually plagued by failures of potato crops that cause hunger. As such, the events in the plot could be relocated to any temporal context, as the novel also implies: "The climate of Ireland is so unsettled, its soil so various in quality and the potato so liable to injury from excess of either drought or moisture, that we have no hesitation in stating the startling fact of this annual famine as one we can vouch for, upon our personal knowledge, and against the truth of which we challenge contradiction."[59]

Shandy M'Guire is a novel by Irish immigrant and priest John Boyce, who wrote under the pseudonym Paul Peppergrass,[60] and was originally published by Edward Dunigan in 1848. The narrative is set in 1822, a year in which, according to the extradiegetic narrator, "by the failure of a single crop, five eighths of the people were reduced to absolute starvation."[61] Likewise, Margaret Percival's *The Irish Dove* (1849) places the story of Reilly's decline and famishing in 1822,[62] which "was marked by a failure of the potato crop; a visitation which, though it falls with the greatest and most fearful weight on the natives of Ireland, can yet draw within the influence of its vortex, the great and wealthy of other less afflicted countries."[63] Finally, Charles Lever's *The Martins of Cro' Martin* (1856), which describes how a "dreadful malady walked the land" and "villages were depopulated," appears to contextualize these events in the famine of 1832: the narrator's opening remark that he or she is about "to speak of Ireland as it was some four-and-twenty years ago" would lead us to the year 1832 if we count back from the date of publication.[64]

The explicit references to years in which earlier famines afflicted Ireland could render an interpretation of any of the above works of fiction as mnemonic expressions of the Great Famine invalid. After all, it could as well be argued that these stories and novels consciously perform the memory of earlier episodes of famine from Irish history. Nevertheless, I would like to argue that these texts reenact recollections of the Great Famine, but they also seek to create a greater distance between its harrowing trauma and the present by relocating recent Famine memories to earlier eras. The main reason to hold on to this view is that these narratives depict aspects of famine that do not match the contexts in which they are set, but rather seem to resonate with the recent calamity. Moreover, many of these narratives set during earlier famines make allusions to persons who played a significant role during the Great Hunger. Carleton's "Owen M'Carthy" relates Owen and his family's degeneration by famine to images of rottenness and disease rather than speaking of weather conditions that damaged the food he cultivated. One can read that Owen faced a year of "disease and scarcity" as a farmer, and the thatch upon the roof of his cottage is described as "black and rotten"—terms that were applied to the condition of the potato crop in Famine reports from the 1840s.[65] Through these descriptions, the narrative evokes the images of pestilence that one finds in accounts of the Great Famine, such as C. A. Rawlins's poem *The Famine in Ireland* (1847), which states that "the Blight, the Famine and the Pestilence / Have been the language of OMNIPOTENCE."[66]

While Carleton's *The Black Prophet* indeed suggests a season of dampness and rain that will bring forth "rottin' crops," as occurred in 1822, the novel is also specifically permeated with the discourses of providential retribution that were employed to explain the Great Famine of the mid-1840s. For instance, Protestant Reverend Hugh McNeile in *The Famine a Rod of God* (1847), a religious tract on the Famine in Ireland, fulminated that the recent calamity was an example of the "plagues, pestilences, famines, wars" that "are used by God as national punishments for sin," and his colleague John Travers Robinson claimed that the Famine should be interpreted as a "vial of wrath . . . poured out by a commissioned angel over a guilty world." Donnel Dhu's vision of the approaching calamity as an expression of the Almighty's anger echoes these discourses of divine punishment: "Isn't the Almighty, in his wrath, this moment proclaimin' it through the heavens and the airth? Look about you, and say what is it you see that doesn't foretell famine—famine—famine!"[67]

The same discourses of providential doom are called forth in *The Irish Dove*, for the omniscient narrator suggests that the visitation of famine upon Reilly's family is translated by his religious enemies into terms of "Divine vengeance, incurred by the hearing of God's own precious word." As such, the novel appears to recall not just the famine of 1822, but also the more recent era of mass starvation, while shifting its focus to a traumatic past that is more remote. At first glance, *Shandy M'Guire* appears to be exclusively restricted to the context of the 1822 famine, for the extradiegetic narrator provides many historical details surrounding the year of disaster, such as the Duke of Cumberland's leadership of Orangeism. Nonetheless, the novel also appears to perform memories and discourses that are more particularly related to the Great Hunger. The scene in which proselytizer Mr. Goodsoul bestows a "small duodecimo Bible" on poor Kathleen Kennedy, who is actually in want of material relief, is strongly reminiscent of images of scripture readers that one encounters in texts dating from the Great Famine.[68] An example is Elizabeth Willoughby Varian's poem "Proselytizing" (1851), which pictures a relentless evangelical who is concerned with winning souls rather than offering relief to the starving Irish: "Thou shalt have food, but first thou must renounce / Thy erring faith, and yield these children up."

A similar temporal displacement seems to manifest itself in Charles Lever's *The Martins of Cro' Martin*. The novel may suggest a setting in 1837, but appears to allude to Charles Trevelyan's mission as governmental overseer of the Famine relief works after the summer of 1846. Trevelyan was assistant secretary to the Treasury,[69] and he was a staunch believer in the economic politics of nonintervention that were adopted by the Russell cabinet.[70] In his famous work *The Irish Crisis* (1848), he not only reported on the conditions of Famine-stricken Ireland but also analyzed the system that, in his view, had led to the severe problems, arguing, for example, that the nation's "universal dependence on the potato" lay at the root of the current calamity.[71] In Lever's novel, the character of Mr. Merll is sent by the absentee Martins to Ireland to investigate whether Mary exaggerates the pictures of devastation that she sketches in her letters: "'In return, I shall ask one favor at your hands,' said Martin, as he folded and addressed the epistle. 'It is that you write me a full account of what you see in the West,—how the country looks, and the people. Of course it will all seem terribly poor and destitute, and all that sort of thing, to your eyes; but just try and find out if it be worse than usual. Paddy is such a shrewd fellow, Merll, that it will require all your own sharpness not to be taken in by him.'"[72]

The scene may remind one of Trevelyan's task: commissioned by a government abroad, he had to examine Ireland's situation and ensure that no unnecessary expenses were made. This reading of Mr. Merll as a character inspired by Trevelyan is further confirmed by the fact that this person, upon arriving in Ireland, compares himself to "some emissary of the Government, sent expressly to obtain this knowledge . . . employed by some section of party politicians." One could therefore conclude that while Lever's novel may recollect the earlier famine of 1837, it simultaneously appears to perform memories of the more recent Great Famine, even though these recollections are transferred back to the late 1830s. The fact that Lever's novel evokes different pasts at the same time appears to underscore Daniel Levy's view that memory "represents a co-existence of simultaneous time transcending multitude of pasts": different layers of past time are connected by similar vortexes of memory and suggest the repetition and circularity of events.[73] By these temporal transferences of memories of the more recent Great Famine to previous episodes of mass starvation, these narratives represent famine as a recurring experience to which the Irish are subjected.

Interestingly, in fiction written after 1870, this idea of recurrent famines, and existing analogies between present and past conditions of starvation, is also strongly present. Thus, in Margaret Dixon McDougall's Irish Canadian novel *The Days of a Life* (1883), which is set during the Land Wars, the conditions of famine that afflicted part of Ireland's population in 1879 are linked to the earlier Great Famine. When discussing the present destitution and hunger among his flock, the local priest remarks to protagonist Ida Livingston that he is not "unused to scenes like this," having been in "the West during the awful time of the great famine, and there I saw miles of country cleared of its inhabitants. I have seen landed proprietors helping to pull down the cabins of the poor people with their own hands. I have seen the people by hundreds on the roadside stricken with famine-fever, dying daily." Furthermore, the idea that Ireland's Great Famine is one of many, almost identical, episodes of starvation in Ireland's history is voiced by the extradiegetic narrator who comments that at present, "the great multitude struggled with death, with famine, were evicted by the thousands, sat in the shelter of the rocks and ditches, drifted into the poor-houses, and the grave. . . . It is strange how history repeats itself."[74]

Famine Memory and Geographical Displacement

A specific form of displacement of the Famine era and its terrifying trauma can be found in several Irish Canadian and Irish American fictional narratives. These texts make use of a strategy that I would like to call geographical displacement, which implies an interaction between spatial and temporal relocation of Famine trauma that can be defined as chronotopic. As many scholars have proposed, migration entails a simultaneous shift in time as well as space. While emigration entails a displacement in space from the homeland,[75] the movement to territories outside the motherland also "implies temporal change."[76] Emigrants are cut off from their native soil, and this process of physical transfer marks a literal passage of time as well as a temporal transition from life in the homeland to residence in diaspora. As Esther Peeren states, "Space is temporal in that movement in space is always also movement in time." In her view, this given legitimizes an extension of the chronotope, as a literary concept of time-space, "into a cultural concept" that aptly describes the experience of diaspora.[77]

Irish diaspora fiction that recalls the Great Hunger appears to express this double sense of displacement of migrant cultural memories, by evoking particular time-space figures that are "typical of certain types of historically instanced plots" as literary dimensions.[78] One of these time-space narrative templates specific to diaspora Famine fiction consists of the main protagonist's encounter with a fellow passenger during the transatlantic crossing that is followed by this traveler's intimation of living memories of Famine. For instance, as we have seen, Sadlier's eponymous heroine Elinor Preston meets Margaret Gilmartin and learns the sad story of her and her mother's reduction "to beggary and starvation" in the past four years.[79] As Elinor Preston and her fellow emigrant travel away from the Emerald Isle, the harrowing recollections of destitution are displaced both in time as well as in space, for they belong to a setting from which the two young women become geographically detached.

This template, which positions Famine recollections in a time-space that is beyond the experiences of the migrating main characters, also figures in "Canada West"'s *Tim Doolan.* On his voyage to North America, the hero meets a fellow countryman from "the parish of Skull, in the west o' the county Cork," who "ontil the bad times came . . . farmed a few acres o' land there," but in the meantime bought a farm in America, where he will settle with his relations.[80] Although the man's speech points to recent hardship in Ireland, the use of the past tense to refer to the calamities, and the implied transition to a different phase of the man's life as the owner of property, suggests a temporal distancing from "the bad times" of deprivation. This impression of temporal distancing is, moreover, bound up with geographical detachment, as Tim and his companion sail away from the places to which the fateful memories are linked. The rest of the narrative does not remember times of want and hunger, almost symbolically consigning them to a far-off space and removing them from narrative "experientiality."

The Dalys of Dalystown (1866), a novel written by Dillon O'Brien, who was born in Tullabeg, County Roscommon, and who immigrated to the American Midwest shortly after the Great Famine, also offers an example of the geographical displacement of the Famine in diaspora fiction.[81] However, unlike the two novels previously discussed, no temporal distancing of the Famine occurs in this narrative. In fact, in this novel, the period in which the son of a ruined landlord, main protagonist Henry Daly, rises in fortune in North America is coterminous with the outbreak of famine in Ireland. After Henry has been in America for twenty years and has settled in the Michigan Territory with his relatives, he receives a letter from Ireland informing him of the dire situation and the failed 1848 rebellion: "I have just had news from Ireland. It is as I expected; those few brave spirits, scorning life, whilst gaunt famine slays their countrymen by tens of thousands, have taken the field. But they will fail; miserably fail! Who could put men's hearts into those famished skeletons, who lie down to die, while the cars laden with grain, on its way to a foreign market, pass their doors—whose hunger is mocked by the sleek skins of the beasts that graze beside them in undisturbed security." While the narrative openly addresses the horrors of the Great Hunger, it also throws up a barrier between the traumatic events and the scope of narrative "experientiality." They take place in a world that is distinct and distant from the American West, where Henry Daly, the subject of focalization, and his family reside. This frontier is "dotted with thriving settlements, growing cities, and cultivated fields" and provides opportunities for "freedom" and social advancement.[82] The painful Famine past is thus placed at a safe divide from the image of transatlantic success that the novel promotes.

The fact that *The Dalys of Dalystown* suggests such a distance between Famine-afflicted Ireland and Irish immigrant existence is not surprising in view of the altering condition of Irish Americans from the mid-1860s onward. During the American Civil War (1861–65), there was vehement opposition to conscription among many Irish from the Famine generation, who engaged in racial violence against African Americans as the socially outcast group with which they were often identified.[83] For instance, during the Draft Riots in New York City in 1863, Irish mobs assaulted blacks and set fire to the Colored Orphan Asylum.[84] However, encouraged by, among others, Archbishop John Hughes, at least 144,221 Irish Catholic newcomers and their descendants enlisted for the Union, forming two Irish American regiments of their own, namely, the Irish Volunteers and the "Fighting 69th," initially led by Colonel Michael Corcoran and later incorporated into Thomas Meagher's Irish Brigade. The heavy losses suffered by these regiments worked in favor of the acceptance and assimilation of Irish Americans of the Famine generation.[85]

At the same time, the late 1860s saw a gradual rise in the social position of an increasing number of Irish Americans. Settling in urban areas in the Northeast and Midwest, most Irish immigrants of the Famine generation had been restricted to unskilled manual work, because they had received little to no education, were often illiterate, and were trained only in peasant labor.[86] As a result, very few experienced occupational mobility. The children of these immigrants, however, often enjoyed better educational opportunities and formed the onset to the eventual emergence of a Catholic Irish American middle class at the end of the century.[87] Additionally, a growing percentage of (post-)Famine immigrants moved away from metropolitan communities to rural settlements along the frontier,[88] which offered them better livelihood opportunities. These developments in the social status of Catholic Irish Americans appear to have affected Dillon O'Brien's 1866 novel, which represents Irish American economic success at the midwestern frontier and, in so doing, displaces the troubling Famine calamities of the past from the major scope of narrative action.

Intriguingly, earlier Irish American fiction, written during an era in which most Irish Famine immigrants had to struggle for survival in urban territories along the East Coast, implies analogies between the wretched living conditions in Famine-afflicted Ireland and the extreme poverty that Irish immigrants were struggling with in urban territories in Canada and along America's East Coast.[89] Representations of the crowded city slums in which newly arrived Irish Famine immigrants settled, such as New York's Five Points—the "focus of New York's misery, squalor and crime," marked by overpopulated, "rickety rotten wooden buildings," according to an 1868 story in *Harper's New Monthly*—are notorious and resonate in Irish North American novels of the 1850s and 1860s.[90] In fact, these texts imply a transposition of Famine memory onto the American urban environment, for tropes of hunger associated with Famine-stricken Ireland are applied to represent the conditions of the Irish immigrants, creating the impression that migration hardly ever leads to an improvement of circumstances.

This phenomenon can, for instance, be witnessed in Mary Anne Sadlier's novel *The Blakes and Flanagans* (1855), which describes how the Dillon family, after a fatal turn in their prosperity, perishes from hunger, while John, the father, succumbs to fever. The image of the old man's "emaciated face" and "thin, wasted hand" is strongly reminiscent of the depictions of Famine victims and implicitly voices a critique of the harsh fate that the Irish sometimes met in the materialistic American city climates. In another novel by Mrs. Sadlier, *Con O'Regan; or, Emigrant Life in the New World* (1864), Famine imagery of hunger is evoked to draw a contrast between the luxuries available in American society and the dire circumstances of many Irish immigrants. While—to the astonishment of newcomer Con—"a magnificent display of meat" is available on the American market, immigrants like his sister Winnie, who settled in Boston, have suffered extreme poverty. The introduction of Winnie as a pale, thin girl, "scantly clothed . . . and rather woe-begone," who "had seen better days," is cast in terms that are also used to portray the physical decay of the Famine afflicted. For example, in Charles Joseph Kickham's *Sally Cavanagh*, one can read: "Mammy, said one of Connor Shea's curly-headed urchins—ah! But where are the rosy cheeks now?—mammy, won't we have anything to eat any more?"[91]

This transference of mnemonic tropes of starvation to criticize the living conditions of Irish immigrants is by no means restricted to Irish American fiction. Miss Mason's *Kate Gearey*, which upon its publication was praised for pointing out the miserable conditions of the poor in the London city slums,[92] conveys the deprivations of the Irish in the Buildings, a district of tenement houses, in words that evoke the recollection of the famishing Irish during the Great Hunger. This characterization is, for instance, the case in the following description of a starving little child, in which the aged, emaciated demeanor of the youngster reminds us of the appearance of Famine victims: "Amidst this tumult was one pale, sickly little thing, the very ghost of a child; whose pallid emaciated countenance bore all the marks of a premature old age, and whose large melancholy eyes seemed eagerly seeking that love and tenderness it had never known. . . . Its little bare feet were bruised and dirty, its thin tattered frock hung loosely on its wasted frame; it was hungry and sick, without spirit even to crave a morsel from its companions."[93]

Food as Screen Memory

In contrast with the earliest North American Famine fiction, which associates transatlantic existence with hunger and deprivation, diaspora fiction from the mid-1860s up to 1870 juxtaposes a Famine-stricken Ireland with a New World marked by abundance of food.

This juxtaposition is, for instance, present in *The Dalys of Dalystown*. Ireland is portrayed in terms of galvanized "skeletons" that are fed "stone soup" in Soyer's soup kitchen; by contrast, on their little farm in Michigan, Henry, wife Rose, and sister Emily get "milk" from their cows and food from their land. Upon arrival in Canada's backwoods, where only on sparse clearings "some solitary settler had built his log-hut," the eponymous hero of *Tim Doolan* and his family are supplied with a "substantial Canadian breakfast" consisting of "rashers, and eggs, and beefsteaks, and molasses, and stewed apples, and pumpkin pies, and whitefish, and what not." This new home for Tim and his loved ones is one where great quantities of "potatoes dressed both ways, both roasted and boiled," can be had for dinner, together with large plates of "sausages, and venison, and roast goose, with buckwheat cakes," and this abundance forms a stark contrast with the Famine-stricken Ireland to which Noonan's tale alludes.[94]

Food imagery also plays a crucial role in Famine fiction written in Ireland as a strategy to dislocate the painful memories of mass starvation. Elaborating upon the Freudian concept of the screen, Stephan Feuchtwang has pointed to the function of specific myths, stories, and representations as "screens for . . . senses of loss." Likewise, Michael Rothberg has drawn attention to the role played by particular images that help displace "a more disturbing or painful memory . . . from consciousness."[95] In some works of Famine fiction, the harrowing recollections of starvation appear to be pushed to the background by enumerations of food articles and long descriptions of lavish dinners. *In re Garland: A Tale of a Transition Time* (1870), a novel by siblings Julia and Edmund O'Ryan, features the wedding banquet of the adoptive daughter of a tenant, Mary Kennedy, who has married John Meany, a local farmer.[96] During the festive meal, which provides ample "eggs . . . ham . . . and roast turkey" to all guests, Father Delany briefly refers to the "bad times" that will "pass away"—a remark that applies to the current potato blight, which, as the ensuing discussion reveals, has also affected Mary's family, whose crops are "gone intirely." Apart from this discussion, the Famine times in which the novel is set are never mentioned in the narrative, and the abundance of victuals that are handed down the table diverts the attention away from the "awful sight" of the pestilence-stricken fields that forebode deprivation.[97]

References to food also diegetically displace the agonizing memories of starvation in Mrs. Hoare's story "Little Mary" (1851). Sally, the autodiegetic narrator, relates the loss of her father, stepmother, and four-year-old stepsister, Mary, in the first year of the Famine. While the narrative exposes the ways in which individual families were afflicted by hunger and fever, it forestalls an elaboration upon the horrifying details of Famine mortality. Young Mary does not die because she has no food at her disposal. Rather, after her mother's death, Mary refuses to eat any of the loaves and cakes that she is offered by the compassionate ladies of the house: "It was almost impossible to get her to taste a morsel; indeed, the only thing she would let inside her lips was a bit of a little white bun, like those her poor mother used to bring her."[98]

Intriguingly, both "Little Mary" and *In re Garland* are narratives that express sympathy for the upper classes as a group that also has to bear suffering. "Little Mary" describes how the lady of the estate loses her child and has to cope with grief in ways similar to the peasant class, which is badly afflicted by deaths of loved ones. *In re Garland* portrays the decline of the once prosperous but prodigal Squire Richard Garland, who finds himself in such heavy debts in the aftermath of the Famine that his house and furniture are confiscated. His demise also marks the disintegration of social bonds. Connor Kennedy dies, and when Mary has taken in the squire, who is her biological father, the ties with her adoptive relatives and former acquaintances are broken: the emotional distance that emerges between Mary, with her genteel blood, and her adoptive mother, Johanna Kennedy, who takes in a widowed sister and her son, makes Mary feel "an interloper . . . a stranger in the house that she was reared in."[99] Thus, the novel appears to lament the "transition time" during which the downfall of the Ascendancy subverts social hierarchies and disrupts social cohesion. The liminal presence of the Famine in "Little Mary" and *In re*

Garland therefore seems to be related to the anxieties that these texts reveal about the position of the landed classes and their subsequent social degeneration during and after the Famine.

Conclusion

In the poem *Desolation: A Story of the Irish Famine* (1869), a forlorn immigrant who has settled in Missouri laments the "barriers" that have arisen between himself and "all that once was home."[100] A close investigation of literary memories of the Great Hunger reveals that one cannot speak of mnemonic boundaries between the homeland and diasporic Irish communities. As the excruciating recollections of hunger found their way into Irish British, Irish American, and Irish Canadian literary traditions, a liminal cultural memory emerged, because it transcended national borders. Moreover, the similarities between the modes in which painful Famine memories are negotiated in homeland and Irish diaspora fiction—through diegetic and temporal displacement and food imagery—suggest that the strategies that were used to cope with culturally shared calamities are transnational. These techniques, which move the acutest features of the Great Famine away from narrative consciousness and thereby create liminal Famine memories, generate narrative traces that enable recuperations of the bleak past.

Various particular dynamics in the displacement of spectacles of starvation in Irish diaspora fiction can be attributed to the status of Irish immigrants in their new homelands. As Jeffrey Alexander has clarified, a cultural trauma not only leaves "indelible marks" upon the "group consciousness" of subjects, but also leads to the creation of "a compelling trauma narrative" that is founded on juxtaposition. Irish diaspora fiction sometimes responds to the double traumatization of Famine and exile by pitting a beloved motherland against an antagonistic New World where the immigrants live in squalor and poverty. In order to uphold an idyllic image of the country of origin, the horrors of Famine have to be toned down, while, especially in early diaspora fiction set in urban climates, mnemonic tropes relating to the cultural legacy of the Great Hunger are transposed to North American environments. However, as Stuart Hall underlines, "cultural identity . . . is a matter of 'becoming' as well as of 'being,'" and, as we have seen, the changing social status of the migrant community also manifests itself as shifts in the cultural memories of the former homeland.[101] Diaspora fiction of later decades mirrors the early stages of assimilation of the Irish: Canada and America are depicted as homes offering abundant food for present and future generations.

2 | Spectacles of Starvation

Rowan Gillespie's two well-known Famine monuments—*Famine* (1997, fig. 2) on the Custom House Quay in Dublin and *Migrants*, which was unveiled by President Mary McAleese in Toronto's Ireland Park in 2007—consist of bronze sculptures of emaciated human beings. As walking skeletons, these life-size figures evoke the Famine past by painfully engaging the viewer with the effects of starvation. Such confronting representations of Famine victims were by no means unfamiliar to Victorian audiences, either. The series of sketches about the conditions in the West of Ireland that James Mahoney made for the *Illustrated London News* in 1847 contains unsettling images of undernourished human beings. Likewise, *Bridget O'Donnell and Children* (fig. 3), published in the issue of December 22, 1849, exposes the gauntness of the mother and her infants, whose lank bodies, which are barely covered by clothes, appear mere bags of bones.

Descriptions of the famished body that convey all its harrowing physical details are notably absent from Irish North American Famine fiction written between 1847 and 1870. In Mary Anne Sadlier's *New Lights; or, Life in Galway* (1853), for instance, the fact that Honora O'Daly is seriously weakened by hunger and fever is not expressed through an elaborate description of a famine-afflicted body. Rather, the narrative suggests that she succumbs to starvation by descriptions of her "faint" voice and her inability to walk if her daughter Bridget does not prop her up. The narrative voice intimates that Honora looks like a ghost, because she is approaching death: the otherwise cold-hearted landlord Ousely is "startled . . . by the sight of a countenance pale as death, eyes sunken and hollow, and lips colorless as those of a

2. Rowan Gillespie, *Famine* (1997), Custom House Quay, Dublin. Author's private collection.

corpse." This description is as detailed as the narrative gets, for the other effects of famine on her body are not touched upon. Even the scene that describes Honora's passing away merely mentions her "cold clammy hands" and "dim and glassy" eyes as signs of impending death. Similarly, in Alice Nolan's *The Byrnes of Glengoulah* (1868), the evicted Norah Cormac, who enters Lord Biggs's house during a family gathering, is described as "unearthly looking" and as having a "slight, girlish form."[1] She looks spectral and otherworldly, rather than emaciated.

By contrast, several works of fiction written in Ireland and England do not shun an explicit and detailed narrative display of the haggard bodies of famine victims, and it is on these texts that this chapter focuses. The thin frames of Famine victims are pictured as emblems of liminality in that they situate the subject of focalization at

3. *Bridget O'Donnell and Children*, *Illustrated London News*, December 22, 1849. Engraving. Courtesy of Ireland's Great Hunger Museum, Quinnipiac University, Hamden, CT.

the borders of normalcy and acceptability. In their explicit exposition of starvation, these narratives exemplify the necessity of revisiting the common identification of the Great Famine with unrepresentable trauma. Rather, these novels and short stories, on the one hand, situate the spectacle of the violated body at the center of narrative consciousness and remove its painfulness, on the other.[2] The unbearable Famine legacy of dehumanization and loss is translated into narrative detachment rather than silence. As this chapter will reveal, early Famine fiction written in Ireland employs three recurring approaches in its attempts to reconcile an exposure of the realities of starvation with a displacement of these acute memories. These strategies are bodily fragmentation, narrative fragmentation, and fetishization. As such, in these works of fiction, the starved body is depicted as a liminal entity: simultaneously present and absent, material as well as spectral.

Traditionally, the famished body was represented in the domestic interior setting of the tenant's cabin. The cover illustration is one such example, as is the engraving *Sketch in a House at Fahey's Quay, Ennis: The Widow Connor and Her Dying Child*, published in the *Illustrated London News* of January 5, 1850, which depicts the dark interior of a cabin in which a mother kneels by her child to pray. The child, almost naked and skin and bones, lies prostrate on the earthen floor. The epistolary narrative *Christmas 1846 and the New Year 1847 in Ireland*, written by "A Lady," reports of the writer's visit to the cabin of a local farmer. Inside, she finds a starving mother whose "skin hung frightfully loose on her bones" and who is therefore unable to suckle her child. Similarly, in Lord Dufferin and G. G. Boyle's *Narrative of a Journey from Oxford to Skibbereen, in the Year of the Famine* (1847), spectacles of starvation are mainly set inside the cottages of the poor: the text describes the two authors entering a cabin to witness an emaciated woman who is "crouching . . . over a few peat embers" and "suffering from diarrhoea."[3] In early Famine fiction, the wasted, hungry human body is also often presented in the private setting of the poor man's home. However, as this chapter will demonstrate, we can also speak of an emerging tendency in Famine fiction to situate the famished body in public settings as a way to expose Ireland's socioeconomic conditions: the ghastly frames of the Famine-stricken serve to express criticism of class relations and colonial government.

Representing the Abject: Famished Bodies on Display

Over the past decades, an extensive interdisciplinary tradition of scholarship has theorized the effect created by the spectacle of the human body, especially in its condition of degeneration. As Lisa Blackman observes, "What defines bodies is their capacity to affect and be affected"; it is the sensory contact with another body that evokes emotion, often translated in physical reactions, in the beholder. Disturbing aspects of the human body, such as excrement, blood, puss, and sewage, may produce feelings of nausea and horror in the spectator, eliciting what Julia Kristeva has called "abjection." Abjection is the desire to cast away specimens of bodily decay that remind one of the inevitability and uncanny nearness of death, because they place the beholder "at the border" of his or her "condition as a living being" and because they represent what is liminal, what is "beyond the scope of the possible, the tolerable, the thinkable." The representations of emaciated bodies of the famishing Irish and the corpses of recent victims of starvation in early Famine fiction can be viewed in light of Kristeva's perceptions of the "abject." As embodiments of approaching death that transcend the boundaries of what is seen as socially acceptable, the Famine victims in these narratives evoke a sense of "uncanniness." They are both recognizable and alien as human beings, simultaneously involving the spectator in processes of identification and repudiation.[4] As such, these starving or starved bodies often evoke strong repulsion in the narrative subjects of focalization, who seek to distance themselves physically and mentally from the liminal scenes of decay that they witness.

Such a sense of repulsion features, for example, in the case in Anthony Trollope's Famine novel *Castle Richmond* (1860). When the novel's hero, the disinherited aristocrat Herbert Fitzgerald, visits the cabin of one of the local tenantry, he is "stricken with horror" by the sight of the "dying woman and the naked corpse of the poor dead child" inside. The bodies of the unfortunate mother and her starved infant are at once recognizably human and estranging: Herbert at first hardly thinks "that the object before him was a human being" in her abject state of destitution and disarray, with a body hardly "clothed, though she was involved in a mass of rags which covered her nakedness." While the suffering woman embodies an unacceptable lack of dignity and civilization from both a class and a gender perspective, her deceased child seems a mere "wretched object." Nevertheless, Herbert can identify the lifeless infant as a fellow man, a sensation that instigates him to cover up its naked limbs with his handkerchief: "Nor was it possible that he should leave the body of the child in that horribly ghastly state. So he took from his pocket his silk handkerchief, and, returning to the corner of the cabin, spread it as a covering over the corpse." This act of restoring some dignity to the little corpse is marked by a sense of abjection, for Herbert—confronted with the limits of humanity by the dead body "covered with dirt and sores"—struggles to overcome his "disgust" at having to "touch the small naked dwindled remains of humanity from which life had fled."[5]

Similar associations of the starved body with the abject can be found in *The Widow O'Leary* (1847) and in Susanna Meredith's "Ellen Harrington" (1865). *The Widow O'Leary* is presented as a series of letters written by an Irishman who returns to his native land to his friend Edward in England. As such, the letters suggest a readership outside Ireland that is not familiar with the conditions of the famishing in Ireland and has to be provided with "a true description of the misery which has been caused" there "by the famine." The first-person narrator visits the home of his former acquaintances Jack and Mary O'Leary and is shocked to witness the "appearance of extreme poverty, disorder, and misery" that their house has attained since the outbreak of the blight. Entering the dark cabin, the narrator can at first not "distinguish" what kind of "object" lies upon the bedstead but, once accustomed to the darkness, perceives it to be "a man, wasted to the greatest degree of emaciation, lying on a litter of straw, and covered only by a dirty ragged quilt." The dehumanized form is hardly recognizable as the narrator's former friend, and the passage that follows displays the narrator's inner struggle between paying his respects to Jack O'Leary, on the one hand, and the revulsion and estrangement he experiences in relation to the skeletal corpse, on the other. The narrator takes the "lifeless hand" in his own and sheds "a few tears upon" it, but the sensation of the "cold and clammy" body is unbearable, and he quickly leaves the room: "I hastened into the kitchen, beckoning Mary to follow me." The famished body is a liminal form in that it evokes both pity and abhorrence, both feelings of identification and desires for dissociation. Furthermore, the famished corpse represents abjection in that the narrator physically and emotionally has to discard his connection with it in order to preserve his mental equilibrium: "This accumulation of death and misery was too much for me."[6]

"Ellen Harrington" (1865) likewise includes a scene that represents the Famine body as abject. The English captain Hartley joins his acquaintance the local physician Neligan to "one of the best looking cabins," which is, however, inhabited by "a man lying on his back, almost naked, and evidently dying; a woman . . . sitting upright near him, rigid in despair; two children . . . dead at her side, and one, in the delirium of fever, . . . tossing and moaning on her lap." The horrendous sight drives Hartley "into the open air," a response that implies a distancing from the spectacle of uncanny human degradation.[7] In *Castle Richmond*, *The Widow O'Leary*, and "Ellen Harrington," these moments of "abjection" affect the narrative "experientiality" of the texts, because, in all the cases, they are experienced by the main subjects of focalization. These characters are torn between empathy with the Famine victims and revulsion for them, between the desire to inspect them more closely and the strong urge to physically and emotionally remove themselves from the spectacle of starvation. As a result, these narratives simultaneously confront the famished body and place its acutest unbearable aspects at a distance from narrative consciousness.

This abjection that the famished body represents in early Famine fiction often connotes critique upon circumstances in Ireland, both in the past and in the present. *The Widow O'Leary*, one of the few works of Famine fiction that is written from an anti-Catholic, providential perspective,[8] presents the Famine as the "curse" of the "Almighty" on Ireland owing to its "sins . . . and iniquities." These sins, according to the first-person narrator, consist of the corruption of the priesthood, who will not offer help to the starving congregation, who will only "anoint" the dying in exchange for "money," who will no longer attend to the villagers now that they "haven't the dhues to give him," and who will deny them access to the Bible.[9] Thus, the text draws implicit connections between the abject state of the starving and what it regards as an abjectness of creed. In other works of Famine fiction, the wasted bodies of the famishing are also described in terms of abjectness as a way to point to social iniquities. Often, the putrefaction and the unendurably foul odor of Famine victims underscore the rottenness of the social system, which is exposed in these narratives.

For example, in Richard Baptist O'Brien's *Ailey Moore: A Tale of the Times* (1856), the "putrid remains" of the starved that were "hardly to be approached when discovered" bear witness to society's negligence of the poor and its failing relief provisions. The starving die "in their houses or hovels unknown to any one," their corpses rotting away, as they are "refused admission to the poor-house" when they collapse at its doorstep.[10] Allen H. Clington's *Frank O'Donnell* (1861) evokes the same image of neglected, "putrid corpses" that lie rotting away in the poor's cabins and send forth an unbearable "stench."[11] Furthermore, in the same passage, the novel describes a throng of "living skeletons . . . with barely the semblance of life . . . poor, emaciated-looking beings, covered with wretched, patched rags, that breathed forth a living miasma." These representations of abject bodies appear to symbolize the rottenness of Ireland's social system to which the extradiegetic narrator repeatedly refers in polemic digressions that mark a generic breach with novelistic discourse. As the narrator states, a "nation's esteem and love are to be gained by equitable and just laws, and not by oppressive ones, that protect the rich and despoil the poor." Although a "rich man's wealth gives him power, so the laws should protect the poor man from every abuse of that power," this situation is "not the case in Ireland." Irish society's abject corruption also extends to the Protestant clergy who, as the narrator observes, fill their pockets with the "immense revenue arising out of church property in Ireland," while the Catholic poor starve.[12]

William Gorman Wills's *The Love That Kills* (1867) remembers the Great Famine by describing a starving, "ravening crowd" over whom hangs the "stifling pauper-stench." There is an interesting analogy between the abject physiques of the evicted farmers and the corruption that, according to the preface by the author, characterizes class relations: "There is something rotten, then, in the whole system, when these clearings advantage the landlord, and convert his tenants into vagrants." During as well as after the Famine, the unstable position of the tenants, which often received no extension of rent despite the improvements they had implemented, was often criticized. For example, W. Neilson Hancock denounces the "folly of the present state of the law respecting tenants' improvements, by which, in the absence of a contract, all improvements, although effected by the tenant, become the property of the landlord instead of being the property of the improver." *The Love That Kills* addresses this concern as well. As the novel argues, the general apathy among tenants to improve their land can also be attributed to laws that make tenure "insecure": "Why should Jack Lynoch improve the land which Tom White may hold by next Ladyday? He may drain the marsh, and build the cow-sheds, but neither the landlord nor Tom White will give him a penny compensation." In the novel itself, there are also several examples of tenant families who are evicted from their cottages, despite the improvements they have made to the land: the widow Carroll and her sons are evicted simply because they "did not pay their rent," despite the "ancestral standing" they have within the tenant community and despite the fact that they have taken well care of the place, having "planted all the roses and jessamines over the cottage herself, just like the cottages in England."[13] As such, the haggard bodies of the starving in Gorman's narrative implicitly appear to convey criticism on a land system that is abject in its demoralizing effects.

Fragmenting the Famine Body

There are several other works of early Famine fiction that, in remembering the Great Famine, explicitly depict starved bodies. In many cases, one of the narrative techniques that is used to alleviate the discomfort and pain that such an emaciated body elicits is physical fragmentation. Here it is essential to refer to Chris Morash's important scholarship on bodily fragmentation in representations of the Famine: in "Famine/Holocaust: Fragmented Bodies," he cites various examples of "decomposition" of bodies in texts that thereby "become an inventory of suffering" that defies narrative coherence. Indeed, in many early Famine writings, the bodies of the starved or starving are not presented as an integrated whole, but rather portrayed through loose images. The narrative concentrates on specific body parts through a snapshot focus on particular physical features that testify to famine and death. Inquests on Famine victims, to establish the cause of death, were quite common: a letter from Robert Bennett Forbes, dated April 20, 1847, refers to an inquest in Kilworth, held over the corpse of one James Carthy, a victim of the Famine. Canon John O'Rourke's *The History of the Great Irish Famine of 1847* (1874) provides an example of a man "found dead on the side of the road one day and a coroner's inquest was held upon his remains in the historic graveyard in Abbeystrowry."[14]

Such a coroner's inquest over the body of a Famine victim is represented in Henry Monahan's novel *O'Ruark; or, Chronicles of the Balliquin Family* (1852). The unfortunate man's body is described pars pro toto. The narrative dissection of the body that parallels its analytical examination by the twelve jurors not only reveals its vulnerability, but also emphasizes specific features: "The shrivelled hands; the sharp-pointed face with the yellow skin tightly drawn over it; the fleshless, worn body; these, indeed, placed beyond all doubt what the poor wretch had died of." In a similar vein, the above-cited description of a throng of famishing peasants who "jostle and cry for food" in Wills's *The Love That Kills* is marked by fragmentation. The effects of starvation upon these human beings are rendered in an impressionist narrative style that singles out their "livid faces," "caverned" eyes, and "fleshless arms" as separate body parts. The dying pauper in their midst is, moreover, merely portrayed through the "slime of death" that settles on his bald head, "its purple around his eyes, its dull ochre hue on his cheek."[15]

As Page Dubois argues, a sense of a disintegrated past, which cannot be incorporated into cultural memories, often finds expression in images of fragmented bodies. Although this approach is certainly valid and enriching, I would like to propose an additional way of reading bodily fragmentation in these early Famine narratives that is more in line with Chris Morash's perception, as a way of coping with the sheer magnitude of the Famine and its dire effects. Scholars such as Philip Shaw and Ross Abbinnett characterize the sublime as "sheer unrepresentability," because it consists of events that cannot be included "in any established doctrine of categories," and therefore lie "beyond thought and language." The Great Famine, which caused major social upheaval at different levels and tore the "entire fabric of the country . . . to pieces," as Emily Lawless wrote retrospectively in 1885, was often represented as a sublime experience.[16] Early samples of Famine writing frequently conjure up sublimity in the form of inconceivable and incomprehensible experience, but also in Burkean terms of the boundless and terrifying in their depiction of famine suffering and mortality.[17] The personification of the Famine as a dreadful, potent monster features quite prominently in texts written during and after the Famine years. For example, in R. A. Shafto Adair's *The Winter of 1846–7 in Antrim* (1847), the Famine is depicted as an omnipotent being whose "iron hand . . . grasped its victims yet more closely." A similar personification of the Great Famine as a sublime, destructive force can, moreover, be found in *O'Ruark*, which describes the Famine as walking "with giant tread over the land," crushing all people "with his iron hoof."[18]

The sense of the Famine as a sublime, uncontrollable calamity that goes beyond representation and imagination may account for the fact that the bodies of victims of starvation are presented not as an integrated whole but rather through loose images. This impression is confirmed when one analyzes the description of the crowd gathering at a soup kitchen in *O'Ruark*. The wretched creatures whose bodies are represented through loose images of their "tottering frames," "bleared eyes, and pinched, and pointed features" are called the personification of "starvation in all its shapes . . . from the child, worn and bent like an old man, to the old man, in his childlike feebleness." The passage focuses on the most vulnerable groups of society, the young and the aged, but suggests that all intermediate generations are equally affected by the Famine. This scene suggests such a grand scale of human deprivation that its catastrophe can be grasped only in fragmentation. At the same time, in the earlier-mentioned scene at the inquest, the fragmentary emphasis on specific physical traits of the Famine victim throws into relief its uncanny state as a corpse that is hardly identifiable as human at all: "The body was exposed to view; though, at first glance it could scarcely be recognized as such; it looked merely like a heap of rags and old bones."[19]

Physical bodies often represent the larger body politics of human collectiveness, and imagined communities, such as states.[20] Inspired by Foucauldian notions of the disciplined body, Margaret Owens, among others, has drawn attention to the ways in which fragmented bodies bespeak awareness of the control exerted over human subjects by authorities. In *O'Ruark* this fragmentary inventory of the deceased's body expresses the powerless status of the famishing Irish peasantry, and it forms the impetus to an explicitly voiced critique on social structures that fail to prevent such human degradation. After narratively displaying various bodily parts of the corpse, the narrator exclaims, "There it lay a ghastly but wordless witness, in its very silence appealing to God from man. Could it be that in a christian country such a thing was suffered to occur?"[21] Speaking for the subaltern,[22] silenced Famine victim, the narrative voice here intervenes to critique imperial Ireland's indifference to the fate of the peasant population, a critique that also resonates in the hard-heartedness of the jurors who are charged with the investigation of the cause of death. There is a grotesque disparity between the hedonism of the officials and the depravity that caused the man's death. While the corpse constitutes an "awful" sight "before them," the jurors, "annoyed at having been taken away from their business at the fair," order "spirits and water," which they "all seemed to drink . . . with as much pleasure as if a corpse did not lie on the table before them."[23] Thus, the poor man's body is treated as liminal, that is, marginal, by the higher classes.

Images of bodily fragmentation also function as a tool to expose the self-centeredness of the upper classes in William Carleton's *The Squanders of Castle Squander* (1852). It occurs in a scene set in a cemetery where the body of a famished peasant is taken. Far from assuaging the painfulness of starvation and mass mortality, the graveyard that is scattered with remains of recently interred Famine victims foregrounds their dehumanization: the man, who is "thrown, coffinless and half-naked, into what was rather a shallow trench, than a grave," is an image of both barbarity and uncomfortable familiarity, for his distorted face constitutes "one horrific remnant of humanity." His fate is certainly to be akin to that of individuals who were previously buried coffinless and whose corpses have been torn apart by ravenous dogs: "Here and there an arm; in another place a head (half-eaten by some famished mongrel, who had been frightened from his prey), or a leg, dragged partially from the earth, and half-mangled, might be seen." While the monstrosity of half-devoured bodies is exposed in detail, the landowning Squander family proves to be less affected by the scene, for, as the narrator implies, "all that we have attempted to describe was taken in by a glance or two of those who were in the carriage, as they passed through this terrific Golgotha into the church."[24]

As the Squanders are simply driving past the exhibited bodily remains, they appear to treat the corpses of the Famine victims with abjection in the form of indifference, and their Christian worship does not open their eyes to the human suffering that, as the reference to Golgotha implies, is not unlike that of Christ. Through this behavior, the Squanders exemplify the "subject/abject subjugations and privileges" that mark colonial hierarchies in general, but also specifically nineteenth-century Anglo-Irish relations. Cast in the role of the uncivilized Other, the rural native Irish population was often associated with physical barbarity that needed to be either reformed according to English models or discarded. For example, Thomas Carlyle's *Reminiscences of My Irish Journey in 1849* (1882) describes the hunger-stricken Irish in the western regions as a "dingy semi-savage population" that is "rough and fierce faced" and that forms a "savage poor republic."[25] In a critical sense, Carleton's novel implies that this imperial ideology of abjectness results in neglect and carelessness of the gentry toward the suffering agricultural classes.

Narrative Fragmentation, Emotional Dissociation

Chris Morash has pointed to the fragmented narrative structure and syntax that frame literary representations of the Great Hunger, arguing that starvation is often portrayed in the form of "dislocated, isolated emblems of suffering."[26] As we have seen, the bodily fragmentation that often marks representations of emaciated bodies in early Famine fiction is accompanied by diegetic fragmentation: the plot-driven narrative flow is interrupted by digressions on human suffering, as epitomized by the abject, starved body, and the ways in which the narrative zooms in on specific physical features effect a faltering style of description. As the following will demonstrate, narrative fragmentation also occurs on another level in these texts: on a diegetic level, the background story of the Famine victim is disconnected from the display of his or her wasted body, which in turn brings about an emotional dissociation from the spectacle of famine.

For example, the previously discussed scene in *O'Ruark*, which exposes the corpse of a starved man to the jurors, is marked by distinct boundaries between the description of his emaciated features and the personal narrative of the hapless man who has succumbed to starvation. The exhibition of the abject bodily decay of the dead man is characterized by an objectification of the victim, who is described as "only a poor crathur that died of starvation, they're goin' to hould a inquest on," whose fate and identity are left unmentioned. It is only later on in the narrative, when the details of the corpse are no longer the focus of the narrative, that the victim is revealed by one of its neighbors to be Owen Moloney and that readers learn about the cause of his death:

"Owen Moloney was a tinant of Misther Elmore's; but when the times got bad, he was turnd out, an ent up a little shed upon the hills. There the starvation an' sickness came on him, an' one by one, his wife and childre died. But, when the last son went, the father's heart gave way intirely, as well it might, for a betther boy never lived."[27]

The elaborate but rather clinical description of the Famine corpse and the tale of individual sorrow are presented at different moments in the narrative. This emotional dissociation, as I would like to call it, places a barrier between the disturbing physical reality of the famished body that seems inhuman and the personalized history of a stricken man that one can relate to. It is in line with the deindividuation of Famine victims that we see in many works of Famine fiction, as the previously cited scenes from William Gorman Wills's *The Love That Kills* and Richard Baptist O'Brien's *Ailey Moore* (1856) also illustrate. While all these texts thus draw attention to the grand scale on which the Famine affected people, their depersonalization of Famine victims also reduces the harrowing effect of bodily decline that they represent.

O'Ruark contains an additional scene in which the personal background of a Famine-stricken man is narrated at a later stage than the lengthy description that is given of his emaciated form and his son's gruesome death of hunger: "Starvation, unmitigated starvation, had bidden the bones to peer fleshless through the frame."[28] It is only several pages after this description that Father Shaughnessy relates the circumstances of the man that had brought him and his family down and appear to refer to the infamous Gregory Clause (1847) that prohibited relief from poor rates to any person who occupied more than a quarter acre of land.[29] As Shaughnessy states, "That man is a tenant of Mr Elmore's; he had a little holding, and when he would not resign it, his name was struck off the relief list." Here, however, the narrative interruption between bodily images of starvation and the personal story of the bereaved father creates a sense of emotional dissociation that has a different function than in the previous scene from *O'Ruark*. In fact, this instance of dissociation underlines the indifference of society toward Famine victims. This point mainly becomes clear from the responses to the suffering father and his recently deceased son: just like the jurors who handle the corpse of Owen Moloney, in this scene the evangelical ladies who visit the cottage with a bundle of tracts are generally untouched by the spectacle of human deprivation. When upon departure one of them, Miss Mulvanny, discovers that she has left her shawl in the hut, having given it to cover the ailing young boy, her companion Miss Stroud remarks, "I really think it would be wiser for you to go back for it for you may rest assured these people will never think of returning it."[30]

This cold, calculating attitude—emphasized by the narrator's remark that she is "a lady of a rather strong constitution, from which a tear could only be extracted like a spark of fire from a piece of flint"—may at first seem to contrast with Father Shaughnessy's revelation that "it's enough to make one's heart bleed to look on such wretchedness." The priest's subsequent observation that he can no longer bear caring for the famishing could be interpreted as a sign of his insupportable mental anguish, but, alternatively, it also suggests that he shirks the responsibility of looking after his starving parishioners. He exclaims that he is getting "too old; it would kill me to be looking on the misery which I cannot relieve" and that therefore "the curate ought to do all this work; . . . I won't, any more, attend such terrible sick calls." Moreover, the women's and the eminent father's attitudes contrast very sharply with the emotion that the extradiegetic narrator seeks to invoke in readers, urging them to view the dead body of the child as an emblem of human potential and feeling: "Who could tell what warm affections, what dreams of future joy, were centred in that frail thing of clay? Who could tell what hopes were passing away with the fast departing spirit?"[31] In this passage, emotional dissociation is undermined by an appeal to emotions and to an identification with the horrendous manifestation of human destitution.

This appeal to emotions on the part of the narrator, which contrasts so sharply with the emotional distance of the women and priest, appears to criticize the overall indifference on the part of the more well-to-do classes with the plight of the starving classes. Thus, the chapter from *O'Ruark* seems to politicize the famished body, making it a vehicle for a social criticism on the ways in which various levels of society fail to deal with the hunger crisis and its dire consequences. This politicization of the Famine body is also illustrated by the social spheres in which the starved body is represented. Generally, victims of Famine were often represented in the enclosed space of dark, gloomy cabins, as the previously discussed scenes from *The Widow O'Leary*, *Castle Richmond*, and "Ellen Harrington" make clear. By contrast, the scene that describes the coroner's inquest on the corpse of Owen Moloney in *O'Ruark* stages the starving body in a public setting, as a way to expose society's indifference to the poor during the Famine years. The fact that the jurors, instead of being bothered by the starvation of the man itself, squabble over the removal of the body from its original location suggests that society is not concerned with the socioeconomic conditions that result in mass deaths in the first place. In another scene in the novel, bodies of starving peasants crowd at a soup kitchen, presenting a disturbing spectacle of "breathing corpses, on their way to the grave," that constitutes an implicit comment on the inadequacy of relief operations that offer food of insufficient quantity and quality to the needy.[32]

In a similar vein, William Carleton's *The Squanders of Castle Squander* reconfigures the condition of the Famine victims as an issue of public concern, by showing how a multitude of famished men and women openly beg for relief on the streets, stretching out their arms "to receive a pittance of meal" and howling for more food. The plaintive, communal wail of the starved villagers suggests a theatrical spectacle, not only because the extradiegetic narrator enjoins that we should "look at them, this sample of Irish population—a throng of livid faces," but also because the jostling, ravening crowd of living skeletons, in begging for food, is said to raise their voices "in shrill, famine chorus."[33] The reference to their "famine chorus" arguably refers to the plaintive screams of the starving crowd that accompanies the clattering of their tins and may be read as an allusion to the communal act of keening, thereby expressing mourning for the many victims of starvation.[34]

As the keen was perceived as a peculiar ethnographic trace of Irishness, David Lloyd explains, the wail of the gaunt crowd suggests a subaltern voice that speaks back defiantly to the authorities that turn a blind eye to the situation of the indigenous population, by treating the villagers as liminal beings. Squire Squander forgets that "property had its duties as well as its rights," and his sons, Harry and Dick, display a "buoyant spirit" at the expense of their starving dependents. Through their clamor, the famishing tenants appear to critique the land and relief policies of their superiors. The extradiegetic narrator, in one of his many moments of narrative intrusion, voices similar critique on the landed classes: "Here, then, the landlords, upon their own showing, are convicted of such gross neglect of duty as gradually occasioned the confusion into which they allowed their property to fall. That is the negative charge, and 'guilty, my lord,' is the verdict."[35] The symbolical significance of the starving mob as an expression of social critique is emphasized by the term "famine chorus," which additionally evokes the dramatic convention of the chorus in tragedy: a group of speakers who, among others, can signify the community, both on- and offstage, and who can express a moral direction in response to the unfolding events.[36]

The Fetishization of Hair and the Negotiation of the Famine Past

Fetishism, the veneration of particular objects, operates as a mechanism to compensate for anxiety and distress.[37] Early Famine fiction often diverts the narrative consciousness away from the display of the emaciated body by a fascination with the beauties of the victims' hair. In a great number of Famine narratives, the descriptions of the starving focus on their locks and curls that often constitute a significant contrast with their decaying bodies and moreover serve as the single markers of the victims' identities as persons and humans. The fetishization of hair in these narratives serves two purposes: hair becomes a vehicle to address as well as displace the atrocities of famine, functioning as what Daniel Miller in *The Comfort of Things* (2008) would term a strategy through which painful "emotions . . . can be objectified." Furthermore, in these narratives hair can also be interpreted as what

Bill Brown in *A Sense of Things* (2003) calls a material objectification of culture: hair symbolically embodies an Irish national consciousness that faces dramatic upheaval and simultaneously seeks consolation in possibilities for cultural survival and regeneration.[38]

Over the past decades, much research concerned with material cultures directed its attention to the cultural significance of hair, which, according to Anthony Synnott, can be regarded as "our most powerful symbol of individual and group identity" on "a religious, political, economic, social and sexual spectrum." According to Elaine Freedgood, Victorian society was a "thing culture," in that material objects played a significant role in rites and social practices as a way to give meaning to and cope with aspects of life. Head hair served as such an object of fixation through which desires and anxieties could be negotiated. Galia Ofrek in *Representations of Hair in Victorian Literature and Culture* (2009) illustrates the ways in which the Victorian obsession with hair can be read against the background of gender relations. Thus, loose hair became a signifier to distinguish between young maidens and sexually active woman and between fallen and sexually virtuous females. At the same time, hair came to be interpreted as a classifier of social status. The vibrant trade in hair in nineteenth-century Europe, as women of the lower classes sold their hair and women of the elite bought hairpieces, bears witness to the fact that hair played a significant role in the "material figuration of power-relations between classes."[39]

Hair also had a prominent function in Victorian mourning cultures. Hair locks of the deceased were often incorporated into mourning jewelry, thereby serving as "mementoes which commemorated the dead," which, worn by a relative or friend, could evoke recollections of the dead beloved.[40] These mourning jewels suggested both loss and consolation and a spectral, liminal state between both absence and presence. On the one hand, the hair in these mourning jewels, as a last remaining trace of the deceased, reminded the holder of its loss, "referring . . . endlessly" to the decomposition of the corpse and the transience of life.[41] On the other, the hair encapsulated in the jewelry suspends "the separation between the holder of the hair and its dead owner," proving that the loved one has been alive and "still exists somewhere, somehow," in the afterlife.[42] As such, in Victorian commemorations of the dead, hair signified a "protection from and a reminder of the fear of loss," as a symbol of consolation and bereavement.[43]

The central and ambivalent role of hair in nineteenth-century traditions sheds light on the fetishization of hair in early Irish Famine fiction. In the portrayal of the starving, destitute rural population, hair sometimes becomes a marker of gender and class positions. This point becomes clear from the earlier-discussed scene in Anthony Trollope's Famine novel *Castle Richmond* (1860), in which Herbert Fitzgerald visits the cabin of one of the local tenantry and is abhorred to find that the starving woman inside is hardly "clothed, though she was involved in a mass of rags which covered her nakedness." The passage draws attention to the woman's hair: her head "was all uncovered, and her wild black hair was streaming round her face." The famished children standing behind her back "were almost absolutely naked," "wild elfish straggling locks" hanging around their faces.[44] While the wild, loosely hanging hair of the mother, together with her nakedness, places her outside the boundaries of Victorian sexual morality, the untamed locks of herself and her infants also underscore the class barriers between the ill-fated family and the Anglo-Irish genteel spectator, making the destitute family seem otherworldly.

As this example shows, the significance of hair in early Famine fiction indeed appears to be rooted in concerns over gender and class. However, as an object of fascination in the description of Famine victims, hair appears to play an even more crucial role in the mediation of the trauma of mass mortality and the radical upheaval of society caused by the Famine. The fetishization of the hair of Famine victims in many early literary narratives can be interpreted as a response to the sense of rupture and loss that the bleak years of hunger generated. For one thing, in these texts the beauty of hair serves to attenuate the horrible suffering of corporeal starvation and to throw into relief the dehumanization of the Famine victims.

In William Carleton's "Owen M'Carthy; or, The Landlord and Tenant," Owen M'Carthy and his family are reduced to starvation, so that he and his wife have become "gaunt skeletons." Their little daughter Alley has also been transformed by hunger, from a rosy-cheeked, healthy girl into an emblem of destitution: "Your colour's gone, your little hands are wasted away, too," her father says. This painful image of starvation and Alley's imminent end are, however, mitigated by Owen's elaborate praise of his daughter's lovely hair: "Your hair is bright and fair, Alley, and curls so purtily that the finest lady in the land might envy it."[45] The radiance of Alley's curls is remarkable, for one of the effects of acute famine is loss of hair, a symptom that Carleton's tale and many early Famine writings seem to ignore.[46] In fact, this focus on Alley's unrealistically beautiful golden curls displaces the more harrowing image of the girl's decaying body from the consciousness that directs the reader's "perception" of the narrated.[47] While Alley's death is fast approaching, her unchanged hair creates the illusion of permanence, suggesting a lasting presence in the face of imminent mortality. Furthermore, the light color of Alley's hair appears to foreshadow her afterlife in heaven as one of God's angels and thereby an existence beyond the grave, even if the story ends on a very dramatic note when Owen returns to find that Alley is dead and buried.

In a similar fashion, *A Tale of the Famine of 1846 and 1847* by "Ireland" pushes previously evoked harrowing images of mortality to the margins of the textual consciousness by the introduction of a young female character, Mona O'Callan, whose golden locks make her seem a "fair angel-like child." While the narrative had earlier touched upon the horrors of the "half mutilated forms" of little famished infants, "lying in frightful fragments, dragged by ferocious dogs from beneath the earth where they had been so recently and so hastily buried," Mona's angelic appearance, as symbolized by her hair, offers relief from the bleak images of death that have been evoked earlier on. Mona herself is weighed down by famine, and her imminent demise signifies the end of an ancient Irish lineage, thereby exemplifying how the Famine ended many native Irish families. Nevertheless, she brings comfort to the bereaved mother Honour M'Carthy, who clasps the "lifeless forms" of her own children "to her heart." It is her golden hair that makes Mona seem this consoling "angel already," ready to "blossom for ever in heaven."[48] The story's recurring focus on Mona's light, angelic hair dispels the confronting images of mortality and imbues the narrative with the promise of an eternal afterlife.[49]

In *The Love That Kills*, the looming, disturbing sense of death that the emaciated body elicits is likewise chased away by a fetishization of hair. The main protagonist, William Clayton, who works as a land agent, finds a girl who dies of starvation by the roadside and decides to carry her to a public house to get her food and thus save her life. The passage that describes Clayton's effort to bring relief to the girl identifies her weak body with the abject: because of her "figure of cork" with limbs that "hung over his arms . . . like sticks," Clayton hardly conceives of the body as "a human frame," and "he sickened to feel how light" she is. This unsettling blend of the alien and familiar that the girl's body represents is attenuated toward the end when Clayton "asked for a pair of scissors, and cut off the white flaxen tresses from the deceased child . . . folding them carefully" and placing them "in his breast."[50] As a token that will always remind Clayton of the deceased girl, the locks suggest a lasting identity beyond the grave.

Various works of Famine fiction written after 1870 show a similar focus on hair as one of the last traces of the humanity and distinct identity of the famishing. Margaret Brew's three-decker *The Chronicles of Castle Cloyne* (1885) contains a vivid recollection of the horrors of famine in the scene that describes how farmer's daughter Oonagh McDermot enters the cabin of her cousin Susie Burke and her family. Confronted with the decaying, haggard body of Susie's deceased husband and the skeletal frames of their starving children, Oonagh is horrified by the "miserable wreck that lay before her" in which she is barely able to recognize her former playmate Susie: "Was this starved-out creature, dying not less surely of famine than of disease on those filthy rags, the soft, fair girl who had been the companion of her youth? Was this wasted woman, prematurely aged, through whose yellow, shrivelled skin the sharp bones were working their way, the beautiful Susie Burke, who, reared in comfort, had never known what pain or sorrow meant, until her wedding day?" The only thing by which Oonagh can still identify her cousin is her "rich golden hair, that even sickness and neglect could not deprive of its silky gloss."[51] Susie's rich tresses are the only features that make her look human rather than a terrifying spectacle, thereby alleviating the pain of degradation that her famished body otherwise evokes.

Hair plays a similar role in two Famine narratives of later date: Rosa Mulholland's story "The Hungry Death" (1891) and Canon Patrick Sheehan's novel *Glenanaar* (1905). In the former, the once beautiful Brigid Lavelle, once known for her luxurious auburn locks, has become utterly disfigured by famine and sorrow. She has become "pallid and worn, the spectre of herself," and when her former beau Coll Prendergast meets her after a long time, he "would scarcely have recognized her in her present death-like guise, had it not been for the still living glory of her hair." Brigid's hair is the only remaining trace of her former loveliness and personality as a strong and proud young woman, now that want has transformed her into a shadow of her former self. In fact, her fiery tresses seem to underscore the "angry despair in her heart," which makes her reach out in charity to help others even less fortunate than herself, through an "unselfishness" by which she makes all her "little worldly goods the common property of the famishing" and which heroically helps her to sacrifice her own chance of survival for that of her love rival, Moya, whom she gives her last scraps of food.[52]

In *Glenanaar* the staggering, "weakened and emaciated form" that blacksmith Redmond Casey discerns outside can be identified as his former betrothed, Nodlag—who had run away from him because she had felt ashamed of her base family background—by only one stray lock of auburn hair that "had freed itself from the hooded shawl." The girl has undergone "a dread change" in appearance owing to the famine she suffered: "Beneath the cheek-bones, her face had sunk in in dreadful hollows, and her neck was thin and withered. There was a blue line across her lips." Looking spectral, by contrast, "her forehead (though her temples were sunken), and the thick masses of auburn hair that crowned it, alone retained their graciousness."[53]

The ways in which these Famine narratives written over a long stretch of time set off these materializations of abject bodily degradation against the fetishization of hair point to a transgenerational strategy to deal with Famine loss, and they also offer interesting anti-imperial connotations. In Malthusian colonial rhetoric, the Great Famine was often depicted as a natural solution to the overpopulation of Ireland and as an onset to bring much-desired modernization to "savage" Ireland. Assistant to the Treasury Charles Trevelyan regarded the Famine as a "remedy" for all "maladies of Ireland," including its density of population, by "the direct stroke of an all-wise Providence." In a similar vein, William Pulteney Allison regarded the blight that affected Ireland and entailed mass starvation and emigration as one of the "positive checks" of nature in areas with a redundancy of population that could not possibly be fed, and Mrs. Maberly commented that Ireland's present problems constitute a solution to its "redundancy of population" and the "total neglect of the proper cultivation of food" that helps to "reduce this monstrous population." The Famine-stricken Irish were thus sometimes cast in terms of the "abject" from a colonizer's perspective.[54] In view of this fact, the humanizing effect of the hair in descriptions of Famine victim may also be interpreted as an implicit response to imperial rhetoric that tended to downplay the humanity of the starving Irish population.

The fascination with hair in these early works of fiction that remember the Great Hunger may also be read from an ethnographic perspective. Long, voluptuous hair has been commonly identified with an authentic, precolonial indigenous Irish culture. As Brendan Kane has argued, in their conflicts with English colonizers during the early modern period, Gaelic tribes would pride themselves on the "the long-hanging fringe of hair, the glib" that was worn as a marker of ethnic identity and was considered to mislead the English opponents in battle who could not see the eyes behind it.[55] A woman's hair in particular played a central role in figurations of Gaelic Irish culture, such as in the Scottish-Irish ballad "The Cruel Sister," where the golden hairs of the girl who is drowned by her envious sibling are turned into a lyre by a harpist.[56] "The Irish Wife" (1855), by Thomas D'Arcy McGee, likens the "golden hair" of his "Irish wife" to a harp, another symbol of Irish identity: "Apollo's harp had once such strings." More famously, Sydney

Owenson's *The Wild Irish Girl* (1806) speaks of the "partiality of the ancient Irish to long hair" that is "still to be traced in their descendants of both sexes, the women in particular," in the form of loose hair flowing "over their shoulders" or worn "fastened up in tresses, with a pin or bodkin." In expressing his admiration for Glorvina, a descendant from an ancient Gaelic family, the narrator, Horatio, displays an obsession with her hair: he appears to be enchanted with "her locks of living gold parting on her brow of snow, yet seeming to separate with reluctance, as they were lightly shaken off with that motion of the head, at once so infantile and graceful; a motion twice put into play, as her recumbent attitude poured the luxuriancy of her tresses over her face and neck, for she was unveiled, and a small gold bodkin was unequal to support the redundancy of that beautiful hair."[57]

In imperial representations, the long, loose hair of the Irish woman was, however, often represented in negative terms, becoming associated with unruliness and lack of civilization.[58] English travel reports such as J. E. Bicheno's *Ireland and Its Economy* (1830) associate the miserable hovels of the western Irish with the uncivilized character of their inhabitants by referring to their "coarse features" and "shaggy hair, looking like the mane of an untamed colt."[59] Moreover, nineteenth-century cartoons in relation to the Irish campaign for home rule would often portray Irish nationalism as a wild young woman with loose hanging hair: *The Order of the Day; or, Unions and Fenians*, published in *Punch* on October 12, 1867, presents a less enlightened parody on the Marianne figure in Eugène Delacroix's famous painting, who is primarily characterized by her long, flowing hair.

However, in cultural expressions from Ireland, and also in William Carleton's Famine novel *The Black Prophet* (1847), the glossy long hair that is invariably identified with Irishness has positive connotations, symbolizing the potential for Ireland's regeneration after the catastrophe of Famine. Early on in the novel, such a reading appears to be problematic, for here head hair is mainly associated with death: when the corpses of a haggard mother and her two skeletal infants are described, the narrative mentions the girl's "light and silken locks blown upon her still and death-like features." However, hair becomes associated with redemption later on in the novel, when the benevolent, beautiful Mave Sullivan, whose "long, abundant hair was beautifully fair," sells her locks to a peddler in order to be able to offer relief to the Daltons, who would otherwise die "wid neglect and starvation": as she says, "for God's sake cut it off, and give me the most you can afford for it. Oh! believe me, it's not on account of the mere value of it, but the money may save lives."[60] As such, the young maiden's hair comes to signify the possibility of regeneration in times of distress.

Head hair has a similar significance in Famine fiction from a later date, so that once again we may speak of a transgenerational mnemonic trope. In Rosa Mulholland's "The Hungry Death," Brigid Lavelle's ever-beautiful red locks symbolize her ardent determination to rescue her countrymen and -women even in the face of famine and sorrow. "Thanks to the timely help," we can read, "Moya lived for better times, and when her health was somewhat restored, she emigrated with Coll to America." Although an existence in a post-Famine Ireland is not imagined here, the promise of future generations through the union of Coll and Moya suggests "New Irelands" in diaspora. In Sheehan's *Glenanaar*, the magical beauty of Nodlag's hair appears to foreshadow her miraculous resuscitation, for shortly after having been taken in by Red Casey and his mother, she is "able to go about again" and "as her strength came back, there came with it a new and more spiritual beauty."[61] Her subsequent marriage to Red, and the birth of their son, Ted, who proves to become very patriotic as he grows up, paves the way for a new post-Famine generation.

Conclusion

In his analysis of narrative effect, Keith Oatley observes that "literature can affect the self and potentially transform identity by suggesting emotions in contexts of understanding" that can be "experienced at different distances."[62] As we have seen, the effect generated by the Famine body in early works of fiction on the Great Hunger indeed implies various levels of experience that range from dissociation to identification and that revolve in the interaction with shifts in narrative focus. At times one can speak of narrative abjection in that the focalizing subject literally removes him- or herself from the display of the decaying, starving body. At other moments, the Famine corpse or emaciated frame is brought closer to the consciousness of the text through the interpolations of a narrator who appeals to empathy and identification.

Thus, the traumatic experience of mass mortality and starvation manifests itself not through silence but rather through layers of affect that are marked by liminality: sometimes they create a sensation of comforting distance and in other contexts demand proximity and engagement. Representing an emblem of uncanniness and liminality, the Famine-stricken body in these texts is also embedded in politicized settings that create an awareness of the implications of socioeconomic institutions and public spheres during the tragedy of the Great Famine. As such, corporeality and the body politics—in their states of abjectness, violation, and fragmentation—are closely intertwined in the cultural remembrance and spatial reconfigurations of Famine atrocities.

The fetishization of hair in these early Famine narratives, moreover, underscores Ron Eyerman's observation that we should not "downplay or ignore the impact of material culture on memory and identity formation," even in discursive representations such as literature. Moreover, embedded in an imperial context that identified head hair, either positively or negatively, with Irishness, references to the locks of the Famine-stricken become tools for anticolonial subtexts that defy the frequent associations of the Irish with savagery and foretell a regeneration of Ireland's people after the severe crisis. As such, the unkempt fastened tresses by which Irish Famine fiction is enthralled illustrate how objects of memory "give shape to the textures of the self."[63]

3 | Beyond Boundaries

Woman Begging at Clonakilty (fig. 4), one of the engravings that Mahoney made for the *Illustrated London News* of February 13, 1847, depicts a devastated peasant woman who is holding her baby up to the viewer—apparently a lifeless infant who has fallen victim to famine and fever, as the accompanying account states. Like many of Mahoney's engravings that picture the harrowing conditions in Ireland, this image is marked by the absence of frames. Composed in the style of the vignette,[1] the boundaries of the image appear to fade out. While this technique effects a focus on the anguished mother, at the same time the boundlessness of the depiction insinuates that the vastness of the calamity cannot be measured. While the begging woman represents one instance of profound misery, the fade-out background creates the impression that an inestimable number of similar cases of deprivation were widespread. As the engraving implies, the extreme hardships take place on a boundless scale that exceeds human comprehension.

The idea that the Great Famine represented a liminal event that went beyond boundaries of conception prevailed in contemporary writings on the severe calamity. Thus, Asenath Nicholson, who traveled from the United States to Famine-stricken Ireland to assist in the provision of relief,[2] argued in 1851 that even from the distance created by the passage of time, the events "appear . . . to myself, more like a dream than reality, because they appear out of *common course* and out of the order of even nature itself."[3] Like Mahoney's engraving, a sermon given by Unitarian minister James Martineau in 1847 points to the boundless scale on which famine and death occurred,

4. James Mahoney, *Woman Begging at Clonakilty*, *Illustrated London News*, February 13, 1847. Engraving. Courtesy of Ireland's Great Hunger Museum, Quinnipiac University, Hamden, CT.

contending that the spectacles witnessed in the open air may provide only a glimpse of the immense degree of privation by which the Irish are afflicted: "If the ghastly look and staggering gait of famine is terrible among the crowds upon the road, you know what must be hidden in the cabins retired from reach."[4] The representation of the Great Famine as a catastrophe that transcends limits of human understanding as well as norms of civilization also features prevalently in early Famine fiction written in Ireland and Britain. Chapter 1 showed that early North American diaspora fiction tends to displace harsh Famine realities from the narrative consciousness in order to uphold the illusion of an idyllic Ireland that can be recuperated after the Famine. In line with this glorification of the motherland, reconfigurations of the Famine in terms of boundlessness are mainly absent from North American novels and stories written between 1846 and 1870.

This chapter will explore the various ways in which early Famine novels and stories reconfigure the Great Famine as an episode that exceeds epistemological and normative frontiers. In so doing, the following discussion will make clear that early Famine fiction, like many other genres in nineteenth-century Irish literature, borrows extensively from Gothic literature. As Jim Shanahan contends, many Irish literary texts, even those works that espouse realist tenets, are infused with Gothic conventions, mainly because Ireland's excruciating past and often turbulent present came to be articulated through Gothic imagery: "The Irish Gothic is not so much concerned about the distant past and imaginary fears, but is better understood as a kind of hyper-realist technique that periodically reveals the truth by laying bare the awful reality behind Irish life and Irish historical experience."[5] As the following makes clear, early Famine fiction takes recourse to Gothic imagery, such as the threshold and obscurity, in its depiction of victims of starvation, as the means to explore abject conditions of depravity.

As this chapter will moreover reveal, these Famine novels and stories identify the bleak years of starvation with crossed boundaries in several other respects. First, these texts give expression to the excess of Famine suffering by employing the register of the sublime. Furthermore, these narratives suggest that the extremities of famine and loss to which the Irish population is exposed provoke behavior that oversteps the norms of civilization. Mentally affected by the inhuman trials of starvation, disease, and death, the people of Ireland are shown to succumb to emotional apathy, insanity, and beastliness. Becoming mere shadows of their former selves, the Famine victims in these works of fiction are often portrayed as living ghosts. The final section of this chapter will discuss the recurring images of spectrality that these texts invoke in order to describe the bodily and psychologically liminal conditions of the starving Irish people and as a representation of a past that persistently haunts the present and future. As will be illustrated, these early Famine novels and stories often reflect upon the nature of traumatic memory itself by allusions to unburied corpses and phantoms that appear to have risen from the dead.

The Sublimity of Starvation

Many who wrote about the Great Famine as the disaster unfolded in Ireland used terms associated with the Burkean sublime to emphasize its powerful impact. For example, the Reverend John Travers Robinson described the woes that befell Ireland by imagining the Famine as a cruel, potent monarch stalking through the land: "Famine gaunt and cruel having taken unto itself other spirits more horrible than itself reigns tremendous over this winter of horrors." Robinson's focus on the powerful, relentless force of "Famine" and his use of terms such as "horrible," "horrors," and "tremendous" come very close to Burke's definition of the sublime. In Burke's view on aesthetics, the sublime encompasses "great objects" that are "vast in their dimensions," but that also trigger experiences of "danger" and "power." The human mind can neither fathom nor understand the sublime: his or her "imagination is . . . lost." When human beings cannot perceive the "bounds of things," "painful" and "terrible" sensations ensue that are rooted in this lack of cognitive control.[6]

A great number of early works of Famine fiction also cast the Great Famine in terms that are reminiscent of Burke's philosophy. In *The Black Prophet*, for example, the devastation that is caused by famine and "the awful fever" of which many die are represented as an experience that surpasses the boundaries of understanding: "There was, we say, all this, and much more than the imagination itself, unaided by a severe acquaintance with the truth, could embody in its gloomiest conceptions." Similarly, *The Squanders of Castle Squander* evokes the idea that the harrowing memories of the Famine exceed all comprehension. The novel presents the Famine as "one of the most fearful and appalling pictures of national calamity and horror that ever the eye of man rested on, or the heart of man conceived," and states that the feelings of unconfined, universal dismay in the country were "beyond all possible powers of description" as well as "unexampled in the history of nations." Moreover, the novel represents the Great Famine as a unique event in that its awfulness is unsurpassable: in Randy's memories, the Great Famine constitutes one of the "most fearful and appalling pictures of national calamity and horror."[7]

In these early Famine novels, the immense scale on which the Famine-stricken die is often depicted through sublime funereal images, which stress the omnipresence of mortality. In *The Black Prophet*, the skies, which according to prophet Donnel Dhu foretell approaching pestilence and famine, have an appearance of "great terror and sublimity, for as it fell on the black shifting clouds, the effect was made still more awful by the accidental resemblance which they bore to coffins, hearses, and funeral processions, as observed by the prophecy-man, all of which seemed to have been lit up against the deepening shades of evening by some gigantic death-light that superadded its fearful omens to the gloomy scenes on which it fell." This expression of Donnel Dhu's vision of starvation in terms of limitless magnitude also characterizes a scene in which the narrator compares blight-stricken Ireland to "one vast lazar-house filled with famine, disease and death."[8] *Frank O'Donnell* evokes a similar image of Famine-stricken Ireland as one boundless sepulchre, stating that the country had turned into "one vast lazaretto."[9]

The many deaths resulting from starvation and Famine-related diseases are thus articulated through funereal images as well as the suggestion that the country has become one vast, timeless space of death and mourning. At the same time, early Famine fiction conceives the prevalence of Famine suffering in terms of massive crowds of walking skeletons that engender fear. Monahan's *O'Ruark* claims that seeing a group of starving farmers, with "haggard faces," "hollow, sunken eyes," and "meagre jaws," could create the illusion that one has "entered Dante's Inferno." "Narrative of Malcolm McGregor," a rather unknown serialized novel by "Ireland," appeared in the English Chartist magazine the *Northern Star* in 1846 and presents the perspectives of a Scottish well-traveled first-person narrator on the conditions in Famine-stricken Ireland as "one of those tourists who set a proper value upon the decent and polite observance of, and deference to, national manners and customs." Accompanied by Captain Burford, Malcolm McGregor is confronted with the grandest scale of destitution that he has ever witnessed. Their carriage is surrounded by "masses of famishing, perishing females" that encroach upon the vehicle in order to beg for food. Additionally, in these narratives, images of the Famine as a mighty, uncontrollable monster also serve to communicate the immensity and intensity of Famine-related distress. In *O'Ruark*, the Great Famine is personified as walking "with giant tread over the land," crushing all people "with his iron hoof."[10]

The Great Famine is recorded in similar sublime terms in Carleton's *Squanders of Castle Squander*, which recalls the event through an intertextual reference to the book of Revelations as "a three-headed monster, which in this shape became the *Apollyon* or destroyer of at least a million and a quarter of people." These three heads are listed as "Famine" and "Pestilence," but also as "Extermination by the landlords," which, according to the narrator, is the most destructive of all: "We question if there is anything in the historical records of civilised life so utterly heartless and inhuman as the system of extermination or eviction, which spread such wide and helpless desolation over the country." The incompetence of the Ascendancy was often addressed in writings dating from the Famine and its immediate aftermath. For example, the anonymous publication *What Have the Whigs Done for Ireland? or, The English Whigs and the Irish Famine* (1851) points out that "the nobleman was generally a recognised and confirmed absentee," imposing high rents while unable to estimate the severity of conditions to which the Famine-stricken tenants were reduced.[11]

Similarly, John Forbes in *Memorandums Made in Ireland in the Autumn of 1852* called "absenteeism of the great lords and lairds . . . one of the main sources of the evils of Ireland," and Rigby Watson complained in an 1847 letter to Prime Minister Lord John Russell that landlords in Ireland were inclined to forget that "property has its duties as well as its rights." By representing the power wielded by landlords during the Famine in terms of the sublime, *The Squanders of Castle Squander* passes a condemning verdict on landowners. By identifying one of the heads of the all-powerful monster with the authority of the landed class, who are free to evict the starving tenantry at will, Carleton's novel points to the very unequal power relationships in Irish society, the lack of rights on the part of the landless, but first and foremost the detrimental agency of the landlords themselves. Examples of the latter's willful abuse of power are provided throughout the novel: for instance, there is a disturbing scene in which an "aged man, hoary and decrepit, even although in health—and still more the poor old companion and partner of all his cares, afflictions, and struggles" are "turned ruthlessly out" without "the least shadow of compassion" on the part of Harry Squander and his agent, Greasy Pockets. At the same time, *The Squanders of Castle Squander* includes an intertextual reference to Mary Shelley's 1818 Gothic novel to intimate that the maltreatment of the tenantry by the landed class unleashes a sublime power of rebellion in society that may turn itself against the landlords: by "suffering such a mass of national misery to accumulate under their eyes," the landlords throw the poor "into the hands of the agitator and the demagogue," transforming the class into an uncontrollable "gigantic and multitudinous Frankenstein, created by corruption," that demands retribution from "their unholy creators," the landlords.[12]

Crossing Thresholds

A "Street Door" in Tarmons (fig. 5), an illustration printed in the *Pictorial Times* of January 24, 1846, depicts a ragged girl with unkempt hair and hollow eyes who stands on the doorstep of a cabin. Returning the gaze of the viewer, the child would have confronted readers of the London-based newspaper with a disturbing image of a human being that they could have regarded as "Other," because the girl was impoverished, famished, savage, and Irish. At the same time, the fact that the scantily clad, disheveled girl is presented as standing on the threshold is significant. The image of the threshold accentuates the fact that the class and ethnicity to which the girl belongs are considered to be at the boundaries of civilization. Furthermore, the spectator is not forced to look into the dire circumstances that have shaped her current condition, as epitomized by the cabin's interior, for a physical barrier keeps them safely apart from the deprivations that are concealed inside. Thus, the readers could abstain from any identification with the unbearable, terrifying penury and inhuman conditions that characterize the infant's domestic life and constitute an example of what David Lloyd calls the "indigent sublime": that which "exceeds conceptualization and overwhelms the boundaries of the subject."[13]

Thresholds also figure in early nonfictional writings about the Great Irish Famine, and often they function as boundaries that keep disturbing, dehumanizing situations at a remove from the narrative consciousness. Thresholds have such a function in, for example, Lord Dufferin and G. F. Boyle's *Narrative of a Journey from Oxford to Skibbereen during the Year of the Irish Famine* (1847). The text describes how the two English travelers join the parson Mr. Townsend on a tour of his parish, where the people inhabit "mere hovels, dark and dismal in the inside, damp and filthy to the most offensive degree." When Mr. Townsend has singled out cottages that are safe to enter, the two Englishmen "stood on the threshold and looked in" to survey a "woman . . . crouching, drawing her only solace from their scanty warmth; she was suffering from diarrhoea."[14] The narrators view the degrading spectacle of dinginess, hunger, and disease from a distance, for they do not enter the cabin. As a result, a narrative barrier is placed between the diseased and starving human being inside and the "experientiality" that the narrative generates.

A "STREET DOOR" IN TARMONS.

Speaking of the hovel to which it belongs, Mr. Russell says, " It was built of loose stones, without mortar or cement, and thatched with half-decayed potato-stalks and rushes. In the front was an opening, about 3½ feet high by 2½ broad, intended as a doorway. Inside, the darkness was so great that it required a considerable time for the eye to discern any thing distinctly.

5. *A "Street Door" in Tarmons*, *Pictorial Times*, January 24, 1846. Courtesy of Ireland's Great Hunger Museum, Quinnipiac University, Hamden, CT.

Such descriptions of Famine atrocities as enclosed, distant tableaux taking place in cabin interiors from which a narrator or focalizer is separated by a literal boundary also figure in early Famine fiction. Such a demarcation between the narrator and spectacles of starvation can be found, for instance, in *Old Trinity* (1867). This novel by T. Mason Jones, a graduate from Trinity College and prominent member of the Reform League that agitated for the reform of suffrage laws,[15] is set in post-Famine Ireland and presents the story of Thomas Stead Butler, who studies at Trinity College. When Mrs. O'Neill and her niece Helen come to visit their sick relative Robert, who resides in halls and is being nursed by Tom, the latter presents the two women with an account of his youth. In this account, Tom elaborates upon the loss of his father, who contracted cabin fever while attending the needs of the starving and diseased poor during the Famine, when "from the fields came the sickening smell of the diseased and decaying potato haulm." The dire scenes witnessed by Dr. Butler in the cabin are not narrated directly: Tom, who is the intradiegetic narrator, waits at the doorstep for his father. The latter, we are told, "remained so long in this miserable hovel" that Tom became worried about "what was keeping him." When, at length, Dr. Butler exits the cabin, he looks "very pale" and subsequently recounts the lamentable scenes he witnessed inside: "'It is as I feared,' he said, stepping into the gig, and taking the reins, 'the others have caught the infection. Last week, the father caught the fever, then the two eldest daughters took it, yesterday the mother was seized, today the other three children are ill, and now the whole seven of them are stricken in that horrid hole, with no one, but a poor old grandmother to take care of them. They have nothing in the place but a pitcher of cold water. No comforts, no medicines, no attendance.'"[16]

The insertion of intradiegetic layers between the scenes in the cabin and Tom's narration of this childhood memory, as well as the fact that the subject of focalization and narrator, Tom, does not cross the threshold of the hovel to witness the miseries inside, ensures a relatively comfortable distance between the almost unrepresentable, unsettling conditions of Famine and the narrative consciousness.

Furthermore, in early Famine fiction, thresholds usually mark the transition from natural to unnatural conditions of humanity: in Mrs. Lorenzo Nunn's *Heirs of the Soil* (1870), for example, one can read that once Phelim M'Carthy and his wife, Nelly, step across the threshold of the workhouse and are separated, God's holy matrimonial laws are transgressed: "What God had joined together, the cruel exigency of hunger, relieved by man's laws, had put asunder."[17]

Reports written during the Famine by travelers who were affiliated with relief and charity organizations, such as the Society of Friends, detailed the miseries that could be found beyond the threshold. Thus, William Bennett described how he and his companions "entered the cabin" of an unfortunate family to find "stretched out in one dark corner . . . three children huddled together, lying there because they were too weak to rise, pale and ghastly, their little limbs . . . perfectly emaciated, eyes sunk, voices gone, and evidently in the last stages of actual starvation." The language and descriptions in eyewitness accounts such as Bennett's appear to have left their imprint on several works of Famine fiction that describe characters in the narrative who visit the cabins of the poor. Often, the characters who cross the thresholds of these wretched abodes come from an entirely different background and are relatively unfamiliar with the extremities of privation that the peasantry endures. In these narratives, the characters who step across the doorway to enter the wretched cabins and huts transcend sectarian boundaries, but the thresholds also symbolize the mental boundary that characters in the narrative have to overcome in confronting human conditions that exceed imagination and conflict with dominant ideas about civilization. As we saw previously, in Susanna Meredith's story "Ellen Harrington" (1865), the English captain Hartley does not have an insider's perspective on the wretchedness of the starving in Cork. His ignorance of the situation of the famishing Irish, however, transforms into a full comprehension of its acuteness that at the same time goes beyond his understanding, when he is faced with a frantic woman, her two dead infants and her feverish child "tossing and moaning on her lap."[18] While ethnic and class barriers had previously separated Hartley from such degrading sights, his stepping over the threshold into the hut initiates him into a sublime terror at the depravity that he witnesses and literally sickens him.

As we saw before, Trollope's Anglo-Irish Herbert Fitzgerald also enters a rather unfamiliar zone when he steps into the "miserable, low-roofed, damp, ragged tenement" of one of the poor cottiers. In fact, intriguingly, it is hinted that Herbert literally goes off the beaten path prior to meeting these starving creatures, suggesting that he has to go out of his customary ways and cross the boundary of his class in order to acquaint himself with the lot of the starving tenantry. Herbert "did not take the direct road to Desmond Court, but went round as though he were going to Gortnaclough, and then turning away from the Gortnaclough road, made his way by a cross lane towards Clady and the mountains. He hardly knew himself whether he had any object in this beyond one which he did not express even to himself,—that, namely, of not being seen on the way leading to Desmond Court." While Herbert's detour can also be read as a response to his disinheritance and loss of prospects among the gentry and in love, the fact that he rides across a road not normally taken also points forward to his transgression of class barriers by his arrival at the cottage. Ironically, while Herbert takes his horse to the hovel in order to seek shelter from the rain, the place itself falls short of every form of shelter for its inhabitants: with "damp, cracked walls," "the old lumpy thatch, through which the water was already dropping . . . and none of those articles of daily use which are usually to be found in the houses even of the poorest." The dreadful place, in its "nakedness," exceeds any notions of the poor man's home that Herbert previously held. Furthermore, the obscurity of the cabin adds to Herbert's sense of disorientation and enhances the shock of the incredible state of human misery that he will witness: "At first, so dark was the place, Herbert hardly thought that the object before him was a human being."[19] In adjusting his eyes to the darkness in the cabin, Herbert at the same time must accommodate his mind-set to the unnatural sights of the bereaved family.

This lengthy description in *Castle Richmond* may have tapped into the existing visual repertoire about the cottier's hut. In illustrations published in the press during the Famine years, it was customary to present the cabins of the rural poor as dim spaces: *Ardcara—Interior of Maurice O'Connell's Cabin*, printed in the *Pictorial Times* of January 24, 1846; *Mullins's Hut, at Scull*, which appeared in the *Illustrated London News* on February 20, 1847; and *Sketch in a House at Fahey's Quay, Ennis: The Widow Connor and Her Dying Child*, published in the *Illustrated London News* of January 5, 1850, are a few examples. The latter engraving, which depicts a woman who prays for the soul of her dying child, pictures a sun ray that falls on the face of the kneeling mother: this small aura of light creates the impression of a spiritual woman who does not neglect her religion in spite of distress. By contrast, in *Castle Richmond*, the glimmer of light that radiates from the mother's eyes does not relieve the distress of the scene: the woman's eyes are "very large and bright as they turned round upon" Herbert, but "a dull, unwholesome brightness,—a brightness that had in it none of the light of life" emanates from them.[20]

The scene from *Castle Richmond* appears to have been influenced by Burke's theory on the sublimity of darkness. As Burke asserted, darkness is "painful" and evokes terror, because in "utter darkness, it is impossible to know in what degree of safety we stand. . . . [W]e may every moment strike against some dangerous obstruction." As the scene from *Castle Richmond* reveals, the obscurity unsettles Herbert's composure, because he cannot immediately identify the objects around him, and the sublimity of the darkness appears to form the prelude to the sublime spectacle of human desolation that he is about to perceive. In *The Widow O'Leary*, the ideas of boundaries and darkness work in similar ways, as a premonition of the sight of dehumanization that the narrator is to encounter. As yet unacquainted with the extent of suffering in his native Ireland, owing to a prolonged stay in England, the narrator comes face-to-face with the agonizing effects of famine once he enters the cottage of Mary and Jack O'Leary. Here the obscurity of the place adds to his sense of alienation: he sees an "object" upon the bedstead, but "could not distinguish what it was, as the room was quite dark." Once his eyes have become "accustomed to the darkness of the room," the narrator can distinguish the object on the bed as a "man, wasted to the greatest degree of emaciation lying on a litter of straw, and covered only by a dirty ragged quilt." The emotional shock that the narrator receives, as the body gradually becomes visible to him, reminds one of the effects that Burke ascribes to sublime objects: "unnatural tension and certain violent emotions of the nerves."[21] The narrator's response therefore underscores the representation of the Famine as a dark event that goes beyond the limits of apprehension and commonality.

The terrifying darkness that accompanies the gradual unfolding of the famished body to the eyes of the subject of focalization in *Castle Richmond* and *The Widow O'Leary* also appears to hark back to the literary Gothic of the late eighteenth and early nineteenth centuries, in which spectacles that invoke terror in their beholder were often cloaked in obscurity. For example, the famous scene in Ann Radcliffe's *The Mysteries of Udolpho* (1794), in which Emily St. Aubert mistakes a waxen statue that is hidden behind a black veil for a corpse "partly decayed and disfigured by worms," takes place in a "dark part of the room." In Charles Maturin's Irish Gothic novel *Melmoth the Wanderer* (1820), the protagonist discovers the dark secret of his ancestor when he sees his portrait upon entering a dark wine cellar at his uncle's castle. He is holding a "dim light," looking around him with a "mixture of terror and curiosity," and these eerie sensations foreshadow his discovery of the painting of the man that inspires "stupid horror" in him. The fact that the scenes in *Castle Richmond* and *The Widow O'Leary* involve the crossing of literal boundaries that symbolize the transgression of symbolical boundaries appears to betray an engagement with Gothic conventions as well. In the above scene from Maturin's novel, young John Melmoth is given a key by his dying uncle to enter "the closet, which no foot but that of old Melmoth had entered for nearly sixty years." The key symbolically unlocks a dark secret: the fact that one of John's ancestors sold his soul to the devil. John's crossing of the threshold into the closet marks his involvement in the plight of this villainous progenitor, which crosses the limits of morality. As David Punter clarifies in his overview of the Gothic tradition, *The Literature of Terror*, barriers (such as thresholds) often signify an exploration of psychological and sociological boundaries between "reality and fantasy" and between the socially accepted and the taboo. In a similar vein, Eugenia DeLamotte has pointed to the symbolical significance of "architecture" in nineteenth-century Gothic literature, arguing that material barriers such as thresholds may signify social entrapment and the transgression of social norms as well as fear of merging with the "Other."[22]

The scenes from *Old Trinity*, "Ellen Harrington," and *Castle Richmond* discussed above invite readings that consider this function of barriers in Gothic literature. The languishing and dead bodies of the starved that are confined in these cabins, hidden from human sight, suggest the entrapment of a class in their poverty as well as society's neglect of the famishing population and their suffering. *Old Trinity* implies that the poor who lie confined in their cabins have become reduced to their current state because they are ensnared by their poverty. As a result of the blight, these people have been constricted to unhealthy food and thereby have lost their physical vigor: "The tubers were rotting before they had time to ripen, and were quite unfit for human food. But many poor people had nothing else, and were obliged to eat them."[23] In one of his many digressions, the extradiegetic narrator in *Castle Richmond* sketches a picture of a country confined to a state of misery by its inability to reform a social system that induces poverty. The absentee landlords left management in the hands of a class of middlemen, "who looked to be gentlemen living on their property, but who should have earned their bread by the work of their brain, or, failing that, by the sweat of their brow." This middle class brings no necessary improvements to land management,[24] thereby discouraging any new methods in "farming . . . any produce from the land except the potato crop." This system persistently "maintained one class of men in what they considered to be the gentility of idleness, and another class, the people of the country, in the abjectness of poverty," the narrator observes.[25]

In "Ellen Harrington," Dr. Nelligan takes Hartley on his tour among the cabins of the sick and starving poor, meanwhile chastising the English for the inadequate relief that they provide. Hartley has brought the Indian meal, but, as Nelligan complains, the people have "no boilers" to cook it. Nelligan therefore wonders why the English Commissariat Department does not send "the bread ready-made."[26] As such, these narratives either wittingly or unwittingly expose the failures of imperial progress—a taboo subject. The emaciated frames of the Famine-stricken evoke horror in the human degradation that they expose, but the fact that the subjects of focalization can withdraw from these scenes that are encapsulated by the interiors of the peasants' dwellings also suggests a reassuring confinement of these harrowing memories of the Famine past within secure boundaries.

Intriguingly, a brief look at Famine fiction written during the last decades of the nineteenth century indicates a growing tendency to blur the boundaries between the focalizing subject and the victim of starvation and between the domestic, contained setting of the cabin and public spaces. In the earlier-discussed *Chronicles of Castle Cloyne* (1885), the heroine Oonagh enters the cottage of her cousin Susie Burke and her husband, Oona's former lover, John Molloy. Initially, similar conventions as the ones in earlier Famine fiction are employed, as Lindsay Janssen has also noted: the cabin is enveloped in darkness, and with the "imperfect light" of her candle, Oonagh can take in only "by degrees" whose bodies are lying inside. The "foul air and suffocating odour" inside almost drive her away, but when Oona discovers the corpse of her once beloved John, she has no further reserves and embraces his dead body with passion: "There was no bashfulness about Oonagh now, no proud reserve, no womanly shame. She knelt down beside the dead man, she twined her arms around his neck, she clasped the wasted body to her bosom, she rained down bitter, scalding tears on the cold, pallid face. He was her own now, at last—this false sweetheart, for whose sake she had rejected many a good man's proffered love—her very own!"[27] There is no separation, but rather a bonding that veers toward immersion between the onlooker and the victim of Famine here.

Furthermore, as Janssen's research has shown, in Famine fiction from a later period, the demarcations between interior and exterior Famine suffering are often suspended: scenes of suffering are often focalized through protagonists who travel freely between public and domestic spaces of suffering and who themselves are sometimes not spared either, "demonstrating that none are safe and that the Famine is in essence an uncontrollable event." For example, in Brew's novel, Oonagh first wanders across roads filled with Famine misery just before she enters the cabin of the Molloys: "The country swarmed with beggars, clad, or to speak more truthfully, half covered by filthy rags, fit for nothing but to be thrown into the fire. The appearance of those wretched people spoke for them more eloquently than any words could have done." Likewise, in the earlier-examined "The Hungry Death," Brigid Lavelle alternately traverses domestic and public spaces of Famine suffering in administering relief to the starving inhabitants of the island Inishbofin. Thus, she enters the cabins of the poor but also passes "prostrate forms, dying or dead, on the heather, on the roadside, and against the cabin walls."[28] One can therefore argue for a development of Famine memory over time in fiction, in that there is a remarkable shift from more enframed Famine spectacles that are dissociated from the narrative consciousness toward representations of more uncontrollable Famine suffering that come closer to the experience of the subjects of focalization.

Beyond Reason

The impact of the Gothic mode on these early works of Famine fiction can be explained by the fact that "the Gothic has flourished at times of actual or potential social upheaval."[29] The use of the Gothic mode in Irish literature has traditionally been construed as an expression of the "repressed fears and anxieties of the minority Anglo-Irish population."[30] However, the widespread use of Gothic traces in Famine fiction that represents a wide spectrum of religious and political affiliations confirms the claim made recently by various scholars that indeed one can speak of a "cross-sectarian" use of Gothic elements in Irish literature that sought to register atrocities.[31] Usually, Gothic literature not only presents pictures of physical deformity, but also tends to explore psychological perversion and unlawful behavior.[32] As the following section will demonstrate, early Famine fiction at times resorts to Gothic themes such as madness, cannibalism, and beastliness in its explorations of the mental effects of famine and loss.

During the Famine years, John Travers Robinson commented that the "famishing multitudes" were but "one remove from madness," and William Bennett observed that in some of the starving, "reason and intelligence had evidently flown." Many of these novels and stories that remember the Great Famine suggest that the trials of being surrounded by starvation and death elicit aberrant behavior among the Famine-stricken. They represent characters whose minds have become unhinged as a result of the distress caused by hunger and the deaths of loved ones. *The Widow O'Leary* represents an afflicted mother who, like a "manic," rushes forward to clasp the "lifeless form" of her child "to her bosom" as his little body is carried out. A similar representation of madness that is connected to mourning can be found in the short story "The Tale of a Tombstone," by D. O'C Townley, which was published in the American periodical the *Catholic World* in 1867. This story is one of the exceptions as a North American work of Famine fiction that explores the extremities of Famine-related suffering through representations of madness. The tale relates the intense bond between a mother, Mary Donovan, and her mentally retarded son, Ned, which is broken by the woman's death of cholera during the "famine and the disease of '47." The loss of his beloved mother triggers a boundless heartbreak in the young man: at times he seems "dead as the dead"; at other moments, his outbursts of uncontrollable grief are "so fearful and so wild as to wring with horror the hearts of all who heard him." When Mary is to be buried, Ned attempts to stop the funeral procession, because his mother should be interred next to her father in Drumbhan, so he utters a "wild unearthly cry" and a "shriek inhuman."[33] The boy's madness, however, culminates when he digs up his mother's coffin in the middle of the night and takes her to the desired resting place. There he is found dead on his mother's grave one day later; his heartstrings seem to have snapped because of his unbearable loss. The disturbing depiction of uncontrollable pain and aberrant conduct in the story is relieved by the narrative layers that are inserted between these depictions of madness and the narrative consciousness of the text. The story is told by a relative outsider, an American tourist who visits the area around Slieve Donard and becomes acquainted with an old sexton, who in turn relates this story to him. This narrative-within-narrative structure and the use of a foreign narrator create a comforting distance between the mental agonies caused by Famine suffering and the "experientiality" of the text.

In *The Black Prophet*, the extradiegetic narrator states that "misery, sickness, and hunger, all together, had brought down the strong intellect and reason of the wretched and famishing multitudes," leading to outbreaks of "temporary frenzy." In its depiction of Brian and Kathleen Murtagh, an elderly couple whose daughter Peggy bore an illegitimate child and died with exhaustion, *The Black Prophet* shows that the combination of bereavement and the pangs of hunger bring on mental delusion. The grief-stricken parents look "white and stony as marble, and their eyes, now dead and glassy, were marked by no appearance of distinct consciousness, or the usual expression of reason." Furthermore, Brian's mind has become so deranged that he holds on to the vision that his daughter is still alive and that all will get well once she marries her suitor, Tom: "'Oh,' he replied, 'I am dyin' wid fair hunger—wid fair hunger, an' I want something to ait'; and as he spoke, a spasm of agony came over his face. 'Ah,' he added, 'if Alick was livin' it isn't this way we'd be, for what can poor Peggy do for us afther her "misfortune"? However, she is a good girl—a good daughter to us, an' will make a good wife, too, for all that has happened yet; for sure they wor both young and foolish, an' Tom is to marry her.'" The passage represents mental instability as a direct consequence of Famine, but Carleton's novel also portrays madness as an angry response to social injustice. It is reported that Peggy's lover, Tom Dalton, has also "gone mad" and is "risin' the counthry, to punish Dick o' the Grange and Darby Skinadre—, the one, he says, for putting his father and themselves out o' the farm, and the other for bein' the death, he says, of poor Peggy there and the child," who in vain asked Skinadre for food and help.[34] As such, *The Black Prophet* imagines madness as the fury of the powerless toward a social system that increases Famine suffering, that is, toward landlords and their agents who refuse relief to the starving and remorselessly evict families who cannot pay the rent.

This depiction of madness in Carleton's novel may put in mind Shoshana Felman's observation that madness is often an alternative form of resistance on the part of those individuals who are culturally and politically impotent. A similar association between Famine suffering, madness, and anger directed at authorities can be found in Charles Joseph Kickham's *Sally Cavanagh* (1869). The narrative was written by supreme executive of the Irish Republic and editor of the Fenian newspaper the *Irish People* Charles Joseph Kickham during his imprisonment for political activism at Woking Convict Prison.[35] Sally has to face hardship by herself, as her husband, Connor Shea, has gone to the United States to look for employment. Initially, she is capable of coping with the trial of starvation, for she heroically withstands landlord Oliver Grindem, who presses her to send her children to his mother's Protestant school so they may be given food: "There was a majesty in her figure and an unearthly light flashed from her dark eyes, as she waved her hand towards the door, and said in a voice of *command*: 'Leave my house! Tyrant, villain, go out of my sight!'"[36]

Eventually, however, the strains of being forced into the workhouse and losing her infants become too much for Sally, and, "stretched upon a pallet in the crowded dormitory," she succumbs to severe brain fever that is accompanied by frenzy: "And then, uttering a wild shriek that rung through every corner of the 'palace of poverty,' and made the good priest turn pale, the broken-hearted woman rushed through the gate—her hands stretched out towards the mountain. Sally Cavanagh was a maniac." Her "reason" being "entirely gone," Sally flees from the workhouse to seek shelter in the churchyard and never recovers. Her lapse into madness almost tempts her husband, Connor, who has returned to Ireland, to shoot Grindem: "and pulling a revolver from his breast, thrust it through the slit; the muzzle was within three feet of the monster's heart."[37] In Kickham's novel, then, madness features on the level of Famine-related affliction as well as in the form of fierce resentment of the landed class, which lets the peasantry starve and does not respect their religious integrity.

Interestingly, this scene, in which Connor almost pulls the trigger to avenge himself on the landlord, not only reflects upon the assassinations of landlords during the Famine that became more frequent after November 1847, when Major Denis Mahon of Strokestown was killed,[38] but also suggests that Grindem himself has become subject to madness as well. When Connor casts a first glance at Grindem, he is "barely able to recognize" him, for his "face was that of a corpse, save that the red glassy eyes glared hideously in the middle of it." Looking quite ferocious himself, ironically, Grindem has come to the churchyard to have Sally, the "dangerous lunatic," removed. Grindem then displays further madness in the sense of unbridled fury, in that he violently thrashes Sally "with the butt end of his whip" and strikes her in the face. Grindem's cruelty is reminiscent of former slave owners in the West Indies or on the plantations in the American South who would frequently lash their slaves, a reading that seems justified in light of the fact that, earlier on in the narrative, Sally's husband, Connor Shea, feels so hunted down by this demanding landlord that he compares himself to a "galley slave" wearing "the flesh off my bones" in his toil.[39] In this way, Kickham's novel appears to respond to writings from the Famine era or its immediate aftermath, which would often compare the fate of the Irish tenantry with the plight of black slaves. For example, John Mitchel, who himself was unsympathetic to the abolitionist movement and in favor of ownership of slaves in the American South,[40] argued that it was "better to be the slave of a merciful master and just man" than "a serf to an Irish land appropriator," pointing to the unfairness of the plight of a white race living, in his view, in greater distress than the black plantation slaves.[41] Thomas Doolan's *Practical Suggestions on the Improvement of the Present Condition of the Peasantry of Ireland* (1847) likened the extensive mortality and destitution in Ireland with the past outrages "in the West Indian and other colonies . . . where slavery reared its black front."[42]

Depicting the relationships between landowners and tenantry in terms that remind one of Atlantic slavery, Kickham's novel not only echoes political treatises about the Land Question, but also transforms the Famine past into "multidirectional" memory, to quote Michael

Rothberg. Interestingly, similar analogies between the fate of the Irish rural laborer during and after the Famine and black slaves recur in fiction from later decades. W. C. Upton's novel *Uncle Pat's Cabin* (1882), which was initially published in Ireland but later reissued in an edition for the American market in 1914, clearly resonates with Harriet Beecher Stowe's *Uncle Tom's Cabin* (1852), depicting a tenant farmer who has to bear with the hardships he suffers through his landlord and agent during and after the Famine. These analogies are further emphasized by the character of Dr. O'Leary, who declares toward Father O'Mahony: "I have seen the negro slave of the Southern States of America whipped at the post; I have seen him chained like a wild beast; I have seen him guarded like a criminal; I have seen him hunted down with bloodhounds, but I fearlessly assert, from all I have studied of the treatment the Irish agricultural labourers are subjected to, they are in as hapless a state as were the slaves of America." In a similar vein, *Scenes and Incidents in Irish Life* (1884), a novel by Irish Canadian writer F. H. Clayton, states that "the Irish poor have experienced more pain than 'the negroes of the southern plantations.'" However, "The negroe was commiserated, but Ireland's population was not."[43]

Kickham's portrayal of Grindem as a man whose conduct exceeds the boundaries of civilization and reason implies severe critique of Ireland's ruling class, which comprises its government, landlords, and justices of peace. In a similar vein, Alice Nolan's Irish American Famine novel *The Byrnes of Glengoulah* (1868) depicts a landlord and Anglican bishop, Biggs, who becomes insane toward the end of the novel. After a failed assault on his life, Biggs suffers from "convulsive tremors" and is plagued by nightmares in which he is haunted by people who were sent prematurely to their graves owing to his policies. Once he settles back in England, he seems to regain his composure, but during a visit from his land agent, Jacob Margin, "frantic Biggs jumped upon him and endeavored to strangle him." Subsequently, the bishop becomes "untractable," is prone to "attempted self-destruction," and spends the last days of his life in a lunatic asylum.[44] A similar dire fate is reserved for the landlord in *Sally Cavanagh*, Oliver Grindem, who, in whipping Sally, falls from his horse and dashes his head against the slabs that are believed to mark the graves of Sally's children. In both Famine narratives, then, the landlords die in a manner that involves the memory of those individuals who fell victim to their lack of compassion and care: Grindem actually dies on the memorial to the children whom he had evicted, and Biggs's madness and eventual death are brought on by the haunting memories of the people whom he had removed from their cottages and who subsequently died of starvation. Thus, both *Sally Cavanagh* and *The Byrnes of Glengoulah* imagine a class system that will crumble under the weight of its innate fallibility, and perhaps these visions of imperial breakdown in both texts can be ascribed to their authors' connections with radical nationalist movements. As already mentioned, Kickham wrote from a Fenian perspective and actually dedicated *Sally Cavanagh* to John O'Leary, and Nolan's text was serialized in John Mitchel's the *Citizen* in 1868, before it was issued in book form.

Beyond the Human

Early works of Famine fiction also reconfigure the Famine past in terms of the dehumanization of the starving population. Several texts suggest that the double plight of loss and hunger leads to deviant behavior, in that emotional responses that are in tune with the circumstances are no longer possible. Some narratives create the impression that the Famine prevents people from mourning their loved ones: the pangs of hunger and excessive distress have physically weakened and emotionally stunned the famishing. Thus, in *Castle Richmond*, the bereaved, "corpselike" mother hardly displays any grief over her dead daughter, Kitty, in contrast with Herbert, who is strongly affected: "But there was no tear in her eye or gurgling sob audible from her throat." In Richard Baptist O'Brien's *Ailey Moore* (1856), the narrator describes how the poor "sat down in a kind of stupor." Whereas during the onset of the Famine people would cling to "the emaciated form of the dead" and lament loudly, soon "the frequency of the appearance of a corpse, or the pangs of hunger, or both, rendered most people insensible."[45]

Similarly, Jane Dunbar Chaplin's *Gems of the Bog: A Tale of the Irish Peasantry* (1869), which had been serialized in the Boston-based Baptist newspaper the *Watchman*, reimagines the time when half-starved and poorly sheltered people were "flying, panic-stricken, in every direction" as one in which people will manifest anomalous conduct. While the main protagonist, Paddy, is credited with some emotional ingenuity in the novel, as he gets "mock" tears "up for strangers," his sorrow over the death of his starved and sick wife, the beggar woman Meg Mannon, proves to be sincere. However, as the narrator states, Paddy's "grief . . . was soon spent," and when the son that he had with Meg who was adopted by a farmer's family passes away, "he himself had had no part in the affliction. He had given the child away, therefore his death was nothing which particularly concerned him." Paddy's rather coldhearted response, which contrasts with the intense mourning of his son's Protestant adoptive parents, John and Peggy, could be attributed to the religious ideology of the novel. However, the narrative also appears to convey the idea that any natural attachment or emotional involvement in these times of Famine is hard: when Paddy wants to lay out Meg in his master's cow house for the wake, the latter does not welcome the idea, fearing that his cattle may contract the disease Meg died of. Furthermore, when Paddy invites the villagers for the wake, "they all fled from him with screams of terror" for fear of contagion.[46]

Many early works of Famine fiction depict the famishing as dehumanized, in that their demeanor is savage and beastly. Casting the starving Irish in such terms was not without the risk of confirming ethnic stereotypes. Traditionally, imperial discourses would identify the Irish peasantry with lack of decorum, unruliness, and lack of self-reliance: for example, John Christian Curwen's *Observations on the State of Ireland* (1818), on the one hand, voiced great sympathy for the dire living conditions of the peasantry; on the other, his account of the "acme of human misery" was uncomfortably infused with traditional bias toward the Irish when it addressed the question of whether the extreme poverty that could be witnessed among the cottagers should be ascribed to "peculiar improvidence, and want of management,"[47] terms that featured prevalently in colonial debates about the Irish Question.[48] Often, this bias of Irish indolence was bound up with the idea that the Irish were by nature barbaric, untamable, and squalid:

Mrs. Maberly refers to what she regards as the unregulated, filthy cabins of the uneducated Irish housewives who are "brawling, idle, dirty creatures" in need of instruction into English domestic "tidiness, . . . cleanliness and industry." This stereotyping of the Irish home as a place of uncivilized dirt also features in North American accounts of travels to Ireland, such as Harriet Vaughan Cheney's "Sketches on a Journey" (1849), which states that the Irish "*native* dwelling" is generally marked by "heaps of dirt outside, offending more than one sense, pigs wallowing before the door, and not a trace of cultivation near them; while at the windows, and through the open doors, are seen all ages huddled together, children without number, and women, squalid and dirty, dawdling about their work, and men, smoking away their time, in stupid idleness."[49]

The works of fiction that resort to images of animalism and brutality as a way to express Famine memory would avoid connotations with such stereotypes by presenting this degradation as a transformation brought about by starvation and disease. Thus, Carleton's *The Black Prophet* evokes the disturbing image of a crowd that looks "wild and wolfish," with the "fire of famine" blazing "so savagely in their hollow eyes." Yet the mob's disturbing ferocity is entirely attributed to the "intensity of their sufferings, and the natural panic which was occasioned by the united ravages of disease and famine," for it is "well known that misery, sickness, and hunger, all together, had brought down the strong intellect and reason of the wretched and famishing multitudes." In *Narrative of Malcolm McGregor*, the narrator's description of "half-naked females" who hunt for "such fragments of food as might have escaped the notice or have been beneath the acceptance of the cat or dog" evokes feelings of regard rather than disgust in the protagonist: "My heart now became brimfull of sympathy." *Sally Cavanagh* initially pictures Sally's children as gentle, angelic, "fair-haired . . . curly-headed . . . rosy-cheeked" beings. However, deprivation changes the infants into savage, uncaring creatures. When the hunger-stricken eldest boy sees one of Brian Purcell's greyhounds crunching a "piece of hard oaten bread," it leaps upon the animal to snatch the bread from between its teeth and to devour "it ravenously."[50]

The Love That Kills (1867), by William Gorman Wills, likewise calls forth the association between the famishing poor and wild animal instincts when the omniscient narrator describes how a destitute family wandering by the roadside stumbles upon a rabbit thrown out of the courtyard: the father's "eyes are wolfish, as he tears it in pieces for them. The children, ever moaning, tear at it too with their lizard-like fingers." When agent William Clayton snatches the animal away from them because it is poisoned with arsenic, the family is depicted as a pack of "yelling hounds." While the novel thus portrays the famishing as dehumanized, beastly beings, its delineation of the terrible fate that awaits the family is completely deprived of any sentimentality. In a rather matter-of-fact tone, the narrator states that when Clayton returns, "the aged children were found dead. It was scarcely worth deciding whether they died of starvation or poison."[51]

As this comment reveals, the dead family has become so much divested of humanity that they no longer seem to be fellow creatures to Clayton. This scene in Wills's novel paints a rather bleak picture of parenthood during the Famine, for the two parents have lost all dignity and composure. In that respect, *The Love That Kills* presents a stark contrast with many of the earliest works of Famine fiction, in which especially the suffering mothers are depicted as selfless and gentle, despite the trials they are facing. For example, in *A Tale of the Irish Famine in 1846 and 1847* (1847), by "Ireland," one can read that Honour "grudged every morsel that she put into her own mouth." Likewise, the first-person narrator in Mrs. Hoare's story "Little Mary" (1851) argues that her stepmother would always give the children "plenty as far as it would go; but 'twas little she took herself. She would often go entirely without a meal, and then she'd slip down to the huckster's, and buy a little white bun for Mary; and I'm sure it used to do her more good to see the child eat it, than if she got a meat dinner for herself."[52] This image of the self-sacrificing mother dominated Victorian gender ideologies in general,[53] and this prevalence may explain why the previously discussed scene from *The Love That Kills*, which describes the animal-like voraciousness with which the family devours the rabbit, specifically focuses on the father and the children.

The impact of gender on representations of Famine-related brutality may also clarify why literary representations of cannibalism within the family during the Great Famine merely feature fathers and sons. The poem *The Famine in Ireland*, by C. A. Rawlins (1847), thus details how a famished son eats the corpse of his father, thereby transgressing the laws of nature and family:

> Within whose stiffen'd jaws half gnaw'd away
> Th fest'ring fingers of the father lay
> The pangs of hunger quench'd the ties of blood,
> And the dead father serv'd the son for food.[54]

Cannibalism also features in William Carleton's *The Squanders of Castle Squander*: a desperate father cuts the flesh from his dead son's bones and partakes of the "cannibal repast," because the "demon of famine had not only hardened his heart, but filled his brain with the savage mania of desolation." The gruesome scene sketches the despair that leads the man to his heinous deed, and the narrative juxtaposes the father's bout of insanity with the willful figurative "cannibalism" of the insatiable land agent Greasy Pockets. In spite of the widespread starvation around him, the agent continuously displays a voracious appetite, as if he were "a shipwrecked mariner, left without food for three days." He refuses to pay for the food that he orders at restaurants and is so self-interested that the community jokes that he will soon be eating everyone, including the landlord himself: "The old villain has lived upon no other victuals during the last five-and-twenty years and generally ends with the landlord himself as a bonne-bouche. Awful as is that enormous mouth of his, and precipitous the throat, into the one and down the other you will go, long before he has done with you, or rather after it. I pledge my honour and conscience, Dick, that the stomach of that monster is nothing more nor less than the sepulchre of landlords." The representation of Greasy Pockets suggests that the real "cannibals" in Ireland are to be found among the landed class and their entourage, because they serve their own purposes over the dead bodies of others. This idea of an unscrupulous, greedy landed class was also conveyed by various nationalist texts during the Famine era. For example, in F. B. Ryan's poem *The Spirit's Lament, or, The Wrongs of Ireland* (1847), written in Montreal for Irish emigrant audiences, the suffering of the Irish is attributed to an Ascendancy with a "great . . . appetite / Unsatisfied still, tho' all sects are his prey," and willing to confiscate any earnings from "the peasant, who's starving."[55]

Famine Specters

Julian Wolfreys has discussed the spectral traces that one can find in nineteenth- and twentieth-century literature, claiming that stock elements of the Gothic such as ghosts are appropriated by texts that do not overly engage with this literary mode otherwise. As the following section will illustrate, early Famine fiction also contains such Gothic traces: it frequently includes phantoms and references to spectrality as well as scenes of haunting. David Lloyd comments that "the phenomenon of haunting . . . seems indissociable from the Famine," and the specter is indeed one of the major mnemonic images that become a vehicle for the memory of the Famine in fiction from this period.[56] In fact, there are three major ways in which specters manifest themselves in these early Famine narratives, namely, as the "living dead," the ghastly, starving bodies of the Famine-stricken; figuratively, as the spirits of the deceased victims who claim retribution as well as remembrance in a post-Famine Ireland; and, finally, as emblems of cultural memory itself.

Ghosts are expressions of a state of liminality: they personify what is "neither present nor absent, neither dead nor alive"; or, as Jacques Derrida put it, the specter is "ce présent non-présent," representing "la limite entre le vivant et le mort." In early accounts of the Great Irish Famine, the extreme deprivation and degeneration of the starving people are often conveyed through images of living ghosts or wandering skeletons. Thus, Asenath Nicholson's *Annals of the Irish Famine in 1847, 1848 and 1849* records the author's reservations about venturing out at night, for fear of stumbling upon some "living walking ghosts." In early works of fiction that remember the great number of casualties, the spectral becomes an image through which the cultural recollections of the harrowing bodily and mental agonies of starvation can be performed. Spectrality figures as an expression of the dire conditions of the Irish: hunger has physically reduced them to staggering corpse-like creatures, who seem to be suspended between life and death. In Henry O'Monahan's *O'Ruark*, a crowd of starved men and women, "with tottering frames, bleared eyes, and pinched, and pointed features," is portrayed as "breathing corpses, on their way to the grave." Allen H. Clington's *Frank O'Donnell* presents the readers with an image of "half-starved, half-naked wretches," "living skeletons, tottering with disease and weakness."[57]

As animated skeletons, these haunting presences in novels and short stories are, moreover, described as ghosts of their former selves, weighed down in spirit by starvation and disease. Writers who reported on the Famine would often stress the mental languidness of the starving population that resulted from malnutrition. D. J. Corrigan, in *On Famine and Fever as Cause and Effect in Ireland* (1846), referred to "the weakness of body and apathy of mind which famine and fever had engendered." Likewise, Nicholson pointed out that the famishing Irish not only were alike to living ghosts physically, but also resembled them in their mental stupor: "The walking skeleton is reduced to a state of inanity—he sees you not, he heeds you not, neither does he beg." This idea that the perishing people are mentally and emotionally spectral also figures in early Famine fiction, which appears to derive most of its imagery from nonfictional representations of the Famine era. In *O'Ruark* the eyes of some of the famishing are said to be "like those of the dead, so lustreless, so sunken, so devoid of meaning from their long fast." In *The Black Prophet*, Brian and Kathleen Murtagh have become emotionally stunned by hunger and grief. The "faces of both were ghastly, and filled with a pale, vague expression of what appeared to be horror, or . . . dull staring stupor," and their eyes have become "dead and glassy . . . marked by no appearance of distinct consciousness, or the usual expression of reason."[58]

This representation of the Famine-stricken as living dead recurs in several works of Famine fiction of the 1890s and 1900s, demonstrating that this mnemonic image has transgenerational impact. For example, Louise Field's *Denis: A Study in Black and White* (1896) describes a spectral body of Famine victims in such detail that they almost seem grotesque: "a crowd that seemed in the white light and dark shadows as though composed of goblins . . . a strange procession of beings so misshapen and so fantastically clad as to seem hardly human."[59] Traversing the public setting of the village streets, these spectral Famine victims, in their dehumanization, are even more disturbing for being in open view.

The above description of a famishing crowd is immediately followed by a discussion between the main characters, Margaret O'Hara and Captain Mervyn, about the poignant "Irish Question," in particular the ways in which "English legislation in the interests of Manchester" implies a neglect of the conditions of the suffering Irish. The image of the spectral population is thus embedded in political critique concerning colonial relations between England and Ireland—an issue that was still topical in the 1890s. Similarly, in Canon Patrick Sheehan's *Glenanaar: A Story of Irish Life* (1905), the starving peasants are described as "gaunt spectres . . . looking at one another out of hollow eyes of despair and gloom. Ghosts walk the land. Great giant figures, reduced to skeletons by hunger, shake in their clothes, which hang loose around their attenuated frames." The fact that in the same passage the many dead that are buried coffinless are described as "ghastly, staring, uncoffined loads" suggests that those individuals still alive are hardly distinguishable from the ones who have perished.[60]

Ross Poole has pointed out that "the role of memory is not simply to provide us with cognitive access to the past; it is also to provide a route by which responsibility for past events is transmitted to the present." His insight can be related to the second way in which spectrality features in Irish and Irish diaspora fiction that recalls the Great Hunger: as the Famine past, neglected by the Anglo-Irish landlords and the British colonial government who wield power over Ireland. As Avery Gordon argues, "The ghost is not simply a dead or a missing person, but a social figure" that bears upon complexities and tensions in social relations.[61] Her observation applies to representations of the Great Famine in fiction: this past, as personified by the mnemonic image of the specter, is represented as disrupting the present in order to claim atonement for the wrongs done to the native Irish Famine victims.

Such representations of the phantom, often in the form of a skeleton that claims retribution from the classes who are responsible for the suffering of the Irish population, can be found in several pre- and post-Famine cultural expressions. For example, the cartoon *Irish Affairs: The Absentee* (fig. 6), published in the London newspaper the *Looking-Glass* on August 1, 1830, shows how a landlord who resides in Naples cannot enjoy a comfortable existence there, for he is haunted by "the Ghosts of starv'd Irish Peasantry" that enter his luxurious lodgings. This chromolithograph probably alludes to the famine of 1822, but similar representations of specters of starvation that haunt the upper classes can be found in cultural memories of the Great Famine. For instance, the lengthy poem *The Feast of Famine: An Irish Banquet* (1870) shows how the "banquet of viands all costly and rare" that is to be enjoyed by an absentee landlord in London and his guests is disturbed by "specters of men, women, children." This throng of ghosts, with "skeleton limbs, cold, frost-bitten, raw," is accompanied by a "spectre . . . superior in horror and height o'er the rest," with a "skeleton finger." Presiding over the table, the giant specter of Famine avenges itself upon the landed classes, forcing them to eat a "poor man's banquet," consisting of dog and seaweed, as well as to suffer the pangs of hunger, because it was "the fare" they left to the poor.[62]

Similar representations can be found in Allen H. Clington's *Frank O'Donnell* and in Alice Nolan's *The Byrnes of Glengoulah*. In Clington's novel, the narrator evokes the image of the specter that will haunt those persons in power over Ireland. He claims that the "millions of corpses that rot in pauper graves, that are tossed about by the ocean waves, or that sleep in far off lands, slain by the miasma of some pestilential swamp, will yet rise up in judgement" to the "despotic landlords" who have driven the peasants from the land and to a conniving government that was set against the "victims" of starvation, because

6. Robert Seymour, *Irish Affairs: The Absentee, Looking-Glass*, August 1, 1830. Lithograph on paper. Copyright, Victoria and Albert Museum, E. 5230-1904. This image is reproduced courtesy of the Victoria and Albert Museum, London.

they were "aliens in blood and religion." The passage remembers the Great Famine in Michelite terms, as deliberate clearance and extermination, and suggests that the Famine dead will be avenged one day. In *The Byrnes of Glengoulah*, specters of retribution can be found at two stages in the narrative, and, in both cases, their anger is aimed at landlord and bishop Biggs. In a scene halfway through the novel that borrows extensively from the Gothic mode, Biggs and his party are gathered for evening pastimes when "without a wild storm was raging. The wind roared up the chimney, crashed furiously against the heavy stone casements, and ran tearing and tumbling along the battlements as if meditating the destruction of the whole building." This description is clearly infused with the pathetic fallacy, for the tempest outside foreshadows the arrival of an unexpected, sinister guest. Suddenly, the door is flung open, and "a slight girlish form with bare and bleeding feet, dressed in a long white gown," is seen standing "on its threshold." Resembling an "apparition" and "unearthly looking being" that terrifies the ladies in the room, young Norah Cormac comes to confront Biggs, for the latter had robbed the girl "of home, kindred, and reason." Biggs had sent her mother to her untimely grave by turning her out on the road, because she refused to have her daughter converted to Protestantism, and it is the spirit of her deceased mother that now instigates Norah to invade the castle. Subsequently, Norah grabs Biggs's arm "in a death grasp," so that the landlord's "teeth actually chattered with dread."[63]

This scene from Nolan's novel, then, depicts a spectral-looking girl who appears to seek justice for the departed. The fact that Norah first pauses on the threshold before entering prefigures the world beyond the boundaries of normality, the intense suffering of the poor at the hand of the landlord, which the girl is about to expose. The ghostly Norah is, however, not the only specter to remind Biggs of his selfish, cruel deeds. In his sleep, he is haunted by the ghosts of former tenants who suffered because of his clearance policies and his religious convictions and now express their grudges toward him. Thus, as he later confesses, Fogarty "walked in to curse me, because his old mother died a lunatic, because she lost the farm and was starving. . . . Then in came thirty-seven that were evicted from the townland of Drismore shortly before Christmas." These spectral presences that visit him at night are quite disturbing, as Biggs confesses: "Sometimes they all come together, and set me nearly crazy with their abuse; sometimes they come alone, but in such rapid succession that they bewilder me. . . . I felt the bed rock under me, and everything was blown about."[64]

These presentations of haunting victims of Famine in *Frank O'Donnell* and *The Byrnes of Glengoulah* also appear to bear out the idea that the Famine past in itself is an episode that will continue to trouble present and future generations. Indeed, scholars in memory and trauma studies have often drawn analogies between processes of remembering and spectrality. For example, Dylan Trigg suggests that in the interaction between remembrance and repression, painful past experience constitutes a haunting presence, like a "specter" that "establishes a portal between the past and the present." Moreover, the specter, the indefinable entity that can disappear and reemerge randomly in different contexts, reminds one of Cathy Caruth's analysis of traumatic memory as resurfacing in "delayed, and uncontrolled, repetitive occurrence."[65]

Indeed, the Famine victims that come to haunt the future, as *Frank O'Donnell* suggests, or return unexpectedly to taunt Biggs's mind in *The Byrnes of Glengoulah*, are important portals between the past and present. In *Frank O'Donnell*, the dead that may rise from their graves appear to predict a resurrected Ireland in a double sense: as a regenerated nation and as a people in revolt. The prospective turn in the extract is complex: it represents a past that has the potential to break loose from its confinement and demand recognition, as symbolized by the dead who may come back to life. Several layers of time intersect here: the narrator points forward to Famine miseries to which the present characters are still oblivious and at the same time remembers this past, suggesting it has implications for the future, in that the nation will become divided by rebellion. The Famine and its memories can travel through different time frames, and in this sense the spectral appears to express the transportability of cultural memory across boundaries of time and space: ghosts from the past are elusive, free-floating apparitions. Moreover, the passage appears to imply that the Famine can never be put to rest unless its past atrocities are redressed.

By contrast, even if the novel itself reevokes the Famine past, *The Byrnes of Glengoulah* generates a sense of closure in that justice appears to prevail when Biggs becomes insane and the new landlord creates communal happiness again, as will be discussed in chapter 4. This sense of closure is also expressed by the peaceful vision of Norah singing among a "troop of angels" that comes up in Clara's dream. On the night when little Norah dies in the snow, Clara is presented with this comforting picture of the girl having been taken up to heaven: "Her face was now radiant as the sun, and a wreath of glory rested on her long dark hair." The earlier examined story "The

Tale of a Tombstone" presents a more ambivalent picture. On the one hand, the pains of Famine suffering seem to come to a close. When Ned lies prostrate on his mother's grave, a "holy peace" rests on his dead "pale, pale face," which speaks of the "mercy of our Heavenly Father, into whose holy keeping the spotless soul had passed." On the other hand, the old man who narrates the tale still appears to be haunted by the memory of the bleak Famine years. This fact becomes clear from the point that he addresses earlier, that the people who "lived through that year of misery and horror" must "shudder at the remembrance its very name reveals."[66]

This idea of a Famine past that must continue to haunt future generations is even more strongly present in Famine fiction from subsequent decades. In these narratives, characters and communities appear to be possessed by the troublesome memory of starvation as well as by fear that the gaunt specter of hunger may reappear. This sense of haunting permeates, for example, Emily Lawless's short story "After the Famine," which forms a framework narrative with its prequel, "Famine Roads and Memories," in the collection *Traits and Confidences* (1898). At the end of the latter story, the first-person narrator encounters an old man who tells her his memories of post-Famine Ireland, where he traveled as a former English estate agent intent on purchasing property. There he meets Eleanor D'Arcy, the only surviving member of her family, who seems to have lost all her relatives, including her sister Ann, during the Famine: "Had this hideous famine swept them all away, as it had swept away hundreds of thousands of humbler victims?" Ann, as the epitome of a Famine victim, haunts not only the old man's narrative, but also post-Famine Ireland, for she still seems to dominate life at Cashla Bay after her death. The servants speak of "Miss Ann's tayhouse" as if she is still alive, and Eleanor often calls out for her sister, looking around her "as if somewhere the person whom she sought must be found." As I have argued elsewhere, as a character both "dead and tangibly present to the other characters, Ann becomes the specter that reminds her sister and the servants of their loss and of the painful Famine years." Likewise, in Katharine Tynan's

A Cluster of Nuts (1894), an old priest in a remote Gaelic-speaking area not only is haunted by memories of the Great Famine, but also confesses his fear that the specter of starvation will resurface to kill his congregation: "But the thing that haunts me is the big famine that will come some day, when all the glen will die of starvation. Year after year we have had help just in the nick of time. But what if the help should come late? This year, or next year! God forgive me for fearing it, but it haunts me all day and every night, and when I go [on] my long walks through the Glen."[67]

The idea of a past that must resurface inevitably and cannot be put to rest is also alluded to in various Famine narratives that portray how the corpses of the Famine victims are not properly interred and are sometimes even dug up by dogs looking for meat. Obviously, these representations of bodies that are buried without a coffin and are devoured by animals appear to have been taken from various sources that recorded such dire circumstances as the harsh realities of life during the Famine. For example, Asenath Nicholson reports how the body of a girl who died "unheeded" is lacerated by dogs that "gnawed the bones, and strewed them about the bog." Similarly, Canon John O'Rourke asserts that of the Famine dead, "three-fourth" were "interred coffinless," and some "left to the many of the dogs which have nothing else to feed on." Almost identical representations can be found in *The Squanders of Castle Squander*: as the narrator states, the cemetery is a spectacle of barbarity, for a body is in "the act of being thrown, coffinless and half-naked, into what was rather a shallow trench, than a grave! Round about, and in this awful cemetery, were numbers of gaunt and starving dogs, whose skeleton bodies and fearful howlings indicated the ravenous fury with which they awaited an opportunity to drag the unfortunate dead from their shallow graves, and glut themselves upon their bodies." *Frank O'Donnell* paints a similar dire picture through the story of the Tobins, who had to bury their son "without a coffin or a shroud to cover him," in a plot of earth near their cabin, because they are both too weakened to take him somewhere else.[68] These pictures of the dead that are not properly interred intriguingly seem to hint at an unburied past that will resurface continuously, a suggestion that is underscored by the fact that these works of fiction are textually haunted by a repertoire of harrowing Famine images that date back to earlier times.

Conclusion

Memories of Ireland's Great Famine in fiction explore liminal zones and liminal discourses. The narratives take us into the liminal physical space of the homes of the Famine-stricken as well as the liminal psychological space of the Famine-afflicted mind, across the thresholds of what people would regard as common or acceptable conditions or conduct. Furthermore, these early Famine novels and stories employ discourses of liminality that are derived from the Gothic mode and Burkean rhetoric of the sublime, thereby giving expression to the idea that the Famine past goes beyond boundaries of conception and humaneness. This chapter has also moved beyond the time frame that is overall central to this study in order to indicate that there are transgenerational developments in the depiction of thresholds and what lies beyond them. Over time, thresholds in Famine fiction no longer serve as markers of disconnection and dissociation on the part of the narrative subjects of focalization, thus creating the impression that the passage of time allows for a more thorough identification with and exploration of Famine suffering.

In the earliest Famine narratives, the legacies of the Great Famine are also shaped by notions of the liminal as well as generic conventions of the Gothic, as a way to engage with a painful past that had deep political resonances. These texts often instrumentalize representations of Famine miseries in terms of liminality, as a way of defying the boundaries of imperial authority. Furthermore, these works of fiction appear to reflect upon the liminality of Famine memory itself, by representing the Famine past as a specter that can erupt and disappear, can be absent and present at the same time. This spectrality of the Famine past also comes to play a crucial role in fiction from subsequent decades. As we have seen, the idea of liminality is seldom explored in North American Famine fiction. This phenomenon may be explained by the reservations that these American and Canadian texts often display to an examination of the acutest Famine memories, as we also saw in chapter 1. When such North American Famine narratives like "The Tale of a Tombstone" and *Byrnes of Glengoulah* do, however, cast the Famine past in terms of the liminal and spectral, they unwittingly testify to the multifaceted fluidity of Famine recollections that cross transgenerational as well as transnational communities of memory.

4 From Wasteland to Paradise Regained

The Discovery of the Potato Blight (fig. 7), an oil painting by Cork-born artist Daniel MacDonald that was exhibited at the British Institution in 1847, is an expressive depiction of the shock and despair of Ireland's rural population at the outbreak of the *Phytophthora infestans* in the early autumn of 1845. Portraying three generations—the aged, people in the prime of their lives, as well as young children—who incredulously contemplate the wasted crops on their patch of land, this work of art not only reveals the ways in which individual families were affected by the potato pestilence, but also suggests the communal panic that followed when the people's main source of nutrition blackened in the bosom of the earth.

The blight-stricken land became an iconic representation of the Great Famine during the years of mass starvation. "The Warning Voice" (1847), by James Clarence Mangan, describes how the "once greenest path" has transformed into "blasted and sterile" soil. His poem "A Voice of Encouragement: A New Year's Lay" (1848) speaks of the "black harvestless fields" through which the woeful "wail" of the peasants resounds, their keen inscribing the scenery as a space of mourning. James Mahoney's earlier-mentioned sketch *Boy and Girl at Cahera* (fig. 1) likewise foregrounds the image of the infertile land. Depicting the famished figures of a boy and girl who vainly turn up the ground as they seek potatoes to still their hunger, Mahoney's illustration not only creates the impression of a rotting wasteland in terms of barrenness, but also creates the impression of a sepulchral landscape

7. Daniel MacDonald, *The Discovery of the Potato Blight* (1847). Oil painting. By permission of the National Folklore Collection, University College Dublin.

where, as the artist comments, "six dead bodies had lain for twelve days, without the least chance of interment, owing to their being so far from the town."[1]

In view of this centrality of the disfigured landscape in cultural (re) constructions of the Great Famine, it is by no means remarkable that images of untilled, fruitless acres and withered crops feature prominently in Irish and Irish diaspora fiction that recollects the successive failure of the potato harvests between 1845 and 1849. These representations of wastelands are, however, often alternated with evocations of pastoral and picturesque settings. As the following discussion will illuminate, in some narratives this pastoral or picturesque scenery is employed to suggest a pre-Famine idealized Ireland that has become irrevocably lost. In this way, these narratives both underline the fact that the Famine was often interpreted as a "failure of the pastoral" and lament the disappearance of a unique Irishness that was traditionally identified with the bucolic.[2] As such, these works of fiction identify the Famine with a rupture of traditional ways of life on economic and cultural levels. Furthermore, these novels and stories envisage the Irish land in terms of liminality, that is, at the edge of civilization.

Other texts—especially those works embodying an emerging postcolonial awareness and ones written in early stages of diaspora—by contrast imagine a post-Famine future homeland in which the traditional Irish pastoral scenery is or can be regenerated. These narratives interpret the Famine as a temporary break that will be followed by a return to earlier forms of living. In these texts, the land simultaneously embodies mortality and regeneration: while the wastelands—scarred by potato pestilence and emptied of population through evictions—seem to imply no hopes of recovery, at the same time they appear to contain a hidden resilience. Thus, the soil is depicted as being in a transitional stage between barrenness and recovery, embodying what I would like to call prospective liminality. Some novels and short stories even represent the actual return of a pastoral Ireland and, in so doing, crystallize an image of a pristine rural Ireland that has remained unscathed by the earlier trials of pestilence and mismanagement by the landed class. As such, these texts signify a country capable of surviving destructive imperial domination. As will be demonstrated, Famine fiction written between 1847 and 1870 thus testifies to the function of landscapes as symbolically encrypted spaces that are invested with "cultural meaning and power,"[3] ones that, as Barbara Bender argues, play a crucial role in the "way in which identities are created and disputed."[4]

Wastelands of Loss

In his pioneering study *Writing the Irish Famine* (1995), Christopher Morash states that cultural mediations of the Great Hunger repeatedly resorted to specific "semiotic systems of representation" to give expression to its trauma. His remark applies to the images of wasteland that early works of Famine fiction employ to reenact the Famine era, for they are generally permeated with notions of decay and death. William Carleton's *The Black Prophet*—while recollecting the 1816–17 famine—clearly resonates with the specific discourses used during the Great Hunger to describe the sudden attack of the blight. The novel describes "heavy clouds" of pestilence that destroy the potato crops overnight, thereby evoking the image of a dark vapor of blight that figures in many contemporary representations of the Great Famine. For instance, in a sermon by the Reverend John Travers Robinson, the blight is compared to a "dark cloud" sent by God that is "intervening between man and his Maker."[5] Moreover, like newspaper reports on the outbreak of blight that generally emphasize the odors of disease and rottenness,[6] Carleton's novel associates the landscape that is destroyed by this dark mist of pestilence with degeneration. Prophet Donnel Dhu reads the smell of "rotten crops, the unhealthy air, an' the green damp" that evaporate from the landscape as certain signs of impending famine, and the extradiegetic narrator comments that "the luxuriance of all weeds and unprofitable production was rank and strong, while an unhealthy fermentation pervaded every thing that was destined for food."[7]

The Black Prophet moreover identifies the barren soil with mortality: when Nelly, Donnel Dhu's spouse, digs for roots to appease her hunger, she literally stumbles upon a buried corpse: "She pushed the spade further down, until it was met by some substance that felt rather hard. . . . [S]he discovered that the spot on which the dandelions had grown, contained the bones of a full grown human body." The fact that the infertile field encapsulates death symbolically portends the population's mass starvation that follows upon the devastation of the land. Likewise, Richard Baptist O'Brien's novel *Ailey Moore: A Tale of the Times* (1856) shows how during the Famine the farmers' fields display degeneration. The narrator recalls a "perfectly appalling . . . condition and appearance of the country," manifested by empty cabbage fields with leafless "reddish-yellow stumps," a wasteland of "an occasional mound of withered grass, or some long yellow weeds." The acres are affected by a disease that has "blackened" the "poor people's food . . . in the bosom of the earth," while rotting weeds send forth a terrible stench of decay, "the odour of the charnel-house."[8] As a site of decay that can no longer sustain the people, the Irish land in these texts signifies a liminal space beyond the boundaries of humane living conditions.

As will be demonstrated in the following section, the pestilence-stricken, rotting acres that figure extensively in Famine fiction written on both sides of the Atlantic are often pitted against an indigenously Irish pastoral landscape that has become hauntingly disfigured by the outbreak of blight. The Famine wastelands in these narratives reveal the population's sense of alienation from their native soil, as well as a crisis of Ireland's rural identity. While these wastelands thus generally underline the dissolution of the symbiosis between man and nature, in some texts the blasted, arid soil conversely suggests a unity between the inhabitants and the land by expressing the condition of its dwellers. Symbolizing a waste of human life and potential, these barren fields embody the physical degeneration of the people living and working on them, functioning as screens that "stand in" or substitute for the "more disturbing or painful memory" of mass starvation and exodus that they displace "from consciousness."[9] By symbolically articulating past traumatic experiences that resist narrative integration,[10] these dismal sites display an interesting tension between a narrative "waste" of words and muteness. The works of fiction that incorporate wastelands as sites of Famine memory are, moreover, marked by a tension in that they translate waste in terms of both the ravaged and the residual. While on the one hand, the barren fields may testify to destruction and appear as evidence of Britain's successful subjugation of Ireland, on the other they present a subtext of colonial resistance: the uncultivable soil challenges the idea of imperial progress,[11] while it also presents "a sublimated and buried history" that contests imperial perspectives of the past.[12]

In many early works of Famine fiction, images of wastelands are incorporated into narrative templates that trace the loss of an Edenic Ireland. The novels and stories that include such a "paradise lost" plotline usually contrast idyllic pastoral scenery, which is invoked in early parts of the narrative, with its sudden transformation into barren wilderness during the Famine years. Indeed, biblical rhetoric of the story of Creation informed some representations of the Great Hunger: John Travers Robinson's earlier-quoted sermon depicts the Famine as a "spirit of destruction" that sets out to "conquer before it . . . the land like the garden of Eden, behind it is the desolate wilderness, the valley of the shadow of death." *A Tale of the Irish Famine in 1846 and 1847* (1847), by "Ireland," echoes this discourse of the Fall. The story intimates that, prior to the attack of potato pestilence, Erin was "a fair country to look upon," its "shamrock covered hills, those gleaming lakes and that soft valley beneath" resembling "a paradise . . . shut out from the rest of the world." However, the "destroying angel" that hovered near has brought "famine and pestilence . . . striding remorselessly over that lovely island."[13]

Although other works of Famine fiction do not refer back to scriptural discourses of a lost Eden so explicitly, they similarly suggest that the potato disease has radically distorted Ireland's pastoral loveliness. This narrative scheme, according to which a prelapsarian landscape is brutally transmuted into blasted, unproductive earth, can be considered transgenerational and transnational, because it appears in Famine fiction written from the 1840s until the 1870s and in narratives written in the homeland as well as diaspora. The novel *The Struggles of Dick Massey* (1860) was published under the pseudonym Reginald Tierney by Thomas O'Neill Russell, who contributed pieces to the *Irishman* to stimulate the revival of Gaelic[14] and to emphasize his allegiance to the Irish nationalist cause. The opening of the novel presents an idyllic scenery, stating that the "country lying around the hamlet of Clonderry was as beautiful as it was possible for mere pastoral scenery to be." When the blight and subsequent famine have badly afflicted the community, the once ravishing environment has turned into a "desert of desolation" and testifies to the broken covenant between man and nature.[15]

Elizabeth Hely Walshe's Irish Canadian novel *Golden Hills* (1865) likewise portrays how the heavenly landscapes of County Westmeath are scarred by the abrupt manifestation of the blight. As the title of the novel indicates, the estate where the Kingston family lives initially resembles pastoral bowers of peacefulness. The adjacent cliffs to which Kingston's daughter Lina retreats are embodiments of nature's loveliness: "crimson, and pink, and bright green, and golden, supplanting the uniform bronze of the winter waifs of algae." The novel even suggests that the scene could have been a place of rest and reflection for the poet Wordsworth, who "would have sat still and idle himself in such a scene, inhaling the surrounding beauty, receiving impressions from the greater Book of Nature . . . open to all the world." Like many texts that recollect the Famine—such as the poem *The Farmer of Inniscreen* (1863), which relates that the "green . . . leaves" of the potato plants wither away within "four days"—Walshe's novel imagines an acute transition from this idyllic scenery to wasteland. The pestilence, which like a "a dark mist creeping along, clinging to the earth in shadowed places," scourges the acres overnight—"while the people quietly slept through all the cabins dotting the country"—changes the verdant lands into tainted, rotten earth: "but the green fields were as if a burning blast had passed over them. Black patches lay where the day previously had been verdure, and the keen odour of decay escaped from them on all sides."[16]

During the nineteenth century, many European (emerging) countries, such as England and Russia,[17] represented a specific national identity in terms of the bucolic, and the pastoral landscape was likewise generally envisaged as the expression of a unique Irish identity. This tendency is aptly illustrated by James Arthur O'Connor's landscape paintings from the 1820s as well as by the poem *Mount Leinster* (1819), which casts the typical Irish landscape in pastoral terms that, interestingly enough, include a vista of flourishing potato crops: there are "undulating fields" where the "young potato-stems" display their green heads in the pleasant sight of "white-washed cottages."[18]

In some works of Famine fiction, this template of a vanished natural paradise underlines the loss of a specific Irish rural culture that is swept away by the wide-scale famine that wreaks havoc among the country people. For instance, in Allen H. Clington's *Frank O'Donnell*

(1861), the heterodiegetic narrator prepares his or her readers for "all the horrors of the famine years" that he or she will shortly describe by offering one last view "of the merry green where the youths and maidens are dancing, hurling, playing hide and go seek, and the like pastimes." While invoking this pastoral of rural leisure and merriment, the narrator foreshadows the transformation of this idyllic countryside setting into a depopulated, ravaged area, stating that "these arcadian scenes are now fast dying away; will some kind spirit rise up and revive them?"[19] Thus, *Frank O'Donnell* represents the Famine as a rupture of rural culture.

Peter McCorry was an Ulster Catholic immigrant to America, journalist, editor of the *Irish People*, and an ardent Irish nationalist.[20] His novel *The Lost Rosary* (1870) depicts damaged pastoral scenery that leads to a loss of specifically Irish customs and traditions. At the onset of the narrative, the heterodiegetic narrator propounds the image of an idyllic, Edenic landscape decked out with spring flowers that is a pleasure to the beholder and provides its inhabitants with a site of delightful labor as well as leisure, in the form of spring festivals: "HAPPY MAY! When the bloom of the hawthorn offers its incense to nature, and gladdens every eye with its milk-white beauties. HAPPY MAY! When the light-hearted youths of Ireland, frolicsome and gleeful, go a-maying over moss and glen, to gather the golden flowers, whose magic spell around the cabin door preserves the humble home from all the spiteful influences and tricks of fairy-land. . . . The whole 'country-side was up.' Young and old were engaged in rambles and athletic sports. . . . Everywhere there was racing and chasing, and harmless amusements."[21] The scene voices the ideal of pastoral *otium*,[22] further emphasized by the dance in a barn that is accompanied by the music of the blind fiddler Darby.

This depiction of pre-Famine Ireland, which foregrounds the physical and spiritual connection of the people to the land, is contrasted with the tropes of infertile land and the descriptions of severe toil that are used to recall the Great Famine. When "the second and third years' crops lay rotting in the earth," the fields are deprived not only of crops that can be harvested, but also of the rural songs that would normally reverberate through the landscape. Due to wide-scale starvation, "the reapers' song was hushed, and the dull workers in the field, from morn till eve, plodded out their lives in the hopeless task of saving their bits of land."[23] While the rural community is no longer a bower of pastoral pleasure, the land no longer functions as a Georgic space, suitable for farming and thus offering "permanence . . . peace and prosperity," either:[24] the toil of farming is a source not of gratification, but of frustration.[25] While the land has become a site of hard, and even useless, labor, the musical traditions of the rural population are also waning. As such, the evocation of wasteland in the novel serves to express concern about the extinction of a unique rural identity.

Laurence Buell contends that nature as a place constitutes a "space that is bounded and marked as humanly meaningful through personal attachment, social relations and physiographic distinctiveness" and is therefore associated with a sense of home and belonging. In view of his claim, it is not surprising that quite a few early Famine novels and stories written on both sides of the Atlantic also juxtapose an originally pastoral landscape with representations of blight-stricken wasteland to point to the experiences of displacement that the suffering Irish population had to undergo. This experience of displacement is often translated into a dislocation from home or the homely that runs analogous to the transformations of the landscape into uncultivable, barren ground. In William Carleton's story "Owen M'Carthy; or, The Landlord and Tenant" (1857), the transfiguration of the land from a pastoral haven to "waste" appears to be accompanied by a similar degeneration of the family house that forms a prelude to the protagonist's dislocation from his roots. While in former happier days, Owen M'Carthy's abode was a "neat white house" that "among the shining branches" of treetops formed an "emblem of contentment, industry and innocence," in the narrative present his house has attained a "wasted, unthriving look like its master" that manifests itself through thatch that lies "black and rotten upon its roof."[26]

This process of dissolution that the house embodies and that runs parallel to the degeneration of Owen and his starving family appears to express metaphorically their suffering and hardships, which are not elaborated upon in detail. As such, the house appears to convey trauma that cannot be narrated. Smelser identifies "projection," that is, the shifting of a painful experience to another object, as one of the major defense mechanisms when coping with trauma. In similar terms, Rothberg argues that a screen of memory "stands in or substitutes for a more disturbing or painful memory that it displaces from consciousness." The description of the dilapidating house can be read as such a screen of displacement, for the site mirrors the deteriorating circumstances of its dwellers. The black and rotten thatch upon its roof moreover seems to allude to the potato blight that caused the Great Hunger, which, as we saw, was traditionally cast in similar terms of decay. Carleton's story thus implies a connection between the withered landscape and the disfiguration of what once was a domestic haven of bliss, while sidestepping a full account of its inhabitants' painful bodily decay. This dramatic decline of the homestead moreover prefigures the family's eventual loss of the cottage: when Owen returns from his fruitless mission to ask his landlord for an extension of payment, he finds that he has "neither house nor home," for his family has been evicted.[27] In Carleton's story, then, images of waste underscore the dissolution between man and his environment, by portraying the rural setting as a site that reflects and embodies the condition of the starving family. By using the scenic image of degeneration to convey a sense of enfeebled bodies, the narrative literally does not waste any words on the painful process of starvation that the family endures.

In other works of fiction, the dramatic transfiguration of the pastoral Irish landscape into Famine wasteland is likewise accompanied by a loss of home. In Clington's *Frank O'Donnell* (1861), the eponymous hero experiences a great sense of belonging and comfort when the rustic beauties of his surroundings are still intact. The pastoral settings even hold a promise of future domestic happiness, for the budding love between Alice and Frank comes to full bloom when they pass "along to the hurling green, floating in the breeze. A thrush and blackbird, from a thicket near, seemed to endeavor to tire each other out. There was a delicious freshness in the balmy air; it was an evening for lovers to breathe forth their feelings of devotion." By contrast, when the outbreak of the potato pestilence eventually reduces Frank's family to such dire straits that they are ejected from their home and his mother dies during the eviction, Frank also feels that all his hopes of a marital haven with Alice are forever crushed: "Oh! I had hopes and yearnings of enjoying peace, and love, and happiness in that old home. . . . Often have I imagined ourselves seated by our own fireside, fostering our little plots and plans of life. . . . But oh! All this, this was but a dream!" Robert Curtis's "McCormack's Grudge" (1862) also reveals that the "sudden and destructive blight which the will of an inscrutable Providence cast upon the potato crops of Ireland in 1846" has resulted in the depopulation of once densely housed communities. Whereas in 1844, according to the extradiegetic narrator, "some hundreds of comfortable dwellings" could be found in the area, "upon the same tour, subsequent to that period," nothing could be seen but "broken-down gables and black rafters" of abandoned cottages. *Irish Diamonds* (1864) is a Famine novel by Emily Bowles, who converted to Catholicism in the Oxford Movement of 1843 and founded a convent in Liverpool. In the text, the image of potato crops "badly tainted with disease" is likewise followed by eviction, as the novel describes how the landlord summons "old Michael Macnamara to quit his dwelling and give up the key."[28]

This plotline of displacement, which is related to the transformation of the scenery into wasteland, is by no means restricted to fiction written in the homeland, for in the Irish American novels *The Lost Rosary* (1870) and *Bessy Conway* (1862), the outbreak of the blight similarly leads to a dislocation from the family home. In McCorry's novel, the blight transforms the land beyond recognition, and Corny O'Donnell, father to main female protagonist Mary, is rack-rented out of his ancestral family holding, losing "a portion of his land." The acres that had been family possessions for years are no longer a site where he may dwell, and Corny dies of the mental affliction that this loss brings him. In *Bessy Conway* the pastoral scenery that the opening of the novel evokes, in the form of Bessy's childhood "cottage beneath the sycamore" surrounded by an idyllic green "pasture-field," is transformed into barren land. When the "dismal time in Denis Conway's cottage, and in many a cottage through the length and breadth of Ireland," sets in, caused by "the failure of crops" during "the terrible year of the Famine," once blooming acres have become breeding places of weeds: "Tall ragweed nodded in the summer breeze, the dock weed spread its broad leaves on the arid soil, and the fiery nettle grew and flourished where a weed dared not rear its head before, to dispute possession with the careful grain stalk." This transfiguration of "fallow fields where in other years the golden grain would, at that season, wave luxuriant, ready for the sickle, and the rugged leaves of the potato stalk covering whole acres with their dark green hue of promise" into desolate soil brings Denis such financial difficulties that the bailiffs come to expel him and his family from their home.[29]

In some texts the sense of displacement that is connected to the lamentable transmutation of the once idyllic landscape is expressed through an uncanny feeling of alienation from natural scenes. In these narratives the once familiar landscape that is characteristic of Ireland is now unsettling and unhomely, thereby representing a liminal space between familiarity and alienation. Basing his ideas on conventional Freudian and Heideggerian definitions, Nicholas Royle claims that the uncanny signifies an unsettling "commingling of the familiar and unfamiliar" that may take the form of "something strange and unfamiliar unexpectedly arising in a familiar context."[30] This sense of an uncanny displacement that is marked by a "sickening estrangement from self, home, and nature" can be found in Dillon O'Brien's novel *The Dalys of Dalystown* (1866).[31] When Henry Daly, who had left Ireland many years before, returns to his former abode in the last trail of the Famine, he finds the bleak landscape both recognizable and utterly strange: "From time to time, he reined up his horse to look around on the familiar landscape, changed but little in the years that had passed, save that it now wore a desolate look—Not a living thing was to be seen in the fields or along the road he traveled."[32] While the scene voices the sense of displacement that would have struck any Irish emigrant returning from diaspora, Henry Daly's ambivalent feelings of rootedness as well as estrangement identify the land that has been scarred by the blight and depopulation with mental dislocation.

Mrs. Hoare's story "The Black Potatoes" also suggests a defamiliarization of the Irish landscape that is a direct consequence of the potato pestilence. The first-person narrator draws a contrast between the "remote district of Munster" of "former years," which was "covered with the rich green leaves and star-shaped purple-and-white flowers of the potatoes," and the present year, in which the fields are covered with "black withered stalks, exhaling a strong offensive odour."[33] This sense of estrangement that the current natural scenery evokes is underlined by references to the figure of the tourist: the narrator, who appears to be native to the area, argues that while the Irish scenery is different from the landscape of "the Scottish Highlands" and "the rural districts of 'Merrie England,'" in former years it would hold out equally extensive pleasures for the foreign traveler: "Yet many and abounding were the points of interest that caught the tourist's attention, including the humours of the light-hearted Irishman, as well as the romantic beauties of his land."[34] While this allusion to the tourists' former rapture at the romantic scenes once again emphasizes the radically altered land, it additionally positions the readers as non-Irish travelers to the region who are guided through its present blight-afflicted, dreary scenery by the all-knowing local narrator.

The narrator's subsequent sketch of blackened crops and rotting weeds reinforces the sense of displacement that the story foregrounds. Before the Famine, tourists' representations of Ireland would emphasize the picturesque scenery of the country. For instance, Thomas Kitson Cromwell's *The Irish Tourist; or, Excursions through Ireland* (1820) describes Loch Bray as a "scene of exquisite beauty and softness," a "land of enchantment . . . always picturesque in its outline and many coloured in its details." Henrietta Chatterton's *Rambles in the South of Ireland during the Year 1838* (1839) praises the "rich and vivid colouring of the scenery in Ireland; when the sun shines after one of the frequent showers, the whole landscape resembles a highly finished and freshly varnished picture, not by any well-known master, for the composition." With the arrival of the Famine, this tendency to describe Ireland in terms of the picturesque persisted, in spite of the prevalence of blighted fields, ruined and deserted cottages, and the widespread presence of starvation. As William Williams argues, "By the time of the Great Famine, the picturesque had so defined Ireland that even some of those who came to observe the crisis . . . or to minister to its victims were drawn to Ireland's scenic landscapes." That indeed tourists to Ireland employed "picturesque techniques to create a comforting distance between themselves and the horrors of the Famine" becomes clear from narratives written by English travelers during the Great Hunger. Spencer T. Hall's *Life and Death in Ireland, as Witnessed in 1849* (1850), for example, alternately describes the conditions of the farmers in need of relief and the "dash of the romantic" in the "irresistibly charming" landscape. Similarly, William Bennett's *Narrative of a Recent Journey of Six Weeks in Ireland* (1847) switches back and forth between detailed descriptions of the effects of the Famine, such as "swollen limbs, emaciated countenances, and other hideous forms of disease," and picturesque scenery marked by "noble vistas into deep, abrupt-looking valleys, alive with the voice of waters, and the motion of many graceful white-threaded streamlets coming down from the heights." "The Black Potatoes" rather suggests what Raymond Williams would call a "pastoral elegy," that is, a picturesque setting that appears forever lost.[35] Hinting that the "romantic beauties" of the scenery that would capture the tourist's gaze belong to a bygone era, the story challenges the stock images that crop up in tourist accounts, instead suggesting an insider's perspective that is entirely demystifying and defamiliarizing.[36]

This sense of alienation in connection to the land(scape) also permeates Famine fiction of subsequent decades and can therefore be regarded as a transgenerational mnemonic template. In Hester Sigerson's *A Ruined Race* (1889), the protagonist, Dam Macmanus, not only literally loses a once "comfortable roomy cottage" with "a pretty flower garden" when the blight sets in and devastates his prospects, but also no longer feels at home in his environment after losing his wife, child, and home, for because of his sorrows he can no longer connect to the pastoral aspects of the landscape surrounding him. While on a beautiful moonlit night, "the rich sweet smell of the hawthorn filled the air, and the fairy laughter of the little brook close by was the only sound which broke the stillness of the night," Dan is so overcome by "mental anguish, fatigue, and long fasting" and "a chill and dreadful sense of loss" that he does not receive consolation from the scene but wishes for death. Similarly, in *Castle Daly* (1875) protagonist Ellen Daly fails to derive pleasure from the Hollow Valley even if at that moment it had "never looked fairer, or showed more like an enchanted region, jewel-paved with emerald and diamond and azure," simply because the landscape is scarred by loss as well: "There was something wanting; the old sights were there, but not the old sounds. A strange silence reigned all about the place that fell like an ache on Ellen's heart."[37] Deprived of population, the landscape cannot retain its former beauties in the eyes of the beholder, who can perceive only traces of loss and death.

Wastelands of Resistance

In an effort to theorize the cultural significance of landscape, Denis Cosgrove argues that "landscape constitutes a discourse through which identifiable social groups historically have framed their relations both with the land and with other human groups." Landscape therefore concerns not only the condition and cultivation of the soil, but also the economic and symbolic value it embodies for the people who inhabit it. The blasted landscapes that prevail in early Famine fiction testify to the close interrelationships between scenery, the economic and social situation of those individuals who labor in the fields as well as those who own the soil. In Mrs. Hoare's story "Little Mary" (1851), for instance, the sudden transformation of "gardens that used to be so bright and sweet, covered with the purple and white potato blossoms," into "black and offensive" remains runs parallel to a symbolic waste of human energy, as the laboring men in vain try to "dig their suppers from under the blackstalks" and have to turn up spadeful after spadeful before "they'd get a small kish full of such withered crohauneens, as other years would be hardly counted fit for the pigs."[38] This analogy between wasted land and wasted labor also occurs in other Famine narratives. However, this section will specifically contemplate the ways in which the scarred natural environment serves as a symbolic platform to criticize the policies of the representatives of imperial power, the landlords and their agents, who deliberately waste the potential of their estates as well as their tenants.

This function of wasteland as an emblem of colonial critique is particularly present in Famine fiction written in the homeland during the 1860s, probably because the problems of exorbitantly high rent rates and evictions were still high on the Irish political agenda at the time: in 1866 Isaac Butt spoke about the "problems of Ireland's condition" in that the tenure system fueled the disloyalty of the people to "the whole system of landed propriety." Furthermore, in 1867 Lord Dufferin complained about the "iniquity of the laws affecting the tenure of land" in Ireland, which, in his view, led to mass deprivation and emigration. These texts recall and engage with the rhetoric of misuse that marked discussions of Irish agriculture at the time of the Famine. Many authors of pamphlets or political letters who entered the debate about the rural condition of the Emerald Isle during the Famine would take issue with the landed class, who, in their view, neglected to exhaust the resources of the land and implement agricultural reform. Jonathan Pym, for example, openly questioned the right of the landowners to keep the lands "waste or untenanted" during the ongoing crisis, asserting that a country "naturally very fertile is left almost unimproved, and only half cultivated; the fields are undrained . . . straggling hedges and uncultivated spots deform the face of the country . . . and much land capable of culture is left to its natural wildness, or is so ill tilled, that it is but little better than waste."[39]

Member of Parliament G. Poulett Scrope similarly wondered why the landed classes were "still to be permitted to lock up one-third of the area of the entire island in a state of barrenness" and expend millions on "much-abused roads . . . almost to no purpose of future utility" instead of "developing vast resources of waste land" that "would afford for the future permanent employment to thousands of labourers." Lawrence Rawsterne and W. W. Robinson therefore recommended reclamation and "drainage of the lands" to "ward off the weight of the poor-rate by opening new fields of labour, instead of supplying relief in kind."[40] In advocating these modes of improvement, Pym, Scrope,

Rawsterne, and Robinson took a stance against a landed class that, made responsible for poor relief by John Russell's laissez-faire politics and often fed by "an instinctive suspicion of relief expenditure,"[41] increasingly set out to clear estates of tenants in order to "make way for graziers."[42] The dire result of these clearance policies, which intensified after the introduction of the infamous Gregory Clause (1847),[43] was a wasteland not simply because the soil was unsuitable for cultivation, but also in the sense of a desolate scenery of vacant farms.[44]

Both Clington's *Frank O'Donnell* and Charles Joseph Kickham's novel *Sally Cavanagh* (1869) use images of wasteland in this second sense of cleared, depopulated fields that testify to the unused residues of the land and the farmers, in order to criticize landlords and their agents who care only for their own benefit in times of distress. In *Sally Cavanagh*, Brian Purcell, son of a comparably well-to-do family of farmers, is dismayed to see "hundreds of acres along the mountain foot, which were a rocky waste till the persevering toil of the poor tenants reclaimed them." The land here is a barren scene of desolation not because of the potato rot, but because the tenants have been evicted and therefore no longer maintain the acres. Expelled from the fields on which they worked, the "poor people were robbed of the fruits of their labour" and left to die by the roadside by the greedy and selfish landlord Oliver Grindem.[45] The wasteland thereby bears witness to the shortcomings of a landowner unwilling to improve the conditions of his estate. Symbolizing the wasted lives of the famishing ejected tenants and the unused potential of the soil, the barren land suggests imperial neglect.

Imperialist narratives conventionally tend to legitimize the colonial power's conquest of the land by emphasizing the improvements and cultivation that the civilized, usurping nation will bring to the barbarous wasteland.[46] As the landed class was often associated with the British Empire, by implication Kickham's narrative appears to point out the failures of colonization: the land embodies a liminal space at the margins of progress and civilization. In a similar vein, the narrator in *Frank O'Donnell* uses images of waste to denounce the landowners' neglect of the land as a primary source for the people's sustenance. The narrator elaborates upon the "unchristian conduct of Irish landlords" such as Lord Clearall "in laying waste the country, in levelling the poor man's cabin, and sending him and his family to a pauper's grave," solely for the purpose of exploiting the mineral resources of the soil. The landscape that has wasted away owing to the policies of Clearall and his covetous land agent, Mr. Ellis, thus functions as a physical site that expresses a subversive critique of the Ascendancy and those persons who represent them. In Mrs. Lorenzo Nunn's novel *Heirs of the Soil* (1870), the agent of the absentee landlord Mr. Alfred Gifford, who "had learned high-pressure farming the Lothians," is eager to "weed" the Glensallagh estate "of tenants in arrear," as if they are useless nettles that disfigure the land, in order to "introduce not only the Scotch mode of farming, but Scotchmen" as "desirable tenants."[47] For the sake of agricultural modernization, he turns out several famishing families without any compassion for their fate.

Criticism of the tendency among the landed classes to clear their property of tenantry, often in order to convert their lands into pastures for cattle, also features in *The Struggles of Dick Massey*. Guided by his immoral agent, Mr. Winters, Colonel Hutchinson is almost convinced that he should turn his estate into one large sheeping farm, so that rent may be more easily collected and the lands that he possesses will look "so nice too, all laid down in grass . . . especially in Ireland, where they are so green, not like the arid-looking wastes of Normandy." Hutchinson's inclination to give in too easily to the whims of his agent and have his lands cleared by shipping his tenants off to Canada and America is criticized by his daughter Clara, who, stepping out of her traditional gender role, instead argues in favor of agricultural reform. Based on the management of estates she had witnessed in Bruges, Clara has concrete visions that she would realize if she had a different social position: "If I were a man, I would, had I estates, a thousand times rather turn them into such populous Edens, than into great deserted sheepwalks." As her remark suggests, a depopulated estate is far less attractive scenery than a well-cultivated and inhabited land such as the Bruges countryside, which "like a garden" with its "luxuriance of crops . . . was the most beautiful sight you ever saw," and would moreover entail a waste of human potential that is likely to be lost by "shipwreck or sickness" on the transatlantic crossing. As such, Tierney's novel appears to recollect the common denouncement of the emigration schemes launched by landlords in the age of the Famine: William Henry Smith considered these policies of forced emigration monstrous, as the country was "requiring agricultural development as much as the wilds of Australia," and G. Poulett Scrope lamented the exodus of industrious people to "Upper Canada or Illinois" while they could have tilled the soils at home.[48]

Clara's observations moreover imply a challenge to the concept of the picturesque. As Susan Egenolf asserts, the traditional idea of the picturesque was rooted in the absence of human work, like agriculture—a claim that is illustrated by William Gilpin's declaration that "from scenes indeed of the *picturesque kind* we exclude the appendages of tillage, and in general the works of men; which too often introduce preciseness, and formality."[49] Colonel Hutchinson's idealization of large green fields that are populated only by sheep fits in with this conventional representation of the picturesque that was especially popular in English perspectives on the Irish scenery, as we saw in the previous section. Clara's redefinition of an idyllic landscape in terms of the Georgic, that is, a human relationship to the landscape that is marked by labor,[50] rather than the conventional pastoral images of pastures and graziers that give her father scenic pleasure, questions the tendency of the ruling classes to reconstruct the Irish landscape merely in terms of what pleases the eye.

Similar critiques of the aestheticization of the Irish land by the Ascendancy can be found in several other works of Famine fiction. In Henry J. Monahan's *O'Ruark* (1852), Mr. Elmore's desire to beautify his estate comes with a deliberate neglect of the conditions of his tenantry, as the sore presence of the dilapidated cottages and deprived farmers must be removed from sight as much as possible: "No dirty cabins, no filthy dung heaps, no wretched tenants shocked the beholder; for though there were such, they were wisely placed in the background; and if a very far-sighted person did catch a glimpse of them, they looked quite picturesque." Rather, Elmore tries to create a pastoral atmosphere in the proximity of his home, marked by "green" land and "immense sheep walls," while he wishes his tenants to be as distant as "the union work-house." Elmore's inclination to see the cottiers and their poor housing conditions as a blemish on the scenery moreover echoes the sentiments voiced by many foreign travelers who in the aftermath of the Famine increasingly journeyed to rural Ireland—most specifically the remote western parts—as tourist destinations. For instance, English tourist Sidney Godolphin Osborne wrote in his *Gleanings in the West of Ireland* (1850) that "to any one, fond of lake and mountain scenery, the road from Oughterard to Clifden will afford a great treat. I confess I enjoyed it the more, from the absence of population, and therefore of misery."[51] In this respect, *O'Ruark* also appears to criticize the conventional English tourist discourses on Ireland's landscape, which often identified scenic beauty with depopulation.

William Gorman Wills's novel *The Love That Kills* (1867) also implies that the picturesque beauties that surround the stately homes of the landed gentry conceal the dire scenes of deprivation that can be found in other parts of the estate and that the lord of the mansion seeks to forget. Rathmount, home to the Armstrongs, "lies in a pleasant site" amid "lakes of pasture rippling in the yellow sunshine," but the picturesque beauties that the grounds at first sight present are marred by the presence of "dirty cottiers, lean pigs, black potatoes, and ruined cabins" elsewhere on the estate. Alice Nolan's Irish American novel *The Byrnes of Glengoulah* (1868) represents a landowning elite and their agents who are indifferent to the state of the crops and the farms on their grounds, because they are mainly concerned with beautifying the natural environment of their demesnes. The narrator shows that the landlord's ineffectual policies compel the cottiers to perform inefficient tasks on his estate and prevent them from maintaining the land. When the narrator comments upon the fact that "gates were seen hanging by one hinge, cattle roaming at will or grazing in the ditches, pigs and poultry trespassing upon neighbors, . . . the whole byre, once so trim and well-kept, dirty and miry, the poor vines and flower-beds drooping and running wild," he or she subsequently states that readers should "wonder no longer" about this overall state of dirt and disorder.

The tenants are forced to beautify Lord Biggs's grounds, thereby losing precious time that they could have invested in planting crops and sowing seeds. Jacob Margin, Biggs's agent, not only takes pleasure in "presiding in person" over the "inhuman" evictions of families on the estate and gloats over the fact that a clearance of tenants' farms will enable a profitable exploitation of the present mines. He also appropriates part of the land on which the former cottages of the tenants have been pulled down in order to make "a smiling garden where this poor home once stood, and beautiful flowers of brilliant hue exhaled their fragrance and opened their petals to the sun, and the birds came there and sang their little hymns of praise, never knowing the bitter sorrow that had wrung burning curses on that very spot from a heart seared with human agony."[52]

Thus, while Margin creates a pastoral bower, this sense of pleasure is undermined by the trauma of eviction that still haunts the horticulturally refined land as what Pierre Nora calls a *lieu de mémoire*.[53] As such, the soil itself and the traumatic recollections that it continues to conjure up challenge the facade of progress and improvement that Margin creates in realizing his horticultural ambitions. While his conversion of the grounds into a garden seeks to eliminate any traces of the former exploitation of the tenantry, the narrator implies that this buried past still manifests itself, even if the warbling birds are ignorant of these past atrocities. The grounds that were laid waste during Margin's reorganization speak back to the imperial narrative of progress that his garden personifies. They express an alternative history of imperial failure that moreover criticizes the aestheticization of the soil that goes at the expense of labor and resources and transforms this Georgic space into a pastoral bower that may be enjoyed by only a specific class.

By contrast, Nolan's novel celebrates the scenic beauties of nature that are God-made and persist in spite of the blight, but even more despite efforts by the landed class and their agents to spoil the natural function of the land as the people's communal sustenance for the sake of profit and personal benefit. When the cottiers by necessity have to neglect the cultivation of their lands, Biggs employs them to aggrandize his grounds. The narrator intimates that the "landscape, however, lost nothing of its beauty, for the hand of God had piled the beautiful hills peak over peak and clothed them with the most exquisite variety of shrubs and trees, and the slopes He covered with the softest and greenest of turf."[54] In this outline of a resilient picturesque scene, Nolan's novel expresses criticism of the ways in which the representatives of empire, the English-born Lord Biggs and his agent, Margin, ruin Ireland's land. This land is a liminal site in several respects. It is a space of decay and death that nevertheless implies the possibility of future recuperation, thereby creating the impression that the Famine era may prove to be a temporary rupture of rural existence. Furthermore, while the land displays traces of imperial usurpation and defeat, it also suggests invincibility: those persons who colonize Ireland's areas cannot fully control its nature, for the landscape has a boundless regenerative power.[55] As such, the land represents a prospective liminality: while apparently stuck in degeneration, it contains the germs of a future recovery and therefore seems suspended between death and rebirth.

Paradise Regained

In fiction written in Ireland during or in the immediate aftermath of the Great Hunger, the loss of pastoral scenery that results from the outbreak of the potato blight often proves to be permanent. Stories such as "The Black Potatoes" by Mrs. Hoare, *A Tale of the Irish Famine in 1846 and 1847* by Ireland, and "Owen M'Carthy; or, Landlords and Tenants" by William Carleton portray a lamentable transfiguration of the once lovely landscape of "renowned verdure . . . a paradise . . . shut out from the rest of the world" into barren soil that appears to be irreversible and irredeemable. In Hoare's story, the evoked idyllic settings of green fields and flourishing vegetation seem to be mere recollections of "former years" that can be neither relived nor regenerated. *A Tale of the Irish Famine in 1846 and 1847* evokes the image of a dried-up stream to underscore the extinction of Irish ancient families owing to the blight, and at the end of Carleton's tale Owen finds his "land . . .

about two years waste."[56] As such, these early works of Famine fiction testify to the fresh traumatic phase of calamity and loss during which a recuperation of Ireland's natural scenery could not yet be imagined.

By contrast, works of fiction written in the 1860s frequently represent the return of an Edenic Irish landscape from which the scars of the blight have been erased, thereby suggesting that the Famine has been just a temporary rupture of rural bliss. These narratives incorporate a template tracing the loss of a pastoral Ireland until the eventual retrieval of this paradisiacal setting, attributing the possibilities for Ireland's recuperation either to a landed class that looks after the well-being of its tenantry and embraces reform or to the investments made by remigrants who have made fortunes in the New World. While this plotline is typical for Irish North American Famine fiction, Reginald Tierney's *The Struggles of Dick Massey* is an example of a novel written in Ireland that features such a "paradise regained" template. The remigrants Tom Neligan and his betrothed, Norah Conroy, who had spent some time in the valley of the Wabash, can resettle into a rural community that suggests the recovery of rural bliss in Ireland. This recovery is largely owing to the pains taken by Tom's former landlord, the empathic Dick Massey, and his beloved, the previously mentioned Clara Hutchinson, to improve the conditions of the tenants in Kilfarney, "in spite of sickness and famine." As a result, while the surrounding areas bear traces of eviction and excessive mortality—containing "depopulated" sites and "roofless skeletons of cabins" that symbolically express the phantom of starvation that haunts rural existence—Kilfarney has been turned into "a green oasis amid the surrounding desert of desolation."[57]

This image of a bucolic haven in the middle of a wasteland constitutes the characteristic pastoral *locus amoenus*,[58] or what Terry Gifford calls the pastoral "aesthetic landscape that is devoid of conflict and tension." The estate radiates beauty and what Donna Potts terms "pastoral harmony," as it is dotted with "trim and whitewashed" cottages inhabited by "swarms of rosy children, and also men and women that don't seem to have suffered from either hunger or sickness." This typical pastoral retreat from the "dark mist of famine and disease, which had overspread all the rest of the surrounding country," dispels the horrors visiting the nation "by the sunshine of love" and thereby displaces the trauma of starvation from the site to which Tom and Norah return. While the trauma of deserted Famine wastelands is thus comfortably pushed to the background of the narrative, the idea of remigration to an idyllic Ireland unspoiled by the miseries of famine is underlined by the fact that Tom and Norah gain a plot of land of their own on which they can establish a pastoral home: they obtain a "neatly thatched cottage with whitewashed walls, that nestles amongst boor trees and hawthorns" for their expanding family. Their new homestead also appears untouched by Famine atrocities, for the fields surrounding the cottage are fertile and rich: "It is a beautiful place, all flowers and fragrance."[59]

Moreover, this regained pastoral Irish scene appears to be a much more preferable alternative to the "finest prairie" in the fruitful valley of the Wabash where Norah's uncle, Martin Conroy, has made a fortune with land that requires hardly any manure. Even if pastoral homesteads may be set up in the New World, they are "not half so goodly or so fair as Ireland." Clonderry is once more a recognizable home, as the omniscient narrator intimates: "Sure we ought to know it?" In Tierney's novel, the retrieval of a pastoral Irish environment is thus accompanied by the characters' reappropriation of their roots. This reconnection to their native soil secures what Greg Gerrard would call the experience of dwelling on the land: "the long-term imbrication of humans in a landscape of memory, ancestry and death, of ritual, life and work."[60]

In a similar vein, the conclusion of Robert Curtis's "McCormack's Grudge" reveals the regeneration of the blight-stricken land, for the "potatoes were 'getting the better' of the disease; and from this very period every year was better for the farmer than the previous one. Corn, hay, potatoes, every article of produce began to look up, and the farmers began to look up after them." Now that the crisis of the blight had passed and the land attained its former function as a Georgic site of rural labor, Ireland "began to gain strength daily, after having been bruised and gored in a fearful manner from one end to the other." Rewarded for his heroic rescue of the land agent's son, Myles McCormack thrives: he "ultimately fell in for Jones's holdings, and became the most comfortable and independent man in the townland of Tullybrin or upon the estate." While crops flourish again, and the once deprived tenant Myles enjoys prosperity, the Edenic vision of the estate is completed by the fact that English landowner Mr. Walcroft takes up "his permanent residence at Curranure" and has even come to adjust himself to the qualities of the Irish soil: "From constant practice, he is enabled to walk the bogs."[61] Cultural differences are erased by a common rootedness in the reanimated land that unites all classes.

The more positive perspective on Ireland's post-Famine future that these narratives by Curtis and Tierney yield can be clarified by the country's gradual economic recovery in the 1860s—even if the position of the tenantry remained very vulnerable.[62] At the same time, it is worth noting that "McGormack's Grudge," though written by an author who worked and lived in Ireland, first appeared in an Irish American periodical: the rather rose-tinted portrayal of post-Famine Curranure fits in with the return-to-paradise motif that one finds in quite a number of Irish American works of Famine fiction. For example, Alice Nolan's *The Byrnes of Glengoulah* (1868) depicts the reinvigoration of a pastoral Irish landscape that runs parallel to the restoration of bonds of kindness and loyalty between the landed class and the tenantry. When the unfeeling Englishman Lord Biggs loses his mind and dies in the "cell of a mad-house chained like a dog to an iron bed," the new proprietor of the Glengoulah estate, Lord Bentley, reinstates the compassionate De Courcy as its agent. Bentley subsequently organizes a communal gathering at the estate: he erects an "immense marquee," puts in "long tables . . . covered with substantials of every variety," and orders pipers and fiddlers to provide repasts for the tenantry of the estate.[63] Thus, he establishes moments of leisure, underscored by bucolic festivities, that can be enjoyed by all classes rather than exclusively by a social elite.

The ensuing "scenes of merriment" are accompanied by elaborate descriptions of a pastoral setting symbolically rejuvenated by spring. As "long tables were spread, covered by substantials of every variety," and fiddlers and pipers arrive to provide repasts for the tenantry of the estate, nature presents itself in all its enchanting beauty: "sapphire and golden tints" of sunset "spread far over the firmament," while the moon sheds a "trail of glittering spangles on the bosom of the Avoca." While this peaceful scene mirrors the enchanting setting that is sketched at the opening of the novel as an image of the authentic Ireland—the beauties of the vale of Avoca, from the "stream of liquid silver bearing the same name" to "the picturesque village of 'Wooden Bridge'"—the reestablishment of harmony on the Glengoulah grounds is emphasized by the regeneration of nature through spring: "May came at last, and with the daisies and primroses came the summons to the landlord's entertainment."[64]

Images of spring are also employed in two other Irish diaspora novels as a way to express the recuperation of a pastoral post-Famine Ireland. In Elizabeth Hely Walshe's Irish Canadian novel *Golden Hills* (1865), the restoration of a post-Famine pastoral setting is also bound up with reform of the estate, although in Walshe's narrative it is effected at the disadvantage of the tenants. While Walshe elaborately pictures the decline of Golden Hills from *locus amoenus* to paradise under threat, she glosses over the last years of the Great Famine, and the end of the novel, which is set in 1850, depicts the estate as a paradise regained. With the "hopes of fair weather" that spring brings, the "horizon was clearing" both in a literal and in a figurative sense, as the season symbolically heralds the dawn of a brighter era: the "lessened agricultural population had more elbow-room, and new systems of cropping the land were introduced among the peasantry."[65] Moreover, in line with the pastoral convention of "convenings,"[66] there is a joyful "summer gathering" at Golden Hills, which, in line with its name, is once more a pastoral bower of bliss.[67]

Golden Hills suggests that the Famine has resulted in a more stable golden world: the catastrophe is described as a scourge and even a "finger of God" that purges the nation of its evils, such as overpopulation, the barbarity of the Celtic peasant who "would never be civilized till he recognized the power of his own hands and brain to raise him higher in the scale of social existence," as well as his rebellion against authority. The sentiment voiced by many characters, including Kingston himself, is that the Famine is "a judicial punishment for bloodshed lying upon" the land, in the form of agrarian outrages. Moreover, *Golden Hills* presents diaspora as a solution to Ireland's problems and as a way to reclaim pastoral peacefulness. For the lawless Ribandmen who threaten Kingston's peaceful existence, migration is offered as a solution: Tom Carmody, who is involved in a plot to murder Kingston, is shipped off to Quebec to "leave the country and never return." The Irishmen for whom there is no sustenance should leave the nation to "purge" it of indolence and starvation: "those hundreds languishing in idleness, while the great plains of Canada and Australia call out for labourers."[68] The call for work on the land in the New World suggests a Georgic rather than a pastoral scene: the future of immigrants involves tilling the land rather than leisure. The joys of pastoral *otium*, by contrast, are exclusively reserved for the landed Anglo-Irish classes staying behind in the regenerated Ireland.

Spring also marks an overnight transition from Famine wasteland to pastoral scenery in Mary Ann Sadlier's *Bessy Conway* (1862). As we saw, the description of "the failure of crops" during "the terrible year of the Famine" that affects Denis and "many a cottage through the length and breadth of Ireland" and leaves merely "tall ragweed" and "dock weed . . . on the arid soil" is relatively brief and instantly followed by Bessy's timely return to her motherland to save her family from eviction and starvation. This representation of a recuperated home extends to nature, for Bessy's financial support appears to form the onset of a sudden regeneration of the landscape that is revitalized by spring: "The green fields of Erin were covered with their spring carpet dotted over with white daisies and yellow buttercups, the pale primrose—'dower of sweetest memories!'—was peeping forth on every sunny bank."[69] *Bessy Conway* evokes an image of blight-stricken wasteland, but represses it shortly afterward by representing a regenerated pastoral Irish landscape, so that the illusion of Erin as a pristine Eden can persist. The question remains, however, why Sadlier's novel shifts the image of a desolate, barren soil to the margins of the narrative in order to foreground the conventional identification of rural Ireland with idyllic green pastures. Moreover, why is the narrative scheme of a recovered natural paradise so central to early Irish North American Famine fiction in particular, as we have seen?

An explanation may lie in the dual process of upheaval that immigrants of the Famine generation to North America had to undergo, as they were doubly traumatized by the calamities on and the exodus from their native soil. As we saw in chapter 1, the enmity that the North American diaspora encountered, which was aggravated, according to Thomas D'Arcy McGee, by the fact that the Irish found themselves "in the presence of those" from English descent "whose fathers were the enemies, or rivals of their fathers," fueled the cultural construction of an idealized version of Ireland from which all recent trauma of pestilence had to be dissociated. The strong emphasis on reappropriating the ancestral land—well illustrated by a nationalist article from November 12, 1864, in the *Irish People* that states its objective to "sweep aristocracy away and give the land to the people"—is manifested in these Famine novels as reclaiming the Irish land from the traumatic Famine past. Paul Alpers's seminal study on the pastoral shows that the bucolic landscape plays a prominent role in nostalgic narratives of a lost past or country. Considering the fact that in the nineteenth century, the "land has long been central to articulations of Irish nationality," and in view of Oona Frawley's illustration of the significance of pastoral scenery in Irish nostalgia, it is by no means remarkable that these Irish North American Famine writings imagine a return of the pastoral.[70]

In fact, a close examination of cultural expressions produced in and for Irish transatlantic Famine immigrants reveals that a nostalgic yearning for a distant Edenic Irish landscape was central to the early stages of this generation's emerging diasporic consciousness.[71] For example, the poem "The Irish Emigrant's Lament," which was published in the *Pilot* on January 23, 1858, and describes the heartbreaking departure of an Irishman from his native shore and his love, Mary, celebrates the Irish scenery in May when the "corn is green" and "the lark's loud song" can be heard. David O'Callohan's "Will He Return" (1869) and John Boyle O'Reilly's "Our Own Green Island

Home" (1870), both published in the *Emerald*, express a heartfelt longing to "wander back" to "old Ireland," with its "simple village church with its open campanile" and the "quaint old cottage."[72] In a similar vein, John Locke's "The Old Homestead," which was printed in the *Emerald* on February 26, 1870, presents an immigrant persona who recollects his former cottage in Ulster "deep in the low, green woods" where linnets and sparrows would fly "out of the blossomy woods" in springtime.

This Edenic portrayal of the Irish land, which lay at the heart of the formation of a shared Irish North American cultural identity and which, according to Oona Frawley, was later "propelled back into Ireland itself," also recurs in many works of Irish North American fiction. These texts often ostensibly idealize Ireland and the virtues associated with the homeland by pitting a pastoral and peaceful homeland against unpleasant transatlantic urban areas that are characterized by a lack of natural spaces. As such, they bear witness to Joep Leerssen's idea that ethnicity is "interculturally produced" in opposition to other groups. For example, in Mary Anne Sadlier's *Elinor Preston* (1861), the eponymous immigrant heroine feels great homesickness for "the natural beauties of that romantic region" of Killarney, as well as "the yellow corn-fields, and green pastures" of County Wicklow, which are such pleasant sites compared to the "wilderness of black, smoky buildings" of the thoroughfares of Liverpool and New York that are marked by the absence of "a decent park for the recreation and pastimes of their municipal children."[73]

In *Bessy Conway* and *The Lost Rosary*, idealized pastoral Irish scenes are diametrically opposed to the squalor and immorality of North American urban climates, which pose a threat to the essentially Irish qualities of the immigrants. In *Bessy Conway* the "cottage beneath the sycamore tree" where Bessy was born and bred stands in shrill contrast with what Sadlier in her preface calls "These Great Babylons of the West," the dirty American cities where Irish immigrants are exposed to all sorts of temptations. It is in New York City that many of Bessy's fellow immigrants lose their faith and morality: Ned Finigan and his spouse, Ally, who set up a pub, are ensnared by the American dream of wealth and neglect the Catholic faith they were raised in, while many of the Irish domestics lose their virtue at the urban dancing halls. In *The Lost Rosary*, McCorry likewise implies that New York is full of the "allurements of the devil," dens of moral degradation where young Irish women will discard their Catholic creed as well as their maidenly honor. As the narrator's invocation to Irish immigrant girls suggests, the city streets will expose scenes to them that will shock their "virgin modesty": "vice will cunningly allure" them, with its "deformities hidden beneath the garb of wealth." These sites of urban degradation are in juxtaposition with the pastoral scenes of May Day celebrations at the beginning of the novel that epitomize loveliness and purity, also in terms of gender: "Girls romping about, neither last in the chase, nor behind at a good spring or hop over ditch or hedge; comely and beautiful, artless and innocent, but withal modest in speech and in act."[74] The fact that these idyllic rural bowers of bliss are described at such length and thereby seem to occlude the later references to Famine wasteland moreover indicates the significance of pastoral landscapes in transatlantic processes of identity formation, as the pastoral land rather than the desolate blight-stricken fields came to be envisaged as the site of real Irishness.

Relocating the Irish Landscape

While quite a few North American works of Famine fiction from the early 1860s depict a restored Edenic homeland from which the trauma of blight has been eliminated, during the period up to 1870 several Irish American novels also imagine "pastoral endings" on North American soil. In these texts the natural spaces in North American cities as well as on the western frontier are conceptualized as pastoral sites where Irish immigrants may establish new Erins as alternatives to the stricken homeland. The idyllic settings associated with Ireland in Irish North American reconceptualizations of its past are here relocated to the New World, both symbolically and geographically.

In this respect, Sadlier's *Bessy Conway* can be regarded as a transitional narrative: while on the one hand, it envisions a homeland that is recovering from the trials of pestilence, on the other it also suggests that transatlantic sites of natural beauty may become appropriate spaces of settlement for Irish immigrant communities. While Bessy returns to her country of birth, fellow immigrant Paul Brannigan does not settle back in Ireland, but manages to find a home in the New World that closely resembles the pastoral motherland. We read that Paul likes to spend his free Sundays in the City Hall Park, which is called "the favorite haunt of all the dwellers 'down town' who loved the verdure and the shade," thus offering a bower of pastoral retreat and leisure in busy New York. The narrator even evokes a comparison between Irish poet Oliver Goldsmith's "The Deserted Village" (1770), which describes pastoral Auburn, and the City Hall Park by quoting the poem: "'With seats beneath the shade,' which if not exactly 'For talking age and whispering lovers made,' like those immortalized in Goldsmith's verse, were none the less most excellent resting places for the sons and daughters of toil when on 'the Sabbath, the poor man's day,' they could sit and listen to the plash of the fountain and think of things past, present, and future."[75] While the City Hall Park thus resembles nature "at home" in Ireland, it is even hinted that the park is not only where nature may bloom, but where the Irish Catholic spirit may be cultivated as well, for it is here that Paul Brannigan meets Irish youngsters in order to teach them Catholic doctrine and morality.[76] In this way, the City Hall Park appears to be a replica of the pastoral scenery that is associated with the motherland, suggesting that the bucolic landscape typical for Ireland functions as a translocatable memory space that can establish a specific Irish Catholic ethnoscape in diaspora.[77]

Other works of Famine fiction that were written in America from the middle to the end of the decade transfer a pastoral setting that is traditionally identified with Ireland to North American territories in the West, thereby illustrating that cultural memory transcends national boundaries and underlining the views currently expressed by memory scholars like Astrid Erll on the "'default' combination of territorial, ethnic and national collectivity."[78] In fact, it can be argued that the configuration of North American pastoral landscapes reminiscent of the homeland in these narratives can be regarded as a specific reinscription of the frontier. As several scholars have argued, during the mid-nineteenth century, the North American West in its emptiness and vastness was generally represented in terms of the Burkean sublime rather than the pastoral mode,[79] and this general tendency to interpret the frontier as sublime is illustrated by iconic landscape paintings from the period, such as Thomas Moran's *Clearing in the Mountains* (1865) and Albert Bierstadt's *A Storm in the Rocky Mountains* (1866).

The Lost Rosary presents a reconstruction of Irish pastoral dwelling in the New World where the same crops may be cultivated as in Ireland, but now without the threat of pestilence: "You just put up five or six sticks in a row, and nail thin ones across them, and the grapes run up them, before they become grapes you know, just like kidney beans at home, an' sweet peas, an' I'm told they pay well. Turnips an' other things are much like as in Magheramore." Through this description of the fertility of the western soil, McCorry's narrative appears to respond to pioneer narratives, which would almost invariably stress the potential of the land at the frontier. William B. Dewees's *Letters from an Early Settler of Texas* (1854) recurrently emphasizes that the land in Texas is "very rich and fertile," and Henry T. Newton's *Canada in 1864: A Hand-Book for Settlers* (1864) contends that in the West, "the variety of its products and abundance of its harvests attest, where proper care is bestowed on its cultivation, the excellence of its soil."[80] McCorry's representation of the frontier as a site of opportunity also appears to be inspired by the Homestead Act of 1862, which encouraged many Europeans to settle in America, as 160 acres of land could be obtained for free, and additional acres could be obtained at favorable rates, on the condition that the settler set up a home and improved the purchased land over a period of five years.[81] Publications in the Irish press thus also sought to persuade Irish farmers to try their luck in the United States. "Canada and Ireland," an article published in *Duffy's Hibernian Sixpenny Magazine* on April 4, 1862, stated that in the West, "cheap and fertile land is to be had almost for the asking, in whatever direction he turns. He is astonished to hear of the immense produce of its harvests, which, when contrasted with the blighted and unfavoured results of those to which he has been accustomed, appears indeed incredible."[82] Emigrating to American frontier settlements was thus presented as a viable opportunity to escape a climate in which failed crops, and by extension famines, were likely.[83]

This sense of recuperation is also implied at the conclusion of *The Lost Rosary*. The characters procure a real home in the American countryside, buying two neat little farms that adjoin one another. Although the recollection of the Famine is traumatizing, "in the shadowy outlines of a memory made treacherous by its conflicts with the world," Tim, Barney, Mary, and Alley will manage to reproduce their idealized image of rural Irish nature and a farming existence in America—an image, moreover, that is untainted by hunger and disease. It is through hard toil in an area where civilization still needs to be laid out—without "hedges" or "roads of any consequence"[84]—that Tim and Barney can achieve this longed-for idyllic rural existence: in other words, the eventual acquisition of a pastoral Eden is shown to rely on the Georgic ideal of agricultural labor. Furthermore, in depicting how Tim and Barney in the end can become owners of an idyllic little Ireland in the American West, McCorry's novel suggests a transcultural blend of the cultural legacies of the former homeland and the North American heritage of the hardworking, self-made pioneer.[85] For example, Major Strickland's *Twenty-Seven Years in Canada West* (1853) asserts that the ideal frontier settler is willing to endure "hard labour, and . . . all sorts of privations . . . dangers and hardships attending the settlement of a new country," William B. Dewees's *Letters from an Early Settler of Texas* describes the "days and nights of toil and fatigue" that settlers need to invest to be able to "provide food for their families," and Mrs. C. P. Traill's *The Canadian Emigrant Housekeeper's Guide* (1861) emphasizes that success in the West can be attained only by "active, hardworking inhabitants who are earning their bread honestly by the sweat of their brow."[86]

Other Famine narratives include similar representations. Sadlier's *Con O'Regan* (1864) hints that living in urban America may entail as much hunger and deprivation as an existence in the homeland, as we saw in chapter 1. However, like *The Lost Rosary*, the novel suggests that a further relocation to frontier regions may involve an escape from the threats of starvation that one would encounter in the mother country, while at the same time providing the opportunities for creating a microcosmic Ireland that feels like home. When Con and his family eventually set up a farm in Iowa, they are blessed with the "promise of a luxuriant harvest" of the planted potatoes. Without the danger that the crops will be destroyed by blight, the family's Iowa acres moreover offer enough space to grow "some roots of Irish shamrock in our garden" and thus create "our little Ireland." That this plot of land comes to substitute for the pastoral homeland is revealed by Con's conviction that his children will grow up there in the "same pure, moral atmosphere" as they would in Erin.[87] The appropriation of the western regions by Irish immigrant pioneers thus entails a reimagination of the American land in line with Irish ethical values.

Dillon O'Brien's *The Dalys of Dalystown* likewise implies that Irish immigrants who move into frontier areas can find and model landscapes that remind them of their motherland. Henry Daly, his sister Emily, and his spouse, Rose, set up a new home in Michigan, plan and lay out a flower garden, and make it "resemble, as nearly as possible, the one it was intended to represent," namely, the gardens they used to have at the Dalystown estate, even though "to have it of the same extent was out of the question, for many a day to come." Upon Henry's arrival, the landscape of the American West initially appears to be dreary and unmanageable: "The blackened stumps and girdled trees, with their long, withered arms extended, gave to some of those clearings, especially when viewed by moon-light, a dreary, desolate look." However, the Irish settlers succeed in converting this traditionally sublime frontier landscape into a microcosmic pastoral Ireland. While the Daly family consciously seeks to re-create their former Irish garden on American soil, the narrator creates the impression that the landscapes of the American West are naturally imbued with traits that are inherent to the Irish scene: in the narrator's opinion, the fields of the West have ever been "the green-carpeted ballrooms of the fairies," for "stretched, with closed eyes, in one of those grassy dells, on a dreamy summer's evening, the little people have danced around me."[88] The narrator thus overlays the frontier landscape with Irish mythology, thereby representing it as a natural habitat for the immigrants from the Emerald Isle who seem to be destined to create little "New Irelands" there.

These evident intersections between cultural legacies of rural Ireland and cultural memories of the countries of settlement that one finds in *The Lost Rosary* and *Tim Doolan* are significant in several respects. In these narratives, the American West, as an area that was regarded as liminal because it was at the edge of civilization, signifies liminality in a second sense: as a site of cross-cultural memories and traditions. This liminality of the frontier in these North American works of Famine fiction mirrors the liminality of the conditions of first-generation emigrants who occupied what Homi Bhabha would call a "Third Space."[89] They belonged completely neither in the host society nor in the former homeland, having "transnational affiliations" and participating in "transnational spaces" shared by both "immigrants and natives."[90] Additionally, the recurring representation of the frontier as a heterotopic New Ireland in these narratives illustrates the development of what Michael Rothberg calls "multidirectional memory": "dialogical interactions" between the memories of different social groups that result from intercultural contacts in the public space and blur "borders of memory and identity."[91]

The existence of these dynamic transfers between Irish and North American cultural legacies in fiction written between 1864 and 1870 demonstrates the malleability of diasporic identities whose ethnic configurations transform under the influence of increasing cultural exchanges with the host culture. From the mid-1860s up to the early 1870s, groups of Irish immigrants of the Famine generation who had initially settled in urban areas such as Boston and New York gradually began to move to the uncleared western interiors of America and Canada. As David Emmons clarifies in his study *Beyond the American Pale*, "Irish America does not mean eastern America," for by 1870 the number of Irish settling in the West had multiplied by ten and extended to new territories such as Michigan, Minnesota, and Wisconsin. As such, the configuration of New Irelands at the frontier rather than in the old country in these works of fiction appears to mirror the changing living circumstances of many Irish Americans and Irish Canadians who moved westward. At the same time, the fact that novels written between 1864 and 1870 begin to conceptualize idyllic Irish communities in the New World can be attributed to the progressive integration of Irish immigrant communities. Not only did influential spokespersons for the Irish transatlantic diaspora, such as Thomas D'Arcy McGee, urge "the Irish man in America to modify his manners . . . and to fit his habits as far as propriety demands to his new relations," but as we saw in chapter 1, the end of the American Civil War also brought the gradual emergence of an Irish American middle class.[92] These developments in the social conditions of Irish North Americans are therefore mirrored by the changing approaches toward homeland and host country that these texts from the late 1860s and 1870 indicate.

In line with the assimilation of the Irish in North America, the plotline that suggests a reconstruction of microcosmic Irelands in diaspora features less prominently in fiction of the later 1870s, 1880s, and 1890s, as Lindsay Janssen has also demonstrated. For example, in McDougall's *The Days of a Life* (1883), Mrs. Mulrooney and her sons soon "sowed and reaped on a snug little farm of their own" in West Canada. The land that they cultivate fails to transform into a New Ireland, however. The "little whin bush" that Mrs. Mulrooney had taken with her "in a flower pot . . . as a reminder of the Donegal hills" is ill-fated in the country of adoption, for "that prickly emigrant refused to flourish under the cloudless skies of Canada, and died of stove-heat the first winter." The land in the North American West may still be identified as an opportunity to rebuild a rural existence similar to that in the homeland, but it increasingly comes to be imagined as a site of multicultural cohabitation in works of Famine fiction. Thus, in John Brennan's *Erin Mór* (1892), the title suggests the creation of a greater Ireland that extends to the North American diaspora, but this conception is not quite how land functions in the narrative. The novel deals with Andy Dillon, who leaves Ireland with his parents during the Famine and grows up in an East Coast tenement slum. After having led an itinerant life for several years, he ultimately discovers gold in California. He buys land in order to establish a utopian community for "his exiled race in their trans-Atlantic home," which he calls "Erin Mór."[93] The settlement actually becomes a community that involves other ethnicities as well, including former slave Tony Sexton and a group of Native Americans.

Conclusion

As Rudy Koshar has observed, cultural communities develop a "a sense of history with reference to specific and tangible objects," such as "specific places and landscapes." Indeed, as we have seen, early works of Famine fiction written on both sides of the Atlantic give expression to the Famine past through symbolically inscribed wastelands and pastoral scenes that, especially in earliest homeland fiction and in Irish diaspora fiction written until 1864, function as spaces of displacement on which the excruciating and often inexpressible memories of mass starvation and degeneration can be negotiated. As such, these scenic sites appear to play a significant role in the narrative representation of fresh trauma and the negotiation of displaced diaspora identities, for the problems that attend integrating into a new society provoke a crisis in identity that must be transcended by what Matthew Jacobson has called "extolling certain virtues, condemning certain vices, celebrating certain kinds of deeds, and advancing certain versions of the heroic, fabricated and enshrined . . . 'national character.'"[94] This fiction actively pushes Famine memory to the narrative margins in order to crystallize an Irish pre- and post-Famine past that may never have existed in reality, but that, through a form of retrospective as well as prospective nostalgia, offered anchorage for ethnic identity construction in exile.

At the same time, in fiction written in Ireland as of 1860, these black patches of land and regenerated pastoral bowers can be read as liminal, heterotopic premises that, occupying a shadowy space between illusionary absence and an invisible, lurking presence, suggest the potential of Ireland, the Irish, and their cultural traditions to overcome the calamity of the Famine and to become reinvigorated against all odds. As such, these landscapes represent narratives about Ireland as either "triumphantly victorious or tragically defeated." The fact that this representation of Ireland's landscape corresponds specifically to the nationalist agenda in Ireland in the 1860s endorses Ross Poole's comment that in cultural remembrance, "we reach into the past, and make that past a presence in our current moral or political agenda."[95]

North American fiction written from the mid-1860s onward illustrates, however, that the relocation of homeland remembrance to diaspora spaces may also involve temporal reconfigurations. Irish American Famine fiction from this later era is still rooted in the unshakable identification of the pastoral with Irishness. Yet these texts envisage pastoral Irish communities as ethnoscapes that can be transported to uncleared American territories in the West that function as blank canvases on which transnationalistic versions of the lost motherland may be projected. The intersections between these mythic versions of Erin and the ideological foundations of the frontier that these later Irish North American narratives bear witness to imply the integration of immigrant communities and their formation of culturally hybrid constellations of recollection. As the narratives suggest, migrant communities affiliate with memory cultures of both the homeland and the host society.

5 | Ruins of the Past

THE POEM "Dream Journeys" (1869), by Thomas D'Arcy McGee, presents the voice of the homesick immigrant who revisits the Emerald Isle in his sleep. In his vision, the persona wanders through its scenery, attending upon sites that evoke recollections of Ireland's past, such as the Hill of Tara, the Lake of Arva, and the mountains of Tirhugh, where

> The sacred strand our fathers' feet
> Have often trod . . .
> The island of the Saint's retreat.

This lyrical exposition of Ireland's history provides prime examples of what Pierre Nora has coined *lieux de mémoire*, in the form of locations where historical events actually took place and are invested with symbolical meaning and a community's "will to remember." Over the past two decades, Irish studies have strongly engaged with the functions of space as a container of memories that specific "imagined communities" identify with and use as sites of commemoration.[1] Scholars from various disciplinary backgrounds working on the Great Famine have turned their attention to the symbolical significance of physical traces of the Famine past in the landscape, such as former workhouses, deserted cottages, and Famine roads, as well as to memorials of the Famine past.[2]

The brutal eviction of tenant farmers from their homesteads, and the subsequent demolition of their cottages,[3] led to the emergence of deserted, dilapidated rural communities[4]—scattered with "plainly ruined cabins," as Harriet Martineau would describe them in "The Famine Time" (1852). In fact, the abandoned, leveled cottage became one of the iconic images in representations of the Great Famine dating from the period itself as well as its immediate aftermath. Illustrations published in the press often depicted uninhabited villages with unroofed cabins: *The Ruined Village of Tullig in County Clare* and *Village of Moveen* (fig. 8), printed in the *Illustrated London News* on December 15 and 22, 1849, respectively, are well-known examples. The remnants of leveled houses are also a recurring motif in literary memories of the Great Famine. In Henry J. Monahan's *O'Ruark* (1852), Tom Connor returns to Ireland only to find that his parents have perished when "the pratees failed," while "what wanst was the house" has turned into "ruins."[5] Likewise, William Carleton's *The Squanders of Castle Squander* (1852) sketches the depopulated villages, "where a few dying wretches . . . are crawling or lying beside the ruins" of their former homes, thereby aligning the wrecked cottages with the devastations of a people ruined by the potato blight.[6]

While ruins in the form of ravaged, deserted dwellings feature prominently in early Famine fiction, this chapter will focus on the ruins of monastic buildings and precolonial fortresses that are represented in early Irish and Irish diaspora Famine fiction. Ruins had played an important role in the romantic imagination, featuring as expressions of the picturesque. William Gilpin had singled out the "*rough* ruin" as one of the most characteristic examples of the picturesque. This image of the picturesque ruin would leave a strong impact on configurations of landscape through the mid-nineteenth century, as in, for example, John Ruskin's essays that were serialized in the *Architectural Magazine* in 1837–38 and would later be republished as *The Poetry of Architecture* (1893).[7] Furthermore, ruins would often function as objects of contemplation about human mortality and the transcendental world that elides the cultural and historical circumstances that led to their ruination. An example is William Wordsworth's "Lines Composed a Few Miles above Tintern Abbey" (1798), in which the ruins enable the persona to see "into the life of things," from his own development as

8. *Village of Moveen, Illustrated London News*, December 22, 1849. Engraving. Courtesy of Ireland's Great Hunger Museum, Quinnipiac University, Hamden, CT.

a grown-up man to man's transformation into a "living soul," when he will be "laid asleep / In body."

However, in Irish cultural expressions from the long nineteenth century, these romantic readings of ruins appear to occur less frequently than interpretations of ruins as signifiers of colonial violence and subjugation. As scholars such as Luke Gibbons, Ina Ferris, Claire Connolly, and Julia M. Wright have argued, during the nineteenth century ruins played an important role in Ireland's negotiation of its colonial identity, as emblems of the devastation of Ireland's indigenous cultures by English invaders and settlers.[8] Indeed, this colonial subtext already figures in pre-Famine representations of ruins: in Lady Morgan's *The Wild Irish Girl* (1808), the "noblest mass of ruins" of the Castle of Inismore, in their sublime vastness and grotesqueness, not only inspires awe in Horatio, a landlord's son who grew up in England; as symbols of "princely grandeur" that are "mouldering into oblivion," they also bear witness to the decline of Gaelic Catholic clans, personified by the Prince of Inismore, who were displaced from the land during the Cromwellian conquest. Similarly, James Clarence Mangan published translations of Gaelic ruin poems into English in the 1830s and 1840s, such as "Lamentation of Mac Liag for Kincora" (1841) and "Lament over the Ruins of the Abbey of Teach Molaga" (1846), which identified the ruins in the Irish landscape with imperial devastation. As Coílín Parsons writes, these poems evoke the ruins of the vestiges of once noble households and monasteries as a way to critique the ongoing "destruction of remains and ruins of archeological significance (and often imagined significance) in an effort to bring more and more of the island of Ireland under cultivation."[9]

As this chapter will reveal, monastic and dynastic ruins feature prominently in early Famine fiction. In many earlier nineteenth-century texts, such as *The Wild Irish Girl*, this colonial subtext takes on the form of imperial elegy, that is, a lament on the disappearance of native traditions. By contrast, in early Famine fiction, ruins convey a more polemical narrative of imperial destruction as well as a sense of anticolonial resistance. The prominence of ruins in Irish and Irish diaspora fiction that remembers this bleak era of deprivation can partially be attributed to the fact that, during the Famine, many monuments to Ireland's precolonial past were destroyed: when the food crisis led to "forced economic modernization" of the countryside and bogs were reclaimed, a great number of ruined ancient buildings were pulled down.[10] Thus, as Máirín Ní Cheallaigh maintains, the "loss of monuments" and the disappearance of narratives caused by depopulation "went hand in hand." Sites of memory, such as monuments, were under threat not only of physical disappearance, but also of losing their symbolical significance. As generations who had invested these places with recollection disappeared, "Irish antiquarians increasingly turned their attention to the study of prehistoric and other archeological remains." Since *lieux de mémoire*, such as remains of monasteries, memorials, or abbeys, would enable future generations to recuperate memories, for them "preserving monuments meant preserving narratives" about the regional past.[11]

As will be demonstrated in this chapter, the symbolical function of ruins in early Famine novels and short stories can be read in light of Ireland's status within the British Empire and also in relation to the inherently liminal nature of ruins. Ruins are physical traces of an evanescent past that evoke cultural remembrance, but they simultaneously impede recollection by the absence that they materialize. As Dylan Trigg claims, because of their fragmentation, ruins represent a mnemonic void, "a puncturing in spatio-temporal presence," in that they evoke a past presence that is at the same time notably absent. The ruin is "not the same as its previous (active) incarnation," but represents "an altered place" that "retains the shadow of its old self." As such, ruins constitute spectral sites that continue to haunt their beholders with the trauma of loss. However, as Stuart McLean and Kevin Whelan have observed, ruins may conversely be viewed as sites that enable a retrieval of memories of former days, in the face of colonial powers that seek to root out the indigenous population's pasts. Ruins can foreclose oblivion, and they can "invoke an otherwise vanished past" that constitutes a form of "counter-memory" of socially marginalized groups, "which answers back to history."[12]

As the following discussion will demonstrate, the dilapidated castles and convents in early Famine fiction testify to the ambivalent nature of ruins. In these Famine narratives, ruins are liminal spaces, in that they signify both death and regeneration, both conquest and defiance. On the one hand, these moldering remnants of once impressive buildings speak to recent Famine trauma: they symbolize the degeneration of the Famine-stricken population and serve as screens or traces that express the pains of mass starvation and penury. Furthermore, they function as heterochronic sites that place the Great Famine in a succession of colonial catastrophes. On the other hand, as symbols of endurance, the ruined sites in these texts also portend the survival and post-Famine regeneration of Ireland's people and its native cultures in spite of a destructive colonial regime. As such, these wasted abbeys and seats of power represent heterotopic spaces that are emblems of both imperial victory and prospective decolonization.

Ruins as Screens of Famine Memory

In contemporary descriptions as well as historiographical accounts, the Great Famine was often identified with ruin, both in a literal and in a metaphorical sense. Asenath Nicholson's *Annals of the Famine in Ireland in 1847, 1848 and 1849* (1851) sketches the material ruin of the "unroofed . . . silent and dreary" cabins from which the tenants have been ejected and suggests that many of the former inmates "were buried under the ruins . . . found starved in a putrid state." John Mitchel, in *The History of Ireland, from the Treaty of Limerick to the Present* (1869), examines the symbolic ruin of post-Famine Ireland, picturing the country as "in ruins," because it no longer possesses "recuperative energy." Similarly, in *Ireland* (1887), Emily Lawless comments that "after the famine followed ruin—a ruin which swept high and low alike into its net," thereby referring to the fact that, although of an entirely different proportion and smaller scale, hardship was also suffered by the gentry. As the Earl of Shrewsbury pointed out in 1847, "The great majority of the Irish landlords are bankrupts," and many were forced to sell their property under the Encumbered Estates Act.[13]

The economical and cultural ruin that the Famine brought to the country and its population is translated into images of battered relics in the Irish landscape that epitomize the decay and degeneration caused by blight and starvation. As such, these works of fiction speak indirectly about the agonies of death and loss, thereby showing that trauma may manifest itself through narrative traces rather than silence. For example, Mary Anne Sadlier's Irish Canadian novel *New Lights; or, Life in Galway* (1853) draws an analogy between the defaced and desecrated monuments of Ireland's Catholic heritage and the Catholic tenantry in County Galway who are devastated by the joint visitations of famine and fever. During a conversation with Eleanor Ousely—the daughter of a heartless Anglo-Irish landlord who, unlike her father, shows empathy with the suffering Catholic tenantry—her father's English guest, Captain Hampton, mentions the religious monuments scattered throughout the county that are "in ruins." Although Hampton here directs his thoughts to the widespread vestiges of Ireland's Catholic past, his remarks conjure up an association between the ruined buildings and the destitute Catholic tenantry of Killany in view of an earlier passage in the novel in which the term "ruin" is used to give expression to the dire state of local farmers: "Here, as in every other district of the south and west, ruin has been busy amongst the farming classes, and many a family has fallen, within the last few years, from comfort and affluence and respectability, to want and penury and utter destitution."[14]

This analogy between the spaces of Catholic devotion, presumably wrecked by British Protestants who sought to root out "Romanism," and the Catholic population who are destroyed by famine is endorsed by the fact that the novel partly ascribes the starvation of the native Irish farmers to religious persecution. English proselytizers like Andrew McGilligan urge Bernard O'Daly to embrace Protestantism, "the true bread of life," so he may save his family from death by hunger: "If you now reject our offers, we are authorized to say that you and yours shall be turned out on the road to starve and die!"[15] In light of other passages in the novel, the images of the ravaged convents, cathedrals, and cemeteries, which may be interpreted as the mournful result of English imperial campaigns such as Cromwell's,[16] therefore prove to symbolize the attempts of proselytism to eliminate Irish Catholicism during the Famine years. The novel thus appears to represent the Famine as an extension of colonial religious oppression.[17]

Similar instances of sites of ruin that symbolize the suffering and downfall of the Irish during the Famine can be found in Sadlier's novels *Elinor Preston* (1861) and *Bessy Conway* (1862), in Charles Joseph Kickham's *Sally Cavanagh* (1869), in Paul Peppergrass's Irish American novel *Shandy M'Guire* (1853), and in Anna Dorsey's *Nora Brady's Vow* (1869). While *Elinor Preston* does not gloss over the miseries faced by the Famine-stricken rural poor, the focus is on how the Famine leads to the decline of a Catholic prosperous family, thus illustrating that all social strata were afflicted during the Famine.[18] As we saw, Elinor Preston, the first-person narrator, recounts how her relatives, like many other well-to-do families in the region, fell from their "high estate in Ireland, during those years of commercial depression—that dismal lull which followed the extinction of the great Repeal movement, and ushered in the Famine." As Elinor recounts, her father's death brings bailiffs to their Dublin house in Rutland Square, sent by her "father's creditors to seize our goods and chattels." The orphaned Elinor and her siblings are eventually forced to give up the family home as well as their father's "small property . . . near the Curragh of Kildare."[19] The Prestons' wane in fortune is symbolized by the consecutive deaths of Elinor's mother, aunt Kate, father, and siblings, who all perish with disease.

The ruins that Elinor visits in the narrative express the demise of the family in the Famine era and Elinor's personal loss, for they embody transience and lost glory. For example, when Elinor travels to Killarney, she meets two descendants of the once powerful MacCarthy clan—John Denis MacCarthy and his granddaughter Ellen—who tell her stories of the "old, old time" when "the MacCarthys ruled as princes, and fought as heroes." The MacCarthys' decline forms a parallel to the downfall of Elinor's once influential kin, and the signs of the Celtic clan's degeneration—its "mouldering fortalice" and its "great Abbey . . . in its ruined state"—also underline the losses experienced by once powerful classes during the bleak years of hunger. In referring to her own age, the Famine era, Elinor speaks of Ireland's severe conditions as the result of Britain's rule: Ireland is the "hardly-used step-child of a Protestant government—the 'Niobe of nations,'" because the Irish refused to yield to the Protestant creed of their English settlers. Britain has made Ireland "powerless . . . because of her fidelity to God and His Church." As the narrative suggests, just as the once potent Irish dynasties collapsed when the English brutally seized their power, during the Famine preeminent families like Elinor's fell from fortune because of England's deliberate neglect of Ireland's situation. The text also draws an analogy between the expulsion of the Irish aristocrats who had to wander "landless and friendless over the broad earth" and the Irish who flee from their beloved Famine-afflicted motherland and are described at an earlier stage in the novel: "There were families of two generations—a venerate grandfather or grandmother, apparently tottering on 'life's narrow verge,' yet breaking asunder at the voice of strong affection the ties of country and of home, to follow the son or daughter and their family into their voluntary exile."[20]

The fact that images of starvation are overall repressed in the narrative creates the impression that the racked buildings serve as "screens" to explore the agonizing losses entailed by the Famine, so that a detailed exposure of these pains can be circumvented. This impression is confirmed by the frequent appearance of regionally specific dilapidated historical buildings in the text, such as "Ross Island, with its historic ruin, once a fortress of great strength," and the "once splendid Abbey" of Innisfallen, "now roofless all and desolate,"[21] fading sites of memory that hint at the destruction of older forms of Irish life during the Famine era. Furthermore, these sites that generate recollections of Ireland's past are places where different moments in time come together: memories of the far-away past of clan rule and the present of the Great Famine converge, thereby suggesting a continuum of imperial destruction. Philip Ethington asserts that history is "literally cartographic," in that change through and in space displays the process of time,[22] and in Sadlier's novel these ruins indeed serve as so-called heterochronies. They embody an accumulation of different "slices in time" that signify "an absolute break" with "traditional time," because the boundaries between past and present collapse.[23] The Famine is thus envisaged as one episode of suffering within one long stretch of defeat.

The sight of the "mouldering pillars of the cloisters," lapsing into decay "in silence and neglect," makes Elinor's companion Ellen brood over the past, during which the English took possession of the property of the Irish aristocracy and exiled these native families from their homesteads: "'Sad, is it not?' said the fair descendant of the local princes, 'to see such fabrics as this of Mucruss hurrying to decay, in silence and neglect, and the chiefs who built them for the honor of God and the good of religion, driven as they have been from hearth and home, wandering landless and friendless men over the broad earth, while strangers,—upstart strangers,—revel in their ancient halls—that is, if they be not too time-worn for them—and lord it over their broad domains!'" Furthermore, the ruins of the former McCarthy estate and the disappearance of Gaelic-speaking ancestry that they express signal a loss of cultural heritage that reminds one of the Famine era, when entire generations perished. Although Elinor's relatives do not die of famine, their decease nevertheless appears to bring about a partial extinction of Irish Catholic cultural memories. The impending death of Elinor's aunt Kate entails an erasure of the lady's thitherto perfect recollection of the past in which her forefather participated in the Catholic gentry's rebellion against English rule: "Her pride of ancestry was no longer the same, and even the glory of that idolized progenitor who figured in the grand Catholic Confederation of 1641, had waxed dim and hazy in the far regions of memory."[24] When Aunt Kate passes away, memories of Ireland's attempt to shake off England's domination also appear to lapse into oblivion, suggesting an erosion of cultural legacies.

Ruins also feature in *Bessy Conway*, for when Bessy sets out on her transatlantic voyage, the omniscient narrator enumerates: "She was passing scenes of old renown, where Danish princes ruled and the proud Plantagenets kept their court, where Strongbow wedded the reluctant daughter of McMurrough, and Cromwell left his Vandal-mark on the sacred monuments of art, and where James II took his last farewell of Ireland—what a world of ancient lore crowded into the annals of one city, yet all unknown to Bessy."[25] These sites are all related to the history of Ireland's occupation, by the Vikings but also by the English, and the reference to Cromwell's destruction of Irish cultural treasures invokes the idea not only of ruins, but also of the devastation suffered by Ireland under English colonization. Whereas the fact that Cromwell's destruction of the Irish rebels' corn led to famine is not mentioned in this extract,[26] the imperial pillage that he represents bears an interesting affinity with the havoc created by the exponents of colonial rule in the novel, the English and Protestant Herberts, during the Great Famine. One can read that when Denis's fortunes are affected and he has to sell his stock, milk, and butter, "the money which they brought—it was little compared with what it would have been at another time—had most of it to go to satisfy the clamorous demands of Mrs. Herbert's bailiffs."[27] The sites of memory in the novel therefore bear out a sense of colonial trauma that is also central to the novel's Famine plot.

Paul Peppergrass's *Shandy M'Guire; or, Tricks upon Travelers* (1853) likewise gives expression to the downfall of the Irish during the Famine, through the image of a ruin that represents a more distant past of colonial atrocities. The novel contains a poignant scene in which Father Domnick laments "the measure of England's hate" to his native country. Pointing to the venerable vestiges of the old castle of the O'Donnells, of which only a "skeleton-like" structure remains, the priest bitterly exclaims about imperial Britain: "But why—why did she not destroy all? Why did she leave us these sad mementoes? . . . These traces makes it impossible for the Irish to forget what we once were. But alas! The old walls bring back again old memories, and as the eye rests on the ivied ruin, the heart yearns for the days that are gone." The fact that Father Domnick remains troubled by the phantom of a painful colonial past that the residues of the castle remind him of points to the persistence of trauma, and the skeleton-like bastion of former Irish power also bears a disturbing resemblance to the emaciated Famine victim. As such, the devastated castle also seems to reflect upon the current condition of the country that is "left . . . starving" by England and represents another instance of imperial indifference on the part of the English toward the subjugated sister isle.[28]

Sally Cavanagh associates the dilapidated state of a temple, once in use for Catholic service, with the ruined mental health of a mother whose infants have perished with the hunger. As was discussed in chapter 3, when Sally is forced to languish in a workhouse, she loses her wits when her severely enfeebled five children die. Having escaped from the workhouse, insane Sally roams around "the mouldering walls of a ruined temple" where she supposes her little ones have been buried, as the site features five little mounds "with . . . brown slabs for headstones."[29] While in Kickham's novel the ruin designates the psychological havoc wrought by the Famine, in Anna Dorsey's *Nora Brady's Vow* the "ruins of the old feudal castle and abbey of Fada-Brae" signify the material collapse of the female protagonist during the

Famine era. American-born Anna Dorsey did not have Irish roots, but, after her conversion to Catholicism in 1840, she became one of the pioneer authors of Catholic literature in the United States, and she contributed regularly to the Irish American periodical the *Pilot*.[30] In her novel, Mary Halloran's fortunes are severely wrecked by the "blight . . . on the potatoes." Consequently, she is forced to sell "the ould McCarthy More siller and jewels" and other possessions, and she seeks shelter in the "ruined halls" of her "ancestors . . . the princely McCarthy Mores." There "scarcely a portion" offers shelter "from the weather," but nevertheless some of the former retreats of the saints can be "rendered habitable."[31]

While in Kickham's and Dorsey's novels the decrepit monastic sites and fortresses mirror the descent of the main characters, whose lives are severely affected by potato rot and starvation, these spaces also personify a long tradition of colonial oppression in which the Great Famine constitutes one fundamental episode. The ruins mark a convergence of different moments in time: the far-away past of defeated clan rule that they evoke reflects upon and is analogous to the imagined present of the Great Famine, which can likewise be viewed as a manifestation of imperial oppression of the Irish. In Dorsey's novel, the mildewed and broken remains of Fada-Brae not only betoken the ruin brought by the blight upon Irish people such as Mary Halloran, but also constitute mournful, fading testimonies of the eliminated power of Celtic noble families, such as the McCarthy Mores, thereby linking episodes in Ireland's colonial history. This point is illustrated by a passage that describes the on-site "tombs . . . all more or less dilapidated" and "quite despoiled" of Mary's far-off ancestors, who had reigned before Ireland was usurped by England.[32]

The neglected and wasted burial places of "the dead of ages,—mitered abbots, monks, princes, and knights" represent the enshrined but forgotten past glory of the Irish Celts that was ruined beyond repair, "since Ireland had become an English province" and since survivors of its lineage had "gone abroad and lived and died in the Catholic countries of Europe, preferring exile to a sight of the grievances and oppressions which they could not remove, and which each year became more hopeless." In *Sally Cavanagh*, the ruins of the temple into which the eponymous heroine flees when she is bereaved from her infants by famine call forth recollections of Cromwell's atrocities. The "mouldering walls" bear witness to the fact that "the Mass had not been offered" there "since the day Father Kenrehan was hewn to pieces by a few Cromwellian troopers who happened to ride that way."[33] As such, the temple ruins suggest associations between the Great Famine and Cromwell's brutal campaign in Ireland: the narrative places the two events in one continuous line of imperial devastation and interprets the Famine as a form of colonial suppression.

Ruins as Expressions of Colonial Resistance

The ruins in Famine fiction simultaneously testify to loss and persistence. Signifying the degeneration of the Irish rural population and their culture during the Great Famine in both homeland and diaspora fiction, ruins function as transcultural tropes that give expression to the traumatic recollections of the Great Famine, as one of the episodes of colonial oppression to which Ireland has been subject. The ruins that are scattered through the narrative landscapes of Irish, Irish British, and Irish North American Famine fiction are, however, ambiguous, liminal spaces: on the one hand, they may signify overthrow and the subsequent extinction of native cultures through the Famine; on the other, they may also embody traces of a precolonial past that can be recalled. These remnants represent what David Lloyd denotes as "spaces of safety" that enable the articulation of a "counterhegemonic discourse" and a form of memory that challenges imperial authority.[34] These ruins imply the potential for a regeneration of preimperial cultural traditions and power structures.

The decayed sites of former Catholic worship in *New Lights* underline the ambivalence inherent in ruins, for they are signs not only of appropriation and degeneration, but also of an age-old Gaelic, Catholic identity that cannot be subdued. As such, these *lieux de mémoire* conjure up counterhistories that defy imperial authority and suggest possibilities for a recuperation of Ireland's grandeur through the evocation of a prospective nostalgia: a glorious past is recalled to suggest possibilities for future revival. The ruined abbeys and churches implicitly gesture to the demise that is caused by the Famine, but they also create the impression that Ireland, the Irish, and "Irishness" will overcome this era of disaster. The relics of Ireland's Catholic past that Captain Hampton addresses may be "all . . . in ruins"; nonetheless, they are conspicuous, covering the country "from east to west and from north to south." As symbols of how ancient Celtic clans defended their creed and country, they prove enduring sources of inspiration for the oppressed and famishing Irish such as Bernard O'Daly, who hold their "names and their actions . . . enshrined" in their hearts and consequently refuse to barter their faith in exchange for food. The passage that best exemplifies the Irish people's faithfulness to Catholicism in the face of starvation records Bernard O'Daly's exclamation that he would rather see himself and his family perish with hunger than betray their religious conviction: "We can get over all that so long as we have the thrue faith, an' if we hadn't it, all the riches in the world wouldn't be worth a pinch o' snuff. My children an' myself are in the hands of God, an' we disregard all you can do! That's the last word, now—go back with it to your employers. Tell them that the O'Dalys are of the ould stock, or the ould rock, your choice, an' they can die *for* their faith, as they have lived *in* it, them an' their fathers before them."[35]

As Bernard's defiant remark reveals, Ireland's past resistance to the English is a much-treasured memory in the minds of the rural Catholic population, but an episode that the English, by contrast, would gladly commit to forgetfulness. This point is demonstrated by the fact that Captain Hampton's remark is followed by his observation that his spouse, Caroline, would not be willing to burden her "memory with anything relating to Ireland." Moreover, the omnipresence of these dilapidated monuments of "Catholic piety and Catholic worship" throughout Ireland bears witness to England's lack of success in eradicating native Irish cultures and, consequently, its failure to impose a firm imperial grip on the Emerald Isle. Despite endeavors by the Anglo-Irish landlords and English proselytizers to root out

Catholicism in Ireland, in particular during the Famine, the rural population will hold on to their faith. This faith is also exemplified by Eleanor Ousely's cynical perspective on her father's support of the evangelicals, who, in her view, are doomed to fail in a land so imbued with the Catholic creed. As she states, "I much fear that after all the expenditure and all the trouble, the people of Ireland, take them as a body, will be just as Catholic—though you keep at them these fifty years to come." The desecrated traces of the past therefore create the impression that the Catholic Irish will also persevere in the face of famine, rising up from the ruins it has wrought and, as the text hints, perhaps eventually overcoming colonial oppression. Thus, signifying a persistent religious resistance to a colonial regime that enforces Protestantism, these *lieux de mémoire* can be considered what Foucault calls "heterotopia," sites that have "the power of juxtaposing in a single real place different spaces and locations that are incompatible with each other."[36]

In Sadlier's novel, this interpretation of the Famine past as a test to the Catholic faith, and its representation of Catholicism as a stoic endurance of famine in the face of religious persecution, appears to reflect the politics of the Devotional Revolution (1850–75). This reform movement in the Catholic Church, led by Archbishop Paul Cullen in Ireland and Archbishop John Hughes in the United States, emphasized clerical discipline and promoted devotional practices such as the rosary, vespers, and devotion to the Sacred Heart.[37] This attempt to regenerate the Catholic faith in Ireland and Irish North America was a response to the Great Famine. The decimation of Ireland's rural Catholic population as a result of starvation and emigration demanded a promotion of worship that would strengthen the stronghold of the Catholic Church on both sides of the Atlantic. As Archbishop Cullen remarked in a letter to Monsignor Alessandro Barnabò, secretary of propaganda, upon his arrival in Dublin in 1850, "The wretchedness among the Catholics is very great, and the population is reduced by a third from what it was six years ago."[38] Furthermore, the settlement of Irish immigrants in Protestant North American communities was perceived as a potential threat to their faith, and therefore Archbishop

Hughes stressed the importance of attending Mass that would provide "some permanent anchorage to Divine faith."[39] The significance of ruins in *New Lights*, as emblems of religious perseverance, can be read against the background of developments in Irish Catholicism at home and in diaspora.

Apart from emphasizing the undying prominence of Irish Catholicism and its cultural heritage, the vestiges in *New Lights* also express a counternarrative to traditional colonial views of Ireland's history. In the novel, the characters who personify England's colonial authority, such as Caroline Hampton and landlord Ousely, tend to think of Ireland as an uncivilized nation in order to legitimize its history of imperial subjugation. The officer's wife does not find any merit in cherishing any remnants of Ireland's past, while Ousely, uttering his chagrin at the ineffectiveness of the proselytizing mission, likens the cultural sophistication of the rural Irish to that of the "Hottentots who, I take it, are just as civilized and enlightened as the peasantry of whom O'Connell, rat him! was so proud."[40]

These characters' denunciation of Ireland's rich cultural legacies is at odds with the "counternarrative" of the past that the ruined monasteries and churches articulate. When James Trelawney—significantly one of the few broad-minded English in the narrative—requests Eleanor to guide him to some of the famous regional monasteries, she proposes that they should take a tour of the "old Carmelite monastery" at Loughrea, which is "well worthy of attention, as a specimen of the ecclesiastical architecture of that period."[41] Eleanor's insistence on the artistic rather than the religious value of this mnemonic site, which dates from before English occupation, challenges the at that time reigning idea of Irish savagery and instead displays the refinement of ancient Irish architecture.[42] A similar association of Catholic *lieux de mémoire* with the invincibility of Ireland's Catholicism can be found in *Elinor Preston*: as Elinor reflects, the ruin of the "stately fortress" at Ross Island, "the last great stronghold of the Confederate Catholic nobles," as well as "three ruined abbeys" of the MacCarthys and O'Donoghoes are "grand and beautiful even in decay." The fact that the spectacle brings Elinor into what she calls "a delicious trance, wherein the past and present were softly, mellowly blended," not only suggests the lasting reverence the buildings inspire in later generations of Catholics, but also insinuates that, like these relics of the past, Catholicism may survive times of adversity such as the Famine years.[43]

The ravaged fortresses, convents, and cemeteries that mark the scene in *Nora Brady's Vow* likewise express a defiance of imperial command and of colonial discourses that associate Ireland with primitivism. The decaying relics of Fada Brae not only suggest an analogy to Mary Halloran's financial downfall and the ruined state of the Famine-stricken country at large; they also, conversely, exhibit the steadfastness of precolonial culture and stress its grandeur. The "architectural beauties" of the "old feudal castle and abbey . . . presented an imposing spectacle from a distance . . . remained intact, were wonderful, and vindicated eloquently the civilization and perfection of science in the early ages of Ireland," and, as such, they undermine the prevalent notion that Ireland's indigenous cultures lacked sophistication. The crumbling walls even appear majestic, as "clinging mosses, no longer brown, looked like draperies of velvet festooned from turret and tower, so rich and green was the tint they wore; while the ivy, with its dark, glistening leaves, garlanded, like deathless memories, the silent cloisters below." As the term "deathless" indicates, the recollections that the monumental ruin evokes resuscitate the bygone glorious days of Celtic Catholic families in such a way that the past heritage appears susceptible to regeneration. In spite of the Famine that kills many among the Irish Catholics, the people's heritage stands strong and manages to survive.

Furthermore, *Nora Brady's Vow* employs the at that time conventional rhetoric of the picturesque to endorse the cultural magnificence of precolonial Irish culture and to suggest a possible future revivification. Dorsey's novel portrays Fada Brae as "situated on a beautiful and picturesque hill-side which overhung the glen of Agerlow," hinting that the charming ruggedness of the site would even attract tourists if they had heard of the place: "Had it been on the Rhine, painters, tourists, and poets would have immortalized it; but here it was scarcely known beyond the obscurity of the valley it overlooked, and the sketch-books of a few antiquarians who had visited it more by chance than intention." By placing the scenic beauties of the ruined estate on a par with well-known tourist attractions on the Continent, the passage foregrounds the richness of Ireland's cultural legacies, thereby countering the common association of Irish heritage with the uncultivated. Moreover, whereas in Famine writings ruins are traditionally dissociated from the picturesque—Lord Dufferin and G. F. Boyle's *Narrative of a Journey from Oxford to Skibbereen during the Year of the Famine* (1847), for example, calls the ruins of "an ancient abbey . . . mouldering away in the midst of the surrounding tombs" where Famine victims are interred anything but "picturesque or beautiful"—Dorsey's novel repeats the otherwise common identification of ruins with pleasing roughness.[44] In so doing, *Nora Brady's Vow* qualifies the remnants of the once august precolonial past as signs that the Irish Catholic culture cannot be overcome by colonial calamities such as the Great Famine.

In *Bessy Conway*, ruins also embody a contestation of England's mastery in that they represent a colonization in reverse: they are spaces where the Ascendancy becomes truly Irish by conversion to Catholicism. This significance becomes clear when one looks at the role played by the ruins of the abbey in Bessy's local village. At the beginning of the narrative, Henry Herbert, the landlord's son who is both a Protestant and of English descent, and therefore an unsuitable marriage partner for Bessy, commits "a sacrilegious folly" in this monument of worship by gambling on its site. However, when Henry's parents and companions all come to a bad end, he once more turns to the "moldering relics of mortality" that remind him of the transience of his once powerful but sinful peers. There, meditating on "the end of man," Henry comes to the insight that he has to convert to Catholicism: "Filled with gratitude that God had dealt so mercifully with me, I so unworthy of His least favor, I humbled myself before His awful majesty, and inflicted on myself for nine successive days, by way of expiation, the penance which you have seen me undergo."[45] While his change of creed enables Henry to marry Bessy, the scene is particularly interesting because the monument is endowed with the power not only to regenerate Irish Catholicism, but even to culturally assimilate the strangers in the land that rule over it.

In Famine novels written on both sides of the Atlantic, ruins thus function as sites that summon up a sustainable cultural heritage that cannot be eliminated even by the destructive dynamics of famine. More specifically, in fiction written in the homeland, the worn structures of dilapidated buildings can also be qualified as heterotopic spaces in that they literally figure as sites of colonial revolt. In Richard Baptist O'Brien's *Ailey Moore: A Tale of the Times* (1856), a novel that relates the sufferings of a Famine-stricken Catholic community hunted down by Bible readers and landlords, it is the derelict old castle "twenty miles from Kinmacarra . . . one of those strongholds of the sixteenth and seventeenth centuries, which stand like the milestones on Time's journey," that constitutes a concealed space of revolt. The ruined castle served as a space of resistance "in times of yore," when "the rude chieftain rioted in conscious strength, on feudal offering or rich rapine." Presently, it is also the location where secret meetings take place during which revenge plots to assassinate the generally loathed justice of the peace Jasper Skerin—responsible for Mary Ryan's death when he turned her and her mother "out to die in the ditch"—are devised. While the battered fortress thus embodies a heterochronic space that conflates different eras of colonial resistance, it additionally constitutes a heterotopic site, according to Michel Foucault's definition. It is a space possessed by and embedded "in the very institution" of a colonized society, as its ravaged nature reveals, but simultaneously it is a "counter" space where imperial power, as personified by Skerin, is "challenged, and overturned."[46]

As a heterotopic site that represents a covert potential for challenging imperial authority, the ruins moreover suggest an eerie likeness to the skulls of the starved Irish whose deaths are "frightful and numerous": "Above the string-course, window after window, or rather aperture after aperture, look down the eyeless socket of a monster skeleton upon the rude rocks below." The semblance of the old castle to an eyeless "monster skeleton" underlines what Dylan Trigg calls the "coming-to-light of spectral past/present" that is characteristic of ruins, in that the famished dead seem notably absent and present at the same time, like ghosts seeking retribution.[47] Furthermore, evoking the image of a giant skeleton, the ruin, with its unfathomable and terrifying "greatness of dimension,"[48] is cast in discourses of the Burkean sublime rather than the picturesque normally identified with ruins, thereby implying an uncontrollable energy of rebellion that is ready to be forced out into the open.

Intriguingly, the ruined temple, which figures as a space of colonial riot in *Sally Cavanagh*, is also dissociated from the picturesque. Connor Shea hides there to murder Oliver Grindem, who is guilty of letting Connor's wife, Sally, and their children waste away, because she refused to accept Grimden's advances and embrace Protestantism. This temple is also the place where the relentless landlord is shot by one of his other enemies, and its decay triggers uncomfortable sensations in Brian Purcell: "There was no one within the ruin, and the utter stillness of the place seemed awful to him."[49] The term "awful" reminds one of the sublime experience.[50] The interiors of the ruins, moreover, seem uncanny in that they signify, in Dylan Trigg's words, a "material reality, which . . . remains the same, as it ever was," but which is at the same time "discontinuous," "unsettled," and "alien":[51] the remains of the temple are familiar to Brian as a former site of worship but appear unusually unnerving and unsettling after the murder incident. The sublime and uncanny experiences that the ruins are here imbued with suggest the possibilities of rifts and ruptures in the existing social structures when imperial command is undermined by the Famine-stricken.

It seems remarkable that early Famine fiction specifically written for the North American Irish diaspora does not similarly picture ruins as sites of insurgency. As David Sim, among others, has argued, between 1850 and 1871 Irish nationalism in America was particularly alive and well organized: both American- and Irish-born citizens "organized funds" to foment "republican insurrection in Ireland."[52] Bellicose nationalist sentiments were very strong among Irish American communities in the late 1850s and 1860s, especially Irish Americans who were affiliated with John O'Mahony and Michael Doheny's

Fenian Brotherhood (1858), which structured a dense network of clubs on American soil[53] that shared the ideal of liberating the suffering homeland from what they regarded as British misgovernment.[54] For example, the broadside *On! On! Erin! On!* (1859), by J. J. Cummins, admonishes its audience to "join our ranks" and fight till "dear Erin" will be free again. However, this ideal of freeing Ireland from imperial subjugation is also voiced in widely read periodicals catering to Irish American readers: the article "The New Year for Ireland," published in the Boston-based *Irish Pictorial* of January 26, 1861, implores every "true man of the Irish race" in America to "labor actively and earnestly for his country" and defy the British policy directed "to the utter abolition of our nationality, and the extermination of our people." Possibly, this specific distinction between the symbolical meaning of ruins in fiction originally published in Ireland and in North America can be clarified by the fact that such sites in Ireland existed as real or "imagined rebel meeting points" in Ireland, as Kevin Whelan maintains.[55]

Portable Ruins

One specific kind of *lieu de mémoire* that is identified with ruin in Famine fiction is the cemetery. In fiction the burial places of Famine victims not only stand for literal ruin in the sense that they are situated on dilapidating sites, but also embody figurative ruin in that they symbolize the decay of once blooming families and the pain concomitant upon Famine mortality. This symbolism is well illustrated by *Nora Brady's Vow*, in which the graveyard where "Mrs. Halloran's parents were slumbering" and "where the dead of ages" found their last resting place is a space of physical and mental decay. The tombs of the "mitered abbots, monks, princes and knights" are all "more or less dilapidated," as "some were quite despoiled of the stone and marble effigies which had decorated them." At the same time, the cemetery is a haunt of mental ruin, as Mrs. Halloran comes to mourn over her little Gracie, who died of fever during the Famine: "Planted by a mother's hand, and watered by such tears as only mothers shed, they were precious memorials of the little sleeper below."[56]

In *Sally Cavanagh*, the graveyard figures as a site where the painful memory of the Great Famine crystallizes and can be kept alive, despite the passage of time in a country under an imperial rule aiming to wipe out traces of colonial atrocities. Two decades after his mother's death, Sally and Connor's only surviving son returns to Ireland from America, intent upon seeking out his mother's grave to place a "new headstone," and thus to erect a monument for her as a victim of the Famine era. He subsequently finds that her history is by no means forgotten. He learns that "there was scarcely a child in the parish who could not show me Sally Cavanagh's grave," a given that indicates the transgenerational persistence of recollections of the Great Famine, even if the ruins on the site of Sally's grave can be interpreted as signs of colonial devastation. Moreover, the fact that Sally's son is inspired by his mother's burial place to serve Ireland in its crusade of liberation with the one "arm" he has "left" implies the transnational appeal of the Famine past. The dilapidated ruins of the temple and the graves of Sally and her infants—indicated by "five little brown slabs"—appear to symbolically instigate a commitment on the part of the transatlantic Irish to restore the country.[57]

Nora Brady's Vow shows a marked contrast with Kickham's novel in that the memory space that is related to the Famine past, Gracie's grave, is depicted neither as a chain that physically connects the Irish forever to their native soil nor as fixed only to Irish soil. When John Halloran has found a new homestead in America and cannot return to Ireland owing to his involvement in the 1848 rising, the rest of the family eventually settles with him in his adopted country. This definite migration to the New World involves a translocation of Gracie's coffin, "marblehead" and "footstone," which, "carefully packed and stowed away" on a transatlantic ship, are taken to John, "that it might be laid where he could sometimes go and weep beside it."[58] This physical reterritorialization of Gracie's corpse and grave symbolizes the transportability of Famine memory to Irish communities in diaspora, implying that its recollections are not tied to the sites where fateful events occurred, but can be transplanted through time and space. *Sally Cavanagh* underlines the rootedness of memories connected to the

Great Famine and mainly emphasizes their transgenerational transposition, whereas *Nora Brady's Vow* stresses their transcultural reverberations. This difference may be attributed to the fact that Kickham's narrative was originally directed toward homeland audiences, as a serialized novel in the *Hibernian Magazine* in 1864, whereas Dorsey's text was exclusively written for the Bostonian *Pilot*. As such, Dorsey's text envisages a more extensive Irish imagined community in which Famine memory may circulate.

Conclusion

Recently, Svetlana Boym has pointed out that "ruin literally means to collapse, but ruins are more about remainders and reminders. A tour of ruins leads you into a labyrinth of ambivalent language—no longer, not yet, nevertheless, albeit—that plays tricks with causality."[59] Her observation may well be applied to the narrative ruins that one finds in early fiction that recalls the Great Famine, for these derelict abbeys and sacked fortresses not only express the collapse of a native Irish culture subject to colonial oppression and particularly imperial calamities such as the Famine, but conversely also constitute remainders that trigger memories of imperial atrocities. The ambivalent spectrality of ruins that these Famine novels testify to moreover extends to their temporal and spatial scope. They evoke absent powers and ages, suggesting their reflection in the present state of Famine-stricken Ireland. Their heterochronic nature therefore blurs demarcations between different episodes of Ireland's fateful colonial past, placing the Famine in a series of wrongs inflicted upon the Irish people by the English.

As such, these narratives do not present the Famine as a unique rupture of life in Ireland. Moreover, in Famine fiction written for audiences in Ireland, images of ruins are embedded in anticolonial discourse: their heterotopic premises are haunted by exponents of anti-imperial resistance, who, hidden from broad daylight in the vaults of ruined buildings, occupy a shadowy space between illusionary absence and an invisible, lurking presence. More than anything else, these ruins manifest the transcendence of boundaries between absence and presence in that they manage to transmit the Great Famine across generations and, as a North American novel like *Nora Brady's Vow* implies, even across nations. Written in a transatlantic context that was marked by traveling Famine emigrants, Dorsey's text undermines the notion that ruins form rooted spaces of memory, demonstrating how these "portable monuments" can become symbols for the transnational fluidity of Famine memory itself.[60]

6 | Recollections of (Re)migration

In a speech delivered at the dinner of the St. Patrick's Society, Toronto, on March 17, 1860, William Halley called the Irish the "Ishmaelites of the earth—wanderers everywhere—discovered 'quite at home' under the burning sun of the tropics—happy in the frozen regions of the globe." Wondering where "the 'exiles' have not penetrated,"[1] Halley ponders the massive exodus of Irish men and women during the Great Hunger and its immediate aftermath. Panic driven, many of them were landless poor who, through the "remittance system" of prepaid tickets,[2] that is, fares paid by American relatives,[3] or, in 5 percent of the cases, "landlord-assisted emigration," tried to escape from starvation.[4] The fact that the Great Famine led to unprecedented emigration manifests itself in recent seminal scholarship that examines the historiography and present-day cultural commemorations of Famine emigration.[5] Moreover, this interconnectedness between the Great Famine and emigration is revealed in Irish as well as diaspora fiction from the period 1847–70: novels and short stories frequently recollect the Great Famine through a plotline that focuses on characters who leave Famine-stricken Ireland in order to seek their fortunes elsewhere.

This chapter will analyze the narrative schemes in which the memories of Famine emigration are organized. First, it will examine the templates in which the Famine exodus is cast, as well as the rhetoric that is used to reconfigure the Famine diaspora. A great number of novels and short stories written on both sides of the Atlantic identify the population's flight from their suffering motherland with traumatic rupture and alienation. However, while it is generally assumed that

Famine emigration was experienced and later remembered as compulsory expatriation by the first and second generations of immigrants, some texts also leave room for a more positive reinterpretation of the Famine past. In these narratives, which are first and foremost written for Irish North American audiences, emigration is presented as a redemption of Famine miseries. Many works of Famine fiction from Ireland and the Irish diaspora explore the appalling conditions of transatlantic emigration by focusing on the harsh shipboard realities of the emigrants' journey to their host societies.

The second part of this chapter will illustrate that in early Famine fiction, the voyage assumes a symbolic role, functioning as an episode that emblematizes the liminal status of the emigrants. The vessels that take the Irish from a beloved homeland to foreign North American shores are liminal spaces, for their passengers are literally and metaphorically suspended between two cultures. The transatlantic passage functions as a screen on which painful recollections of starvation can be projected and as a rite of passage for the characters and their sense of ethnic identity. The voyage often foreshadows the trials with which the immigrant characters will have to cope upon arrival, and the emigration plotlines almost invariably imply that ethnic separatism is a condition for survival and success in the host societies. Finally, this chapter will discuss recurring narrative structures that feature returning emigrants. As will be demonstrated, these templates of remigration can be interpreted as responses to the social upheaval caused by the Famine and as expressions of the nostalgia for a lost homeland that informed the transatlantic diaspora.

Famine Emigration: Exile or Deliverance?

In enumerating characteristics of diaspora culture, Robin Cohen emphasizes the traumatic, involuntary "dispersal from an original homeland," a trait that in his view even more strongly marks "victim diasporas" such as those of the Irish Famine generation whose reluctant departure from the mother country is the result of "scarring historical calamities."[6] Cohen's claim is substantiated by the terms of forced exile by which the Famine exodus was conceptualized in a great number of texts written in Ireland and its diaspora between 1847 and 1870.[7] For example, in Lady Helen Dufferin's poem "The Emigrant Ship" (1848), the persona speaks on behalf of fellow emigrants who will forever be separated from country, family, and mother tongue: "For us alone (poor exiles!) those words of kindly cheer / Shall fall no more, in Irish tongue, upon the longing ear!" Thomas D'Arcy McGee's "The Exile's Meditation," published posthumously in 1869, presents a persona who laments the fact that his fellow countrymen are "wiled and cast away, / And driven like soulless cattle from their native land a prey," because those individuals in power compel the tenant farmers to leave their communities.[8] The anonymous poem "The Emigrant's Mother," published in the Canadian magazine the *Literary Garland* in June 1850, similarly imagines the emigrant's parting from Ireland as an inescapable fate imposed by "evil days" at home. Leaving the Emerald Isle causes pain to the expatriate as well as close relatives who stay behind: while the mother weeps and wishes herself in her "grave" when her son Dermot is about to sail for America, he will forever be severed from the beloved "threshold, and . . . the old hearth-stone" of his childhood home.

This representation of the Famine diaspora as forced exile from a cherished homeland that has become uninhabitable is foregrounded in several works of early Famine fiction. "The Emigrant Ship," an anonymous sketch that was republished in the *Literary Garland* in November 1850, which had originally been written for a Protestant orphan bazaar raising funds to aid children who had lost their parents on the transatlantic passage, emphasizes the severe despondency of the emigrants on deck who utter "a wailing cry . . . so sad and plaintive" when they "take a last look of their native land." Wills's *The Love That Kills* (1867) likewise identifies the transatlantic diaspora with unwilling banishment, by incorporating a departure scene that stresses the desolation of the passengers who are "sullen with gloom," while "the friends whom they were leaving behind, mothers, sisters, and little children" give full vent to their grief. Screaming cries like a "caoine"—the mournful notes traditionally sung at an Irish wake—the old women on the quay suggest that the emigration of their loved ones, who are in quest of "good beef and bread instead of black potatoes," involves a loss of community and identity that equals death.[9]

Two early Famine novels, both published around the same time by Dublin-based house James Duffy, situate a plotline of forced exile in the context of colonialism. These texts create the impression that the huge outpour of emigrants should be interpreted as a forced banishment that is the direct consequence of the policies adopted by the London government and its representatives, the landlords. Thus exemplifying Robin Cohen's assertion that groups traumatized by unwilling diaspora are inclined to construe this exodus in terms of "victimhood at the hands of a cruel oppressor," these narratives furthermore demonstrate the significance of nationalist politics for the perception of the Famine in the motherland.[10] Perhaps partly under the influence of Fenian rhetoric, these narratives represent the Famine as a forced expulsion that can be attributed to imperial mismanagement.[11] In Allen H. Clington's *Frank O'Donnell* (1861), the eponymous protagonist suggests that most emigration from Ireland is imposed by the government, which by "law will transport a poor man for stealing a sheep to keep himself and his family from starving."[12] Famine victims who transgress the law, because their dire conditions force them to do so, are punished by expulsion from the land they love.

In *The Struggles of Dick Massey*, Reginald Tierney suggests compelled emigration by showing that the failure of the landed class and the British administration to alleviate Ireland's misery leads to panic among the people who are "flying away from the beauteous isle as though it were the hot-bed, the birth-place of some cursed plague that fastened with deadly gripe upon its victims." Tierney's novel, moreover, emphasizes that it is not just the blight but particularly landlordism that leads to the massive outflux of population. Landlords clear their estates with the selfish object of getting their tenants "out of Ireland" in order to relieve their own responsibilities.[13] As a result, the Irish, once "rooted by chains as strong as adamant to the old soil . . . have to leave for ever the spot of earth where they first saw light . . . and go out amongst strangers, forlorn, desolate, ruined, maddened, shamed!" Tierney's description bears great resemblance to the words used by John Mitchel in 1871, in *Ireland since '98*, for the latter would represent the Famine emigrants as urged on by "a deep and prevailing anxiety to fly—to escape any whither!" Mitchel's suggestion that the country was "made too hot to hold its inhabitants," who felt as if "pursued by wild beasts," conveys criticism at a government that bears responsibility for the panic-driven exodus that is very similar to the anti-imperial rhetoric that pervades Clington's and Tierney's reconfigurations of the Famine diaspora.[14]

Furthermore, early works of Famine fiction—and especially those works by immigrant authors—convey a sense of exile in terms of broken ties that lead to feelings of alienation and isolation. Some texts symbolize this severance of treasured bonds with the motherland and its heritage through the character's physical separation from the motherland. A good example is offered by Charles Cannon's novel *Bickerton* (1855), a text that is rooted in prosthetic experiences of diaspora, as the author, the American-born son of Irish Catholic intellectuals residing in New York,[15] was himself unfamiliar with the experience of emigration. In the novel, Manus O'Hanlon experiences his crossing to America from a destitute Ireland as a sure route into exile. He feels "cast out" of his native land to settle "in the land of the stranger." This loss of ties with his Irish "inheritance" is expressed by the way the ship carries Manus away from the Irish shore, making Ireland disappear before his eyes as he watches the coast from the ship's deck: his "straining eyes were turned towards his native land, which, becoming every moment less, seemed now a mere speck between sea and sky."[16]

The anonymous story "The Emigrant," published in *Catholic World* in September 1870, likewise portrays Famine emigration in terms of broken ties and loneliness. The story relates William Leyden's departure from his local community and family when "the crops failed, the cows died," and the family could no longer pay the rent. Hoping to find employment in America that would enable him to provide for his family, William endures several years of utter loneliness: "His heart would almost fail him when he thought of the ocean that intervened between him and his dearest treasures." When he has finally saved enough money to be reunited with his wife and children, calamity strikes: after surviving the passage, Mary and the children die in a train accident, and William is once again left to face the world alone. His earlier premonition that his emigration would entail eternal separation from his kin proves to come true: the day before he left, William had dreamed about America as a place that could be a pastoral haven, with the "purtiest greenwood": "The birds were singin' and the daisies growin' as they wud be in heaven."[17] However, this dream vision of a paradise turns into a nightmare not only when William finds that a river separates him from his approaching wife and infants, but also when the latter disappear as they try to cross over to him.

In other novels and stories that are imbued with Famine remembrance, the theme of alienation that is associated with emigration takes on the form of utter isolation in the host society. Miss Mason's novel *Kate Gearey* (1853) shows that the heroine feels homesick for her "little cabin on the banks of the Awbeg" when she has moved to London, not only because she has to face as much penury as in her Famine-stricken homeland, but also because she finds herself in a climate that shows little sympathy for her native creed. As a result of the company she keeps, Kate neglects "to approach the Sacraments" and finds herself "what is so emphatically termed 'an out-church Catholic.'" Her feelings of exile and nostalgia for her childhood home are imbued with memories of the person who embodies the religion of her native soil, "Father Phelim." In a similar vein, "Ellen Harrington" (1865) describes how young Ellen, who has escaped the Famine miseries of her native country and settled in London to "earn a competent income" through lace making, is a "lonely girl" leading a "stranger's life." Even after having lived in London for four years, Ellen has "few acquaintances in the wide, wide world of London, and no sympathisers." The rare sight of "a familiar face from her native land" is "greeted with showers of tears," filling her with a pervasive melancholy and homesickness.[18] It is only during her married life with a compatriot in Australia—another part of the world where many Famine emigrants settled—that Ellen eventually regains a sense of home and belonging.

Similarly, in Mary Anne Sadlier's novel *Elinor Preston* (1861), the heroine feels "very lonely" upon her emigration from Famine-stricken Ireland, first to America, then to Montreal, and finally to the Canadian backwoods. Even if in the latter she begins to "relish the soothing stillness of all around," she still misses the "warble of the linnet and the thrush, and the musical whistle of the blackbird" of her "Fatherland." As Elinor states, the adopted country can "never be to us like the land of our birth" to which emigrants will always be bound by "tender ties."[19] While Elinor's idyllic representation suppresses her own as well as Ireland's painful experiences of loss during the Great Famine, this crystallized image of a pastoral landscape expresses a nostalgic longing for a lost homeland from which the main character feels exiled.

Elinor Preston additionally translates the sense of diasporic displacement that permeates the narrative into a sense of lost identity. This point becomes clear from the scene in which Elinor witnesses the funeral procession of a number of Irish emigrants who have not survived the perilous transatlantic crossing to Canada, having died of various epidemic diseases. Elinor is emotionally affected by the fact that these funerals are not well attended, furnishing "pictures of such utter loneliness that it made my heart ache to see them, especially as I all along noticed that the loneliest and most affecting were of the emigrant class—mournful fragments of what has been called the Irish Exodus." Her heart particularly goes out to the "bereaved husband or wife, or the orphan children left friendless and alone on a foreign shore."[20] The passage expresses the sentiments of isolation and alienation that the novel relates to emigration, but also provokes the idea that migration to the New World involves anonymity, as immigrants and their stories of suffering and exile will not be remembered. Sadlier's novel thus conveys anxieties that were often associated with the Irish Famine diaspora in North America. For example, the poem "The Stranger's Grave" (1847), which was published in the *New Brunswick Courier* and appears to respond to the many casualties of shipboard fever that arrived in Canada,[21] pictures a dead Irish immigrant who is "buried unwept, and alone": no "friend there came to weep at his bier," and no "tablet was raised to point out the spot / Where the lone stranger slept, unhonoured—forgot."[22]

This notion that the exodus of the Famine generation implies an erasure of identity, as those emigrants who die in the foreign lands will often receive no memorials by which they may be remembered, also surfaces in *The Struggles of Dick Massey*. The chapter "Sunny Memories" contains a long intervention on the part of the narrator in which he addresses novelist Harriet Beecher Stowe, requesting she consider Famine Ireland and Famine emigration as suitable material for future writing: "Look at this Mrs. Stowe . . . You need all our heroism now, for this is a scene upon which devils would rather not gaze." Famine memories are presented as multidirectional, because they intersect with the (literary) legacies of African American slavery: the landlords are likened to Stowe's cruel slave owner Simon Legree, and the starving mother, with her "hollow eye," is compared to the wretched Uncle Tom.[23] The passage also outlines the painful exile of Irish American immigrants. The narrator observes that, cut off from the soil on which they were raised, these immigrants will never belong in their new countries: "They are in a strange land, and strange people gaze and wonder at them but there is pity in their gaze, although thousands of miles of deep sea rolled between their birth-places. . . . They die without knowing where they are. Their very names are unknown to the men who bury their bodies in the frozen glebe."[24] Dislocated and disoriented strangers forever, these Irish emigrants pass away without any recognition of their histories and memories.

While the above discussion makes clear that the Famine exodus is often reconfigured in terms of exile and alienation in these early works of fiction, some narratives convey a different interpretation. These texts represent emigration to the New World as deliverance from Famine suffering in several respects: they suggest that emigrants to North America will be able to relieve distress of the famishing in Ireland, and they create the impression that comfortable homes will be found in transatlantic territories rather than on Irish soil. As we saw in chapter 4, Irish North American novels such as McCorry's *The Lost Rosary* (1870) and *Tim Doolan* by "Canada West" (1869) do not express fantasies about returning to Ireland. Rather, new settlements at the western frontier are imagined as better dwelling places than Famine-stricken and post-Famine Ireland—even if these new homes imply microcosmic little Irelands. The novella *Paddy's Leisure Hours in the Poor House* (1849) creates the impression that a sense of home is irretrievably lost during the Famine: in the "ould times," a sense of homeliness would be evoked by the "petaty-pot biling on the fire," but the cottage inhabited by Paddy and his family has meanwhile turned into a desolate place of deprivation and hunger. Their domestic life has become disintegrated for good when circumstances force Paddy, his wife, and their children to resort to the poorhouse.[25] In fact, as an inmate who is separated from the rest of his family, Paddy feels "like the ould exile of Erin."[26] While experiences of banishment are thus attached to the Famine-stricken homeland, the New World offers Paddy opportunities to rebuild a family existence. When his sister from America sends Paddy a thirty-pound note, he is reunited with the rest of his family, sailing with them to American shores.

A similar view of emigration as deliverance can be found in "Captain Patrick Malony; or, The Irishman in Alabama," a novel by T. L. N. that was serialized in the *Pilot* in June 1860. The main protagonist, Patrick, leaves for America when "the times were growing worse and worse" and "there were many mouths to feed, and little work and poor pay." Once there, Patrick has to overcome severe bias against "the idolatrous Church of Rome," and his employer, Captain Satford, initially takes offense with his "Popish superstition." However, the moral uprightness and excellent work ethos that Patrick displays lead to several promotions, which enable him to send for his "mother and family by a cotton ship coming to Mobile" when "times grew darker in Ireland" and starvation prevailed: "Millions of the poor children of Ireland perish. . . . [A] million of her Majesty's subjects . . . were left to perish." Patrick can buy his relatives "a pretty cottage in one of the sweet alleys of Montgomery" and himself finds a "comfortable, genial and even elegant home."[27] Thus, emigration is shown to offer better prospects than staying behind in the unfortunate motherland.

As we noticed, some early Famine narratives, especially those texts written in the North American diaspora, represent emigration as a solution to the food crisis in Ireland: returned emigrants help relieve the distress of their relatives or former communities by the wealth they have acquired. Sadlier's heroine Bessy Conway, who thus prevents the eviction and starvation of her family, and Dillon O'Brien's Henry Daly, who manages to restore the happiness of his childhood community by purchasing the ancestral estate, are earlier-discussed examples. A story published in the Canadian periodical the *Literary Garland* in October 1850, "Rose McCarthy's Sorrow," by M. B., also suggests that the dire effects of the Famine are alleviated by the financial support that emigrants can give to their families. Bridget, the protagonist's sister, is said to have "worked faithfully until she had accomplished bringing half the family to New York." However, now that Bridget has decided to follow her own inclinations and to indulge in a more luxurious life for herself, Rose carries the burden of earning money so that "brothers and sisters, escaped hitherto from the maw of famine and disease, be not long exposed to their fangs." The story thus associates emigration with redemption of suffering relatives in the motherland, but the sketch that is given of these circumstances is not quite positive: Rose is almost weighed down by her responsibilities, which compel her to take on too many duties, and this heavy yoke of care is symbolized by Rose's "red-covered prayer-book, with the gilded cross on the back" that is alternately opened at "the place of Devout Prayers in time of Famine and Pestilence" and "Meditations on Christ's Passion."[28] The Famine and its dire effects on her siblings haunt Rose's mind and demand perseverance and self-sacrifice.

The identification of Famine emigration with exile that still prevails in the earliest Famine fiction shifts to the background in favor of more positive views of transatlantic relocation in texts of later date, especially those works published in North America. Such a shift marks, for example, "From Killarney to New York; or, How Thade Became a Banker," a novel by Margaret Anna Cusack, also known as Sister Mary Frances Clare or "the Nun of Kenmare," who played an active role in raising and distributing relief funds during a local famine in

1871. The novel first appeared in *McGee's Illustrated Weekly* between May and November 1877 and was subsequently republished by Burns in London and by McGill in Dublin.[29] This serialized narrative first focuses on Thade O'Halloran's trials during the Great Famine: his father, Tim, dies "of famine fever," his grandmother perishes after several "months of starvation," and Thade himself is kidnapped by a group of Soupers. His fortunes change when he returns a lost wallet to its rightful owner, wealthy American banker Mr. Maxwell, who is visiting Ireland. Impressed by Thade's moral uprightness and looking for a successor—for Mr. Maxwell has no sons—Maxwell gives Thade the opportunity to join him to America, receive an education, and learn the trade of banking. As a result, Thade becomes a very successful banker in New York City several decades later, a rise in status that is attributed to "his admirable conduct" and "quiet, patient religion."[30]

The plot bears many similarities to the previously discussed *Tim Doolan*, but whereas in this novel by "Canada West" Noonan's reward for returning a lost wallet consists of a plot of land in Ireland, Cusack imagines reward in terms of emigration to the United States. Emigration thus signifies opportunity and, additionally, the possibility to stay true to one's native Catholic creed rather than exile and religious oppression, as earlier novels by Sadlier and Cannon suggested. A similar approach to Famine emigration can be found in Mary Synon's "My Grandmother and Myself" (1916), published in *Scribner's Magazine*. The story deconstructs nostalgia for the homeland of yore as well as the conventional interpretation of emigration as exile that one finds in many of the earliest Famine novels and stories. The narrative centers on a clash between the young protagonist's grandmother, who arrived in New York after her father and sister Brigid had died of starvation, and the boy's father, John Stutton, who plans to side with Germany in the First World War, as their victory would lead to Germany's liberation of Ireland from England's imperial rule. John has never been to his mother's homeland but, ironically, wishes he "had been born in Ireland," positioning himself as an exile from the country where he should have been raised. His aged mother, however, chastises him for betraying his country of birth, which gave him the opportunity to become a shopkeeper, and demystifies his idealized view of Ireland by reminding him of her own narrow escape from famine: "And if I'd stayed in Ireland I'd have starved . . . and little chance you'd have had of being born anywhere." The old grandmother shows her grandson Shauneen that he should be loyal to America, for not only did it bring food to the Famine-stricken Connaught shores, but it also gave her the opportunity to "come here with the promise of work to do" and to bring her surviving siblings to the New World, where they were forever free from "famine and persecution" by landlords.[31] Reflecting the social mobility of the descendants of the Famine generation, these works of Famine fiction from subsequent decades move away from the traditional diasporic exile myth.

The Transatlantic Passage as a Narrative Template

In *The Struggles of Dick Massey*, the narrator's imploring of novelist Harriet Beecher Stowe's empathy with Irish emigrants specifically goes into their sufferings on board of the ships that transport them to North America, "down in file steerage of a plague-stricken ship, that is tossed like a nut-shell on the angry billows." Detailing how these spaces belowdecks are crowded with "dead and dying men, women, and, alas! little children" who are "wallowing around in filth and wretchedness," the narrator brings the generally dire conditions on the transatlantic passage to the central consciousness of the text. The voyage on the coffin ships was notorious, as many passengers lost their lives and were buried at sea; as *Grosse-Isle Emigrant Station: A Letter Addressed to the Inspectors of Hospitals, Prisons and Asylums* (1861) argued in retrospect, passenger ships on their way to Canada commonly "arrived at Grosse Isle with the remnant of a phantom crew," while "the Atlantic Ocean was dotted" with the corpses "of upwards of five thousands immigrants thrown overboard in the middle passage."[32] Many of the poorer emigrants, who could afford only the lowest fares or whose emigration had been subsidized by landlords seeking to relieve their overburdened estates, were already "sick or infected with disease" when they embarked upon their long journey, facing a stay of six to seven weeks belowdecks in overcrowded and unsanitary spaces.[33]

In consequence, as a leading article from the *Cork Examiner* of December 29, 1847, states, "Many of their class have already died from want of the means to bear up against the hardships of their journey." As John Francis Maguire claimed, it was "no unusual occurrence for the survivor of a family of ten or twelve to land alone . . . on the wharf of New York."[34] On average, up to 30 percent perished during the crossing,[35] as the work of such historians as Michael Quigley, Susan Campbell, and Ciarán Ó Murchadha has revealed, but as also becomes clear from documents of the Famine era that record the number of casualties on board.[36] For example, Robert Whyte's fictional autobiographical account of a journey on a coffin ship, *The Ocean Plague; or, A Voyage to Quebec in an Irish Emigrant Vessel* (1848), alleges that "in only ten of the vessels that arrived at Montreal in July" of that year, "out of 4,427 passengers, 804 had died on the passage, and 847 were sick on their arrival," and from the "60,000 shipped for Quebec; 5,293 died at sea; 8,072 at Grosse Isle and in Quebec,"[37] in the quarantine stations or so-called fever sheds.[38] Likewise, Theophile Hamel's painting *Le Typhus* (1848), which is exhibited at Chapelle Notre-Dame-de-Bon-Secours in Montreal, represents the many ill-fated Irish who lost their lives during or shortly after their journey to Canada.[39]

In some early Famine novels and stories, the destitution suffered on board of the overpopulated vessels and the concomitant high mortality rates play a prominent role in the recurring plotlines of transatlantic emigration. These representations of the dire conditions belowdecks and the passengers who waste away with hunger and disease suggest that the crossing is an extension of the trauma of Famine: it is implied that the emigrants cannot escape the fate that would probably also have awaited them in their homeland. For instance, in the previously cited "The Emigrant Ship," the passengers are shown to be subject to starvation, as the captain doles out "a scanty supply from his private stores, for which he exacted a most unjust compensation, and those who had no money to give, became a burden on the charity of the compassionate." As a result, the majority of the emigrants turn "pale, dispirited, worn by fasting and confinement." The fact that "those who had been cleanly and robust, were but the shadows of their former selves" reminds one of Famine victims who, as we saw in the first three chapters, were conventionally portrayed in terms of decay and spectrality.[40] As such, the story implies that the emigrants unsuccessfully try to flee the atrocities of hunger and disease in the homeland as they are exposed to the same perils during their passage.

That seeking better opportunities in the New World is to no avail, because coffin ships are sites where the Irish are as much subject to imperial oppression as on their native soil, becomes clear from Reginald Tierney's *The Struggles of Dick Massey*. This novel draws attention to the many victims during the crossing, mainly as a vehicle to condemn England's defective colonial rule over Ireland. The novel's protagonists, tenant Tom Nolan, Mrs. Conroy, and her daughter, Norah, whose lease of land has expired and who are therefore essentially homeless, embark on a voyage to America, where they expect to find better prospects. As the title of the chapter "Dolores Maris," or "sorrows of the sea," already reveals, on board conditions are miserable. The ship is overcrowded, an epidemic breaks out among the enfeebled travelers belowdecks, and the corpses of the dead are thrust overboard. What makes the conditions even more unbearable is the fact that the "water was getting bad, too, and was doled out with as bad grace, and amid as terrible a torrent of blasphemy, as the food." While the emigrants thought to have escaped the Famine, they are once more facing starvation during their passage, and "the numerous deaths made not the slightest impression on either captain or officers; such sights of wretchedness made them even more brutal." While the chapter reevokes and criticizes the treatment of passengers on board of the emigrant vessels, it can also be interpreted as a form of screen memory to negotiate painful memories of the Famine in Ireland, for *The Struggles of Dick Massey* depicts the transatlantic crossing as an extension of the tyranny faced by the tenantry at home. The narrator compares the ship to a "butcher's yard," where the helpless passengers are led to be "slaughtered" by the landlords who deliberately chase them away from Ireland.[41]

As Christopher Cusack and I have argued elsewhere,[42] the novel moreover represents Famine memories as "multidirectional,"[43] in that it draws analogies between the deaths of Irish emigrants during the transatlantic voyage and the brutal and ruthless conduct of owners toward their slaves. Such a comparison was more common, as is illustrated by Robert Whyte's claim that "the worse horrors of that slave-trade which it is the boast or the ambition of this empire to suppress, at any cost, have been reenacted in the flight of British subjects from their native shores." In a similar vein, the narrator in Tierney's novel informs his addressee, novelist Harriet Beecher Stowe, and his readers that "for the one slave that has been lashed to death by his master, there have been a hundred Irishmen drowned by their landlords."[44]

The novel may comment on two episodes of slavery here: either Britain's past as an important slave-trading nation or the American issue of slavery, which had just plunged the United States into civil war at the time of the novel's publication. Following the first possible interpretation, it seems that *The Struggles of Dick Massey* situates the oppression of the native Catholic Irish by Anglo-Irish landlords during the Famine in a series of imperial atrocities. Famine remembrance thus intersects with and is shaped by other painful memories that are related to Ireland's colonial history. If we read this address to Stowe as proof that the novel responds to the politically tense situation in America, then the coffin ship functions as a "multidirectional" mnemonic site that connects the traumatic Famine past with present circumstances and recent developments in America's political landscape. It must be noted that the narrator does not compare the suffering of the Famine emigrants with the Middle Passage, even if this analogy would have been evident. However, the fact that the narrator tells Stowe that the hardships endured on the coffin ships may supply as harrowing material for a best seller such as her *Uncle Tom's Cabin* suggests an allusion to the cultural memories of slave transportation that feature similar instances of death and disease.

As Homi Bhabha explains in *The Location of Culture*, diasporic subjects find themselves between two borders in a liminal space, in between assimilation to the cultures of the host society, on the one hand, and persisting ties to the cultural identities and memories of the motherland, on the other. The coffin ships in these early works of Famine fiction also express the liminality of the migrant experience, which Angelika Bammer calls the "split and double existence—stretched across the multiple ruptures between here and there."[45] In many of these narratives, emigrant ships are places not merely of literal death but also of transition, in that the emigrants' harrowing maritime experiences, such as the loss of loved ones and tempestuous weather, often prefigure the tribulations that await the passengers upon arrival in the New World. These experiences are moreover liminal, because they symbolize a figurative death and rebirth that foreshadow the trials that they face in their quest of transatlantic identities, thereby exemplifying the fact that emigration could mean "either new life or a certain death to the individual emigrant."[46] The on-board communities in these plotlines therefore function as heterotopic spaces where the immigrants undergo a rite of passage and can negotiate in advance the forces of assimilation and cultural problems that await them. The coffin ships point not only back to the trauma of the Great Hunger that forced so many Irish into exile from their cherished motherland, but also forward to the migrants' encounter with multicultural America.[47] As such, these vessels express a sense of temporal liminality.

Many novels depict deaths resulting from the dreadful circumstances on board the coffin ships to symbolically prefigure the struggle to establish new lives that the Irish emigrant characters will have to confront on American soil. In Charles Joseph Kickham's novel *Sally Cavanagh*, for instance, it is the death of Mary Mulvaney "of fever on the voyage" to America that forebodes the temptations that her younger sister, Rose, will be exposed to in urban America. In fact, her arrival in New York leads to the figurative death of the old Rose who back home had been a virtuous, bashful girl, marked by "reserve," but in America is drawn into prostitution: "Rose Mulvaney, the beautiful, the innocent, the pure, is a lost polluted thing . . . lost to virtue and to God."[48] Kickham's novel thus intimates that emigration to the New World may involve not only literal death but also a moral demise caused by disconnection from the ethical values of the homeland.

In many early Famine narratives, the death of emigrants during the transatlantic passage also serves to prefigure the material difficulties that those emigrants who survive the journey will encounter. In Father Hugh Quigley's *The Cross and the Shamrock* (1853), for example, it is the great number of victims to "ship fever and cholera"—diseases that break out owing to "the crowd on board, the lack of proper arrangements, and room, or ventilation, as well as on account of the cruelty of the inhuman captain"—that point forward to the deprivations of those migrants who reach the post of destination. When Arthur O'Clery is attacked by the epidemic and dies after "attending on, and ministering to, the wants of the poor steerage passengers," his widow and children are forced to rely on themselves. However, once they arrive in New York City, the bereaved family is robbed of "the thousand pounds in gold and Bank of England notes" by a fellow traveler and consequently "reduced from competency to poverty . . . by the villainy of a pretended friend and associate."[49] The personal loss that the family suffers on board of the ship thus portends the material destitution that awaits Mrs. O'Clery and her infants as newcomers in America.

In Charles Cannon's novel *Bickerton*, death as a result of shipboard conditions also functions as a sign of future loss on an emotional, material, as well as ethnic level. Manus's spouse cannot endure the crowded, ill-ventilated atmosphere belowdecks and is on death's doorstep when the ship dumps its passengers on a remote beach to avoid custom duties and without offering them assistance in collecting their luggage or finding their way to the city. While Mrs. O'Hanlon does not perish during the crossing, she dies almost immediately upon being carried ashore. Mrs. O'Hanlon's utter forlornness when she breathes her last—a situation that is slightly relieved by the arrival of an Irish American priest who can administer the last rites—parallels the misery of all the emigrants who have been abandoned on the deserted beach, "a long low stretch of sand, backed by a country which, in that light, looked anything but invitingly to the poor stranger." While these fellow passengers had thought to escape death by leaving their Famine-stricken country, many perish during or immediately after the harrowing crossing: those passengers "who had not the means of paying for even the poorest conveyance, and, either by age or illness, were unable to walk, sat themselves down in sullen despair, to await the death from which they had fled in their own land, to meet it in a more appalling form where they had not even the consolation of friendly sympathy for support." This early disillusionment implies an emotional breakdown for both the desolate emigrants and Manus, whose "hopeful spirit . . . seemed for a moment to die within him" and whose frustrated expectations are a premonition of his solitary literal death later on.[50]

Moreover, the distress that the Irish face upon their landing in the New World presages the prospects of a painful, destitute existence in America. Upon arriving in New York, Manus is robbed of his best suit and conned out of his savings, and when he collapses with fatigue and hunger, hardly any American citizens are willing to offer a helping hand. Instead, they are blinded by prejudice against the Irish newcomers.[51] Believing him to be the conventional Irish drunkard "who's taken too much of the 'cratur,'" passersby leave the dying Manus out in the cold on the pavement. Manus's fate illustrates the trials of destitution and discrimination that the Irish endured in America, and the trials that his orphaned daughter, Aileen, has to brave in her childhood and adolescence reveal the opposition that the Irish meet in their adherence to their own ethnic and religious identity. Aileen is adopted by wealthy Protestant Americans—the "Fire-and-Brimstone" Reverend Scroggs and his wife—who persistently try to "stifle the small germ" of Aileen's only "inheritance," her Catholic birth. The fact that the couple rebaptize Aileen Deborah and thereby endeavor to disconnect her from her own Irish background implies that emigration to the United States imperils the Irish's ethnic identities, as the predominant Protestant environment in which they settle seeks to eradicate their Catholic roots. This idea is underscored by the violence that is used by a group of "Thugs" toward the Irish Catholic community of Bickerton. Inspired by their fierce dislike of Irish Catholics, this mob of nativists sets fire to the houses in this "little Dublin," which subsequently becomes "a blazing ruin," and next direct their fury to the "beautiful church of St. Mary," where they destroy "many of the exquisitely stained windows of the sacred edifice" and mutilate "the fine statues of the Apostles Peter and Paul."[52] Reminiscent of several nativist riots that took place in the 1840s and 1850s, such as the Louisville attacks on Irish Catholics in August 1855,[53] *Bickerton* reveals that the atrocities that the emigrants suffer on their transatlantic voyage foreshadow the religious persecution that they will encounter in their host country.[54]

In a similar vein, the dire shipboard conditions in *The Cross and the Shamrock*, which result in massive deaths among the passengers, appear premonitory signs of an American religious climate that seeks to root out the Catholic creed of their newcomers, for in the so-called land of liberty, "many and violent . . . were the arguments that passed between Catholic servants and their heretical masters and mistresses, on one hand to ignore, and on the other to assert, the right to worship according to one's conscience," and "Catholic servants are not only denied the right to attend their duties in many families, but actually forced to hear the disgusting ranting or ludicrous prayer of any impostor who may take on himself the office of preacher." Furthermore, after their father's death on the voyage and their mother's subsequent collapse with penury and fever, the orphaned O'Clery children are adopted by Protestant families. Here they constantly have to withstand the pressure of bartering their faith. They are forced to attend Sunday school and told "to eat meat" on Fridays: "Accordingly, a 'big dinner' was prepared, a turkey cooked, and Friday fixed upon—the appetite being chosen, after a very ancient pattern in paradise, as the channel through which to 'open the eyes' of these blind young Papists!" Ironically, the memories of the Great Famine are part of the rhetoric that is used to make Paul and his siblings break their religious decrees: the stern minister urges Paul "to eat meat, and use the good things of our glorious country, or you will fail and die."[55]

The Narrative Symbolism of Storms

In Tierney's novel, it is not only the many casualties on board, the fact that "half the passengers were absolutely starving," and the many fights between a remorseless crew and furious passengers that make the three travelers' passage to America arduous. The large ship becomes the plaything of the "wild, tumultuous, storm-tossed sea" and gets so severely damaged that it sinks, leaving many passengers shipwrecked or drowned. In works of fiction that reflect upon the Great Famine, tempests are a central motif in the narrative templates concerning the emigrants' crossing to their receiving countries. These storms that buffet the coffin ship and constitute an ordeal to the Irish emigrants on board also symbolize the ways in which the Irish emigrants will be tossed about on waves of adversity and insecurity and will feel unsettled in their new existence. In Margaret Percival's *The Irish Dove* (1849), for instance, Pat Reilly's account of his voyage to England, where he hopes to have better means of sustenance, emphasizes the "storm blowing all the time, and the rain pouring on us the entire night" through which the ship almost capsizes and the travelers get seasick. The storm that Pat has to face upon his exodus from his motherland prefigures the hostile reception that he and his fellow Irish immigrants have to bear in England. As the disillusioned Pat wonders, "But why do they abuse us as they do, and make us dislike them whether we will or no? Wouldn't it be more Christian-like in them to receive us as if we were fellow-creatures, than spurn us like dogs, sending us back full of hatred to them, often for nothing at all but their looks and words?"[56] The fact that Pat and many of his compatriots are denied the opportunities to better themselves by employment shows that England does not offer the Irish a climate in which they can settle. Rather, the sister kingdom provides an unsteady existence to the Irish, just as the maddened winds and waves during their passage swirl around the passengers.

Other early fictional Famine narratives also feature a stormy shipboard crossing to prefigure the tempestuous livelihood that awaits the Irish emigrants on foreign shores. In the earlier-mentioned story "The Emigrant Ship," the storms that arise during the passage "bent the ship about, while drenching rains swept the deck, which only experienced seamen could tread in safety" and "struck terror into the hearts of the ignorant and superstitious." Thus, these tempests point forward to the miseries that the travelers encounter after landing. Widowed Bessy and her young children end up in a squalid, overcrowded tenement house in New York. Hardly able to find any employment, Bessy earns too little to keep "want from the door, and to pay the rent of her little room." When "the long, long Winter came on fast," the poor family faces cold and hunger, and Bessy ultimately perishes with want and disease. In Anna Dorsey's *Nora Brady's Vow*, "the stress of rough weather" that tosses the ship and strains the cordage and leaves the eponymous emigrant heroine "deadly sick and terrified beyond measure" foreshadows the difficulties that Nora meets in looking for her former employer, John Halloran, in the New World. The "restless and fathomless sea" that stirs the emigrant vessel bears an analogy to the wide American continent on which Nora initially feels lost, just as the eventual outbreak of sunshine "spread[ing] a mantle of sparkling gold far and wide over the waves" foretells an eventual hopeful future for the servant girl who succeeds in her mission of reuniting with her boss and mistress and gets married to a successful shopkeeper.[57]

Many Irish American novels portray America and Canada as societies where Irish Catholics have to bear opposition and even proselytism. For instance, Mary Anne Sadlier's *Elinor Preston* (1861) shows that even in Montreal—a city dominated by an impressive Catholic cathedral—the female protagonist finds herself frequently exposed to evangelicals of the "French Canadian Missionary Society" who ostensibly denounce the Roman Church and aim to convert "the Catholic people of Lower Canada," especially "Irish papists."[58] In some works of Famine fiction that are ideologically infused with North American radical and conservative Catholicism, the rough tempest at sea portends the temptations that the Irish emigrants will have to withstand, such as the threats of conversion or neglect of their Catholic creed.[59]

In Peter McCorry's *The Lost Rosary* (1870), for instance, Alley and Mary's transatlantic journey is accompanied by a "storm" that "raged with ruthless fury" and through which the "mainsail was rent in a thousand pieces, and the mast that gallantly bore it was snapped in twain, as if a cannon ball had struck it." The threat of shipwreck, which is eventually averted, closely resembles the tempests of opposition that the Catholic immigrants will encounter in their host country. The narrator explicitly makes a comparison between the weather-beaten ship and the severe tests to their faith that the Catholic Irish will have to overcome, stating that the fateful passage of the St. Patrick is "like to the voyage of life" and invoking Irish immigrant girls to "remember" their "night of storms upon the sea," as "temptations will surround you; sin will encompass you; aye, as the dark waters surround you now." It is by clinging to their Catholic faith as an "anchor . . . like the tempest-tossed mariner who feels his heart grow stout and warm within him, as he gazes on the anchor of his ship" that these young emigrant women can save their souls. A similar analogy is made between a metaphorical tempestuous passage and the immigrants' difficulty of remaining steadfast to their faith in the New World in Mary Anne Sadlier's novel *New Lights; or, Life in Galway* (1853). Cormac and Daniel O'Daly write a letter home from America in which they contrast their current condition, in which they feel "tossed about on the restless waters of this great commercial world," with the "old ark of peace at home."[60] The New World with all its materialist temptations seems a place of turmoil where immigrants may lose their ties with their native creed, as opposed to the homeland, which epitomizes an enduring covenant between the Catholic congregation and God.

Mary Anne Sadlier's eponymous heroine Bessy Conway also has to endure seasickness and storm on her way to America. After they have left Liverpool, Bessy's employer, Mrs. Walters, the ship captain's wife, offers to her a remedy "that would settle your stomach, but if you take my advice you will let nature take its course, for a little suffering now may save you a great deal more hereafter in a strange climate." Bessy's seasickness appears to portend a test of Bessy's Catholic faith in America. Throughout the heavy storm that breaks the ship's mast, Bessy must rely on her faith in the protection of the Virgin Mary, by kneeling down and praying to her. As Lawrence McCaffrey states, "Catholic worship was a bridge of familiarity between rural Ireland and urban America, providing psychological as well as spiritual comfort in a religious taste of home." Bessy's steadfast belief that "God never deserts them that don't desert Him" and her reliance on the intercession of the Virgin Mary prepare her for the trials in America where several employers seek to convert the servant girl to Protestantism. For example, Bessy openly has to contradict her mistress, Mrs. Hibbard, when she and the rest of the domestic staff are entreated to join in Protestant prayer: "Catholics are forbidden to join in prayer, ma'am, with any except people of their own persuasion." In this climate that is hostile to the native faith of the Irish immigrants, many of Bessy's fellow servants, such as Bridget, who is not willing to get up earlier to attend service, indeed start to neglect going to Mass, and many are reduced to a "half-heathen state" during their residence in New York. Thereby, they not only drift away from the fold, but also lose their ties to an essentially Irish identity that the novel explicitly identifies with Catholicism: Bessy's eventual Catholic employer, Mrs. Delaney, indignantly judges the Irish immigrant women who discard their religious duties to be "a disgrace to their country," and in her preface Sadlier addresses the "simple-hearted peasant girls of Ireland" who are to "retain their home-virtues and follow the teachings of religion" in the corrupting Protestant American cities, just like heroine Bessy Conway.[61]

In Sadlier's novel the tempest at sea therefore points not only forward to the future test to her faith that Bessy will have to undergo, but also to the temptations to her virtue that she will have to resist. In fact, in many narratives about the Great Hunger, the emigration of a young Irish woman leads to her moral and spiritual downfall. This recurring narrative template of the fallen woman features in *Sally Cavanagh* in the narrative about Rose Mulvaney's loss of faith and virtue, as we have previously seen. In Miss Mason's *Kate Gearey* (1853), the immigrant heroine comes under the spell of a wicked young man who makes her neglect "to approach the Sacraments" during Lent and Easter, and who also involves her in fencing stolen goods and bigamy. Moreover, Richard Baptist O'Brien's *Ailey Moore* suggests that Irish maidens who flee Famine-stricken Ireland and move to London to look for employment often end up in prostitution, owing to extreme poverty or because they are unwittingly "drugged," while they also "stay away from mass" and "give up their prayers."[62]

Bessy Conway warns its female immigrant readers against cultural intermarriage that may lead to young women's loss of their Catholic, hence Irish, identity: they who fall in "with Protestants and Jews, and everything that way . . . in the course of a little time forget themselves altogether; at least they forget that they have a soul to be saved, or a God to judge them."[63] Many of the Irish immigrant girls whom Bessy meets in New York are enticed by the dancing halls where they become acquainted with immoral young men who lead them astray both sexually and religiously, and Bessy herself also has to withstand such an unsavory alliance in the form of Henry Herbert. Herbert, who repeatedly seeks contact with Bessy during the tempestuous voyage, and who frequently accosts her in New York, is not only the son of an English landlord but also a Protestant, and therefore an unsuitable partner for Bessy, whom he would probably use for bad ends. This point is made clear by Denis Conway's letter, which, after rumors about Bessy and young Herbert, admonishes his daughter to stay away from the landlord's son, who would merely seek to ruin her: "But you know well enough, Bessy, that it isn't for a good end he'd be talkin' to you, and you know the dirty drop that's in him." Trusting that the "Holy Mother of God can protect you in America as well as at home, and will never let you open your ears or your heart to a scape-grace like young Herbert," Denis Conway expresses his conviction that the Catholic faith will offer protection to the simultaneous perils of sexual and religious temptation.[64]

As in *Bessy Conway*, in *The Lost Rosary* the stormy crossing that Alley and Mary have to undergo points forward to both the threats of religious and the sexual degeneration that the New World harbors. The passage that describes the anxiety of the travelers on the storm-wrecked ship foretells the metaphorical "storms and trials" that the brave immigrant girls will meet: the young unspoiled Irish women will be surrounded by "temptations . . . sin . . . as the dark waters surround you now," because their "virgin modesty will be shocked, and thy ears assailed betimes with language unknown to thee before." As the digression by the narrator intimates, these daughters of Erin will be able to withstand the vice that will "cunningly allure you, with its deformities hidden beneath the garb of wealth," in the same way that they survived the tempest at sea. As long as they will remember their native creed, symbolized by "the Old Chapel and its humble Cross" at home, they will be safe from such perils. Indeed, upon their arrival in New York City, Alley and Mary narrowly escape being entrapped in a house of ill repute that seeks to "ensnare young men, as well as young women, into every vice . . . before they're very long on American soil," thanks to their inner moral compass.[65] Mary subsequently has to ward off the obnoxious attentions of her Scottish employer. By remaining devoted to the emblem of their faith, the rosary, the two young women ultimately manage to retain their religious and moral purity.

The Coffin Ship as a Space of Ethnic Solidification

In his speech, William Halley emphasized that the Irish immigrants' "love of country . . . love of the soil from which we spring is strong and enduring; but love of kind, love of blood and brotherhood, is, if possible, more potent and imperishable." It is this love of kind that, according to Halley, inspires the Irish expatriates in North America to reach out to fellow citizens with the same ethnic roots and to chase back inquiry to "history and tradition."[66] Halley's remarks illustrate current insights about diaspora cultures that are believed to "*mobilize a collective identity*, not only a place of settlement or only in respect of an imagined, putative, or real homeland, but also *in solidarity with co-ethnic members in other countries*,"[67] thereby forming both physical and cultural enclaves[68] that are rooted in a shared sense of distinctiveness, a common history, and the belief in a common fate. The often geographical and cultural segregation of the Famine generation in America is mirrored by the symbolic function of the coffin ships in early Famine fiction: as we saw in the previous section, the coffin ships in these works of Famine fiction constitute symbolic spaces in which Irish immigrants are prepared to respond to the trials of the New World and the pending pressures of assimilation, learning that they have to remain loyal to their religious origins. The Famine narratives that incorporate an emigration plot, however, also reveal that the emigrant vessels function as microcosmic spaces that underscore the urgency to develop Irish transatlantic cultural identities that are bound together by shared values.[69] Providing a transitory space that enables emigrants to prepare themselves for life on the other side of the Atlantic, these ships become what Peter McCorry's *The Lost Rosary* describes as "a miniature of the world's life" and what the narrator in David Power Clington's *Frank O'Donnell* calls "Ireland in miniature"—a place to cement their Irish identity before they pass into diaspora.[70] By positioning themselves against other ethnic groups, the Irish on board of the emigrant vessels do not only (re)negotiate Irishness, but are also in the process of forming transatlantic ethnic identities as the ship progresses.

This development of a transatlantic, socially cohesive Irish identity during the crossing that helps the immigrant characters to attain success in the New World figures in Anna Dorsey's novel. During the tumultuous passage, her heroine Nora Brady is prepared for her new existence in America during which she will need to maintain close connections with compatriots and specific Irish American organizations in order to achieve happiness. When many of her fellow travelers fall ill during the voyage to America, Nora administers care to them, cleansing "the sleeping-places of the sick and preparing food for those who were unable to prepare it for themselves." This solidarity with her compatriots appears to anticipate Nora's reliance upon coethnic community networks in the New World. It is through her close ties with other Irish men and women in diaspora, such as Mrs. McGinnis, that she hears of a "respectable situation" as a domestic, and it is with the help of employees at the Boston-based newspaper the *Pilot* that Nora eventually manages to track down John Halloran.[71]

In *Bessy Conway*, there is only "a small sprinkling of Irish" on board of *The Garrick*. Nevertheless, they remain mostly together as a group, mainly because some passengers already know each other from home. Ned Finigan, for instance, is Bessy's cousin. Moreover, the Irish take care of each other: Ned Finigan and hunchback Paul Brannigan protect Bessy from the advances of Henry Herbert, for example. The religious ties that bind these characters are strengthened by the presence of a Catholic priest on board. "Father B," who consoles Dolly Sheehan when she learns during the voyage that her son has died and acts as intermediary to procure the money the latter left for his mother, is devoted to caring for his flock. However, once the characters have settled in America, their cohesion as a group diminishes: "Of the hundreds who had crossed the great sea within her 'wooden walls' very few remained together. Scattered abroad over the face of the country they were lost sight of amid the surging waves of the population." As Christopher Cusack and I have argued previously, "Once landed in the New World, community becomes diaspora, making it increasingly difficult for the characters to sustain their ties with their compatriots." Many of them stray away from the fold. Ned, who establishes a pub in spite of Paul's warning that "it's a bad way of makin' a living an' the money that's made at it never wears well or does much good to them that has it," comes to neglect his religious duties, and dies because of severe drinking.[72]

By contrast, the characters who remain engaged in the ethnic nexus that was forged on board, such as Bessy and Paul, thrive overseas. Bessy manages to uphold her Catholic morality and to secure a good income as a domestic in a Catholic household, partially thanks to the network of acquaintances she had made on board: "She had an excellent place secured with another friend of Mrs. Walters, a Catholic lady whose family was as small as her means were large." Paul Branigan, who also stays in close contact with his former fellow passengers and moreover forms a little group for Irish immigrants' children to train them in Catholic doctrine, also finds bliss in his new country of residence. He sets up a "nice little business, and is so taken up with his Sunday School class in St. James' Church, and various other works of charity in which he is engaged, that he is content to forego the pleasure of seeing the Old Land again."[73] By depicting Irish immigrants whose success in America is closely tied up with loyalty to their roots and to the microcosmic ethnic communities that were constructed on board, the novel underscores the importance of establishing distinct little Irelands within the New World.

In some early Famine narratives, this strong emphasis on racial communality that the emigrant vessels embody is accompanied by a sense of ethnic segregation. In ways similar to *Bessy Conway* and *Nora Brady's Vow*, Reginald Tierney's *The Struggles of Dick Massey* stresses the importance of close interethnic ties, thereby illustrating the tendency of Irish Americans to stick to the indigenous ethnic group in diaspora as a way to cement the ties with the homeland. The novel presents an idyllic picture of a closely knit Irish community in New York, where "you'd a'most imagine you wor in Stonybathther, by raason ov all the people you'd hear talkin' wid the *brogue*."[74] In the valley of Wabash, Michael Martin advises Tom to marry the Irish Norah rather than an immigrant of a different ethnic background. In this respect, the novel reflects the separatism of the Famine immigrant communities who established Catholic institutions, social services, and parochial schools to support the construction of an exclusively Irish American Catholic community in the face of virulent opposition and the pressure for assimilation.[75]

This resistance to ethnic mixing is epitomized by the coffin ship in that Tom here cultivates a sense of ethnic consciousness. Tom encounters a number of black people on deck, including "a fair sprinkling of Negresses." As the narrator states, though, Tom is "evidently . . . not much taken with either their colour, face, or figure." His decision not to marry a "Negresse" can be interpreted as a way to dissociate the Irish immigrants from the African American population and underline their whiteness. Irish immigrants of the Famine generation were often perceived as nonwhite and even lower in ranking than African Americans, because of their willingness to perform the dirtiest jobs for the lowest payment. As Noel Ignatiev argues, the Irish finally became accepted as white by displaying "the highest degree of race consciousness," which is what Tom does in this passage by his act of racial differentiation.[76]

Similarly, the eponymous heroine of *Nora Brady's Vow* dissociates herself from her black fellow servant in Mrs. Sydney's household, Phillis, who has been rescued from bondage in the South. While she is willing to help the "coarse and ignorant black woman" who is tickled in her vanity by the abolitionist ideal of racial equality, Nora tells the girl "not to interfere with her," making Phillis aware of "how widely they differed." The sense of ethnic bonding that Nora developed on board the emigrant ship thus appears to manifest itself in ethnic separatism in the New World, in particular from a race with which the Irish were often identified.[77]

Additionally, the function of coffin ships as spaces of ethnic consolidation becomes clear from the fact that they are literally transitory spaces that transport Irishness to the New World. In David Power Clington's *Frank O'Donnell*, an elderly poor passenger carries a "small box of earth with a few shamrocks in it, taken from behind the old house at home" on board.[78] By literally bringing a bit of Ireland, the man is trying to transport his identity on his transatlantic voyage, and the coffin ship plays a crucial role in the transference of Irishness to American soil.

Remigration: Revisiting the Great Famine

Desolation: A Story of the Irish Famine (1869) presents a forlorn Irish immigrant who has settled in Missouri and laments "earth's barriers and ocean's bilious foam" that have arisen between him and "all that once was home."[79] Although this poem voices a strong desire to return to the "happy home of other days,"[80] very few emigrants of the Famine generation were in the position to remigrate to their native country.[81] In contrast with these historical realities, homecoming emigrants are recurrent figures in Irish, Irish American, and Irish Canadian works of fiction that recall the Great Hunger and that were written between 1860 and 1870.[82] As the following section will demonstrate, these returning natives feature in three specific narrative templates that can be analyzed as responses to the social upheaval caused by the Famine and as expressions of the nostalgia for a lost homeland that informed the transatlantic diaspora. The fact that similar narrative schemata are used in fiction written on both sides of the Atlantic validates the common assumption that diasporic societies share a cultural legacy with the country of origin and can therefore be viewed as its extended communities.[83]

While Irish and Irish North American works of Famine fiction share a specific set of transcultural narrative templates that feature the physical return of the emigrant to Ireland, some works of transatlantic fiction written after the mid-1860s also incorporate a plotline that interprets return in a symbolic sense. Thus responding to the changing status of Irish immigrants in the New World, these texts also suggest the emergence of a specific diasporic memory of the Famine that evolves in distinct ways. The idea that the Famine caused social and economic rupture is notably absent from narrative templates about remigration in Irish and Irish North American works of Famine fiction that were written in the immediate aftermath of the sorrowful events, until the mid-1860s. While these texts represent the Ireland from which their emigrant characters depart as a nation devastated by blight and starvation, the expatriates' return to their native soil forms the prelude to the restoration of an idyllic homeland unscathed by the Famine atrocities of the past.

This template according to which the remigrant's arrival represents an overture to a recovered Irish home can, for instance, be found in *The Struggles of Dick Massey*. The Famine-stricken country from which Tom Nolan and the Conroys set forth has turned into an uninhabitable nation. The infertile, blighted fields and the excessive rents demanded by "tyrant landlord or sneaking rent-noticers, or prying agents or blustering tithe men" have led to the excessive outpour of population. Despite the fact that the American West offers ample opportunities for prosperity, Tom and Norah remain emotionally attached to the old land. They feel that the "fair and goodly land" in "the fertile valley of the Wabash" is not "half so goodly or so fair as Ireland."[84]

While Tom and Norah reminisce about their country of birth, their former harrowing experiences of plague and oppression in Ireland are committed to oblivion. The picture sketched of Ireland upon the couple's remigration similarly pushes the agonizing realities of destitution to the background, as we saw in chapter 4. When Tom and Norah return, Ireland still suffers from wide-scale deprivation, but the rural community in which they resettle holds out the promise of a recovery of rural bliss for the nation at large. This template, which traces what Caroline Brettell would call a "rite of passage," involving "departure, the liminal status of being away, and the reintegration of return," describes the Irish emigrant's flight from the calamitous events at home and, after trials in the New World, his or her resettlement in a remedied, Edenic region of origin.[85] As a common narrative pattern that also recurs in other Irish and Irish North American Famine novels, this template can be regarded as a transnational narrative scheme. In most of these narratives, however, the country has not yet recovered from the joint afflictions of pestilence and hunger when these remigrating characters disembark. Rather, the pastoral "motif of transformation,"[86] which in these narratives concerns the revitalization of the Irish land and its people, is embedded within the tale of diaspora: it is the wealth acquired by these Irish emigrants in North America that helps reestablish the motherland as a paradisical home. In Mary Anne Sadlier's *Bessy Conway* (1862), as we saw, Bessy's flourishing fortunes help her to secure the family's residence in their cottage, and she can put a bountiful dinner on the table. This sense of retrieved domestic bliss is emphasized by the fact that after many days of destitution, the house is warmed once more by "a fire blazing on the well-swept hearth that suggested the idea of a grand pyramidal turfstack somewhere in the immediate vicinity."[87]

The nineteenth-century Irish domestic hearth was viewed as "the focal point around which household activities revolved," such as "the daily collection and arrangement of the bedding" and the cooking of oatcakes,[88] thereby symbolizing not only "family continuity and . . . hospitality towards the stranger,"[89] but also "a sense of warm security."[90] Illustrations from the 1840s, such as Caroline Elizabeth Hamilton's engraving *Irish Fireside* (ca. 1840), and *Interior of a Peasant's Cottage* and *Irish Cabin*, published on February 7 and August 22, 1846, respectively, in the *Pictorial Times*, manifest the centrality of the cabin fireplace as a space of relative comfort amid wretched living conditions. Moreover, in depictions of the high rates of mortality caused by famine and its related fevers, writers would use the image of the extinguished or deserted fireplace as an emblem of social disintegration. For example, in R. A. Shafto Adair's *The Winter of 1846–7 in Antrim* (1847), the mass starvation among the rural population is cast in terms of once "happy hearths whose lights are quenched." In Trollope's *Castle Richmond* (1860), there is "no fire on the hearth" in the house of the famishing family that Herbert visits, and this lack is represented as a sign of the extreme depravities of Ireland: "though a fire on the hearth is the easiest of all luxuries for an Irishman to acquire, and the last which he is willing to lose." The previously discussed novella *The Widow O'Leary* similarly associates the Great Famine with the disappearance of the lit fireplace. The narrator, who returns from England to Ireland during the height of the crisis, looks "in vain" for the "brightly blazing fire" that had illuminated his friends' cottage in former days.[91] In this light, the stress that the passage from *Bessy Conway* lays on the cleaned and blazing hearth suggests the recuperation of a domestic happiness marked by family reunification and prosperity.

Similarly, *Frank O'Donnell* presents the main protagonist's success in recovering an Edenic home in motherland Erin, as a result of the wealth he has acquired in the American West. Frank acquires considerable wealth by toiling "in the golden fields of California." Although it would enable him to "buy a nice property" in America, Frank is determined to return to the old land: not only because of his "talisman"—his beloved Alice Maher—but also because "love of country has become strong" with him during his residence in the West. While Frank's homesick musings appear to have expelled any painful recollections of starvation and ejection—rather, they idyllically summon up a pastoral childhood dwelling where he and his sister Kate were wont to pull "wild flowers" and listen to "the rippling of the stream and the merry notes of the birds"—his arrival back in Ireland is marked by a retrieval of the longed-for homestead. While Frank had initially thought that his Famine-induced pauperism had forever shattered his prospects of setting up a family residence "hallowed" by a "fireside" and Alice's "loving, greeting smiles," he can realize this nuptial haven through the fact that in America, everything he "touched seemed to turn into gold." Returning to Ireland as a rich man, Frank has sufficient means to acquire Alice's hand, and he can buy her the cottage that she "loves so dearly" and is "richly furnished with Turkey carpets, rich papers, costly furniture, and splendid drawings and paintings."[92] Despite the fact that Frank and Alice's home is very near the graves of Frank's parents, the scars of the Famine past do not impede a happy resettlement in his native community.

These transcultural templates of return can be perceived as subversions of the chronotope of progress characteristic of narratives of migration. Emigration implicates a spatial displacement from the homeland,[93] but the movement to territories outside the motherland at the same time "implies temporal change."[94] While the emigrants' transfer to their new countries is marked by a literal passage of time, their settlement in diaspora also signifies the entrance of a new temporal phase in their lives. While in most narratives of relocation one may discern a linear development on both levels of time and space—as the journey to a new country marks progress in time—in the above-explored works of Famine fiction, the characters' return involves a reversed pattern. The regression in space from host to native settings additionally involves a symbolic backward movement in time, as the Ireland in which they land resembles a pre-Famine society.

Why does this transcultural plotline of remigration to an idyllic Erin occupy such a prominent place in Irish and Irish diaspora Famine fiction until the mid-1860s? The stock character of the remigrant in the novels written in Ireland *Frank O'Donnell* and *The Struggles of Dick Massey* can perhaps be read as a nostalgic response to the radically altered social conditions of a post-Famine society.[95] As Cathy Caruth asserts, early stages of trauma involve "a phase of forgetting or denial," and David Lloyd expounds that frequent responses to trauma and loss consist of "the representation of a restored wholeness and harmony."[96] While the Famine narratives discussed above acknowledge the Famine and its atrocities, the painful memories that they conjure up are displaced and put into relief by the conclusive images of a recuperated dwelling in a revitalized Ireland.

In contrast with Bessy's turbulent journey across the Atlantic to America, which is described in detail, her return voyage is omitted from the narrative and appears to have been relatively quiet. This calm passage is in tune with the happy family life that Bessy can bring back to her native community. This contrast between an eventful voyage to North America and a return journey that often remains untold or passes in quietude is by no means specific to the context of diasporic nostalgia that underlies *Bessy Conway*. In fact, similar plot patterns can be found in Famine fiction written in Ireland. In *Frank O'Donnell*, the eponymous hero's voyage on a crowded yet "noble vessel" is beset by tribulations. When a storm sets in, and "the angry seas hissed, and boiled, and foamed," tossing it about "like a plaything," the emigrants utter fearful "shouts and screams and cries for mercy," and two ill-fated passengers are swept off deck by the wild waves, meeting their untimely end. However, Frank's sudden reappearance on his native soil is not preempted by an account of his voyage back. Likewise, in *The Struggles of Dick Massey*, the crossing by Tom and the Conroys is a journey of suffering for them and their fellow passengers. Although here the ship also ends up in tempestuous weather, and "pitched and plunged a good deal," it causes mild hardship compared to the "floating hell" in the steerage. While the perilous voyage to America emphasizes the horrifying conditions that the Irish flee from, Tom and Norah's apparently uneventful return voyage seems to adumbrate the more blissful circumstances of existence that await them upon their resettlement: "So we'll leave the cousins to find their way across the Atlantic."[97]

The centrality of the return motif in fiction from both sides of the Atlantic may also be clarified by the conditions of colonization to which the Emerald Isle was subject. As Oona Frawley asserts, the development of a postcolonial consciousness runs parallel to "processes by which cultures must imaginatively repossess land and customs." This notion of reappropriation of the land features prominently in the above-discussed narrative endings in both a literal and a metaphorical sense. Sadlier's Bessy Conway and Clington's Frank O'Donnell literally reclaim the land that representatives of the colonial power have taken away from their families. Bessy takes repossession of her parents' land and home when she manages to put an end to her family's eviction by representatives of England's colonial rule: the officials working for the originally English landlord Herbert. Frank likewise manages to retrieve the house and grounds of Glen Cottage where he grew up and from which he and his family had previously been expelled by "magistrate and sub-sheriff" Mr. Ellis and "a large military and police force." These all-powerful men represent a class of landlords, such as Lord Clearall, who "unthinkingly follow the advice and example of political economists" making colonial policies.[98] Therefore, Frank's success in purchasing back his childhood house in the Encumbered Estates' Court, where Clearall's property is sold by auction, implies a retrieval of territory from imperial ownership.

The fact that Frank's acquisition of Glen Cottage helps him to realize his childhood dream of a family home "made cheerful" by a "fireside" and that Bessy has the family hearth swept clean can furthermore be viewed as conscious responses to imperial discourses that associated the Irish peasantry with uncivilized domesticity. For instance, in *The Present State of Ireland and Its Remedy* (1847), Mrs. Maberly pleads for improvements in "the domestic conditions of the Irish peasantry," who, in her view, live in squalor, because the woman who manage the households are "brawling, idle, dirty creatures" requiring English examples of "tidiness . . . cleanliness . . . and industry."[99] Sadlier's and Clington's translation of recuperated homes in terms of neat fireplaces around which social life is centered therefore seems to voice an alternative domestic discourse that challenges imperial bias.

Recently, memory studies have increasingly explored the convergences of time and space in the dynamics of remembrance. Dylan Trigg's research into the aesthetics of decay has engaged with the interactions between time and space in recollection and, moreover, has specifically addressed the issue of return to familiar space after the passage of time, pointing to the intertwined sensations of recognition, disorientation, and alienation that arise in this process. Traveling back to a place of the past may further trigger the memories of bygone days that belong to that setting, but inevitably also summon up feelings of estrangement as the spaces that are revisited have inevitably changed over through time.[100] The returning individual will be confronted with recognizable traces of things that have become lost, marking the site of return out as a spectral place imbued by simultaneous absence and presence. These spectral spaces subsequently evoke an uncanny "sense of fragmentation and isolation" that "disrupts" the returned spectator's "sense of being unified in place."[101]

Trigg's exposition of processes of spatial return sheds an interesting light on the second template of return that will be discussed, one that describes the return of the native Irishman to a country that—subject to the joint visitations of mass starvation, eviction, and depopulation—has changed beyond recognition and therefore can no longer provide a sense of home. This plotline of an emigrant's return that is marked by loss and alienation is particularly inherent to Famine fiction written since the mid-1860s and builds forth upon Gothic traditions in earlier nineteenth-century Irish literature. At first glance, *The Dalys of Dalystown* (1866) appears to repeat the template that stages the Irish remigrant's recuperation of a pastoral home. Son of a landlord, Henry Daly, whose family had been forced to give up their heavily encumbered estate during the 1820s, decides to return to Ireland as soon as news about the Famine reaches him. Not only does he wish to take stock of the conditions of his former tenants, but first and foremost he wants to buy back his childhood mansion and its surrounding land, now that the property is for sale and he has gained sufficient means to become its owner. Despite having established a successful farming career in America, Henry cannot forget Dalystown, even if it is now "desecrated" by misfortune, and upon reacquiring the estate, Henry considerably improves the conditions of the suffering tenantry. The narrative's ending with Henry's fulfilled promise to "wall round my property with the smiling cottages of a tenantry whose interests and mine shall be as one" suggests the creation of a harmonious Edenic estate as of yore, which is underlined by cottier Anthony Kelly's remark that with the arrival of Daly, he finds at least "something unchanged in Ireland." However, Henry's recourse to Dalystown is also fraught with sensations of disorientation and disillusionment. He finds that the once vigorous tenants "that remain . . . in a very wretched condition," and the place itself bears the signs of degradation. While upon seeing his former home "Henry Daly could have shouted, in very joy," a closer inspection of his house reveals "the look of neglect and desolation which the place wore" and fills him "with a sudden, indescribable gloom . . . and his whole soul vibrated with thoughts of the past—of things and beings that could never be restored."[102]

This sense that the past as it was cannot be recuperated and that the scars inflicted by the intermediate era may alienate a person from his former home is also foregrounded in the scene that describes Henry's entrance into the mansion. Finding the rooms empty of furniture, and "cold" and "desolate," Henry can no longer "picture it to myself as it was of old." This sense of defamiliarization is significantly underlined by "the personification of a deserted hearth," as "the ample grate had been torn from its setting and carried away, leaving a dark, cave-like opening, while the top slab of the marble mantle piece, lay broken in two across the hearth." The fragmentation of this emblem of homely comfort accentuates the feelings of despondency and alienation that Henry is oppressed by, leaving him with sadness instead of rapture upon beholding the place for which he had "sighed" many an hour. Henry's disenchantment is underlined by an evocation of the uncanny. Sigmund Freud's concept of the *unheimlich*, which in Nicholas Royle's words signifies an unsettling "commingling of the familiar and unfamiliar," exactly corresponds to Henry Daly's emotions.[103]

The dwelling of his childhood that in some respects resembles the place of his memories is at the same time most unfamiliar. Its rooms are marked by a notable absence of objects and atmospheres that used to belong there but have disappeared under the strains of the Famine era. This haunting presence of a dead past that informs the scene can moreover be interpreted as a reconfiguration of the Gothic tradition of the first part of the century, which, as Claire Connolly has pointed out, is characterized by an exploration of the boundaries between being and nonbeing and "between life and death."[104] While in early-nineteenth-century Irish Gothic novels the *unheimlich* constitutes an integral feature of the Anglo-Irish mansion to convey the Ascendancy's estrangement from the indigenous Irish culture as well as the fear of a waning imperial power,[105] in *The Dalys of Dalystown* the uncanny atmosphere of the big house does not epitomize the anxieties and sorrows of one specific class. Rather, the spectrality by which

Henry's former abode is infused symbolizes how all layers of society are affected by loss during the Famine.

While representing return in terms of disillusionment, O'Brien's novel nevertheless ends with Henry Daly's reintegration into the Dalystown community. By contrast, in Charles Joseph Kickham's *Sally Cavanagh* (1869), one can speak of a plotline picturing the frustrated expectations of a returned native who feels mentally displaced from his former abode, followed by his remigration to transatlantic territories. Connor Shea—who made a good living in America—returns to his Famine-afflicted motherland to find that he no longer has a family home there. As was discussed in previous chapters, his wife, Sally, and his infants have been evicted from their cottage; his five infants have succumbed to starvation; and consequently Sally has become deranged with grief. As in *The Dalys of Dalystown*, the former abode is here associated with the uncanny. This point is revealed by the sentiments of one of Connor's closet friends, Brian Purcell: while Connor's presence in the community instigates feelings of familiarity, they are immediately contrasted with a dramatic sense of infinite loss and change as Connor's family residence will never be restored again to its completeness. The spectral memory of the once happy family circle haunts the present, for in Brian Purcell's view, "it seems but yesterday, when he saw the manly peasant in the midst of his blooming children, while the radiant smile of Sally Cavanagh threw a glow of rosy light upon the picture. He can scarcely believe that the reality is not a hideous dream." Now that the homestead has become disfigured, the returned emigrant cannot resettle in his former community. When Captain Dawson tells Connor that he can have "a lease at his former rent" of land and a house, Connor declines, stating that "I could n't live there now." Even though Connor states that he hopes to "see ould Ireland again," he returns to the "land of liberty" never to set foot again on the soil from which he has become estranged.[106]

Instead, return is reserved to the following generation: in the concluding pages, one can read that Ned, the only son who joined Connor Shea to America, travels back to visit the grave of his mother and siblings and to erect a headstone on it. Ned Shea's mission creates the impression that memorialization of the Famine trauma can be borne only after a sufficient lapse of time, thereby underlining the painful processes of reworking trauma. Moreover, interestingly, Ned Shea comes to Ireland to have a home to fight for after he has gone through a traumatic experience in his adopted country. Ned has fought in America's Civil War and has literally become scarred by the experience, having "lost an arm" in the service of the Northern states and being marked by a cicatrix on his forehead, "which gave him the look of a veteran."[107] While this passage bears witness to Ireland's lasting hold on successive generations of Irish Americans in diaspora—as epitomized by the prominence of organizations such as the Fenian Brotherhood in the 1860s and 1870s and Clan Na Gael in the 1870s and 1880s[108]—it appears as if Ireland can materialize again as a home only when the land of promise has turned into a site of nightmarish trauma of its own.

As trauma theorist Dominick LaCapra maintains, a second step in working through a painful experience is "mourning," which "involves a different inflection of performativity: a relation to the past which involves recognizing its difference from the present."[109] The two novels by O'Brien and Kickham stage New Irelands that bear the marks of the Famine age in the form of lost lives and homes. Pervaded by a sense of absence, these works of fiction not only acknowledge the dramatic upheaval that the Famine era entailed, but also suggest a more advanced stage in the processing of its trauma. Perhaps it is a sign of the later date of their composition and publication compared to the earlier texts that deny these profound reconfigurations of a society shattered by mass starvation and imagine an unspoiled, timeless place of return. In so doing, these novels from the late 1860s exhibit alternative versions of return that demystify the homeland.

Conclusion

The Famine past and migration are inextricably connected in early works of fiction that recollect the years of mass starvation. Narratives of emigration not only address the frightful conditions of the Irish who fled the wide-scale hunger in Ireland, but especially North American texts also represent the transference of Famine memories to new territories, thereby revealing the fluidity of remembrance. Narratives of remigration, moreover, testify to the complex negotiation of the Famine era: by a nostalgic reconfiguration of Ireland that contradictorily lies between restoration and regeneration and between longed-for, bygone eras and desired futures. Works of fiction from a later date display a growing consciousness of new homeland realities that acknowledge the scars of the past and the rupture caused by the Famine at various levels of society. In these texts, the Ireland that remigrants face is in a liminal stage toward future developments.

In Famine narratives, migration is placed in the contexts of present concerns: fiction written in Ireland specifically situates the mass outpour of Irish during the Famine in relation to issues of imperialism. Novels and stories written in both homeland and diaspora, moreover, use the Famine exodus to foreground questions of cultural identity formation in view of more globalized Irish communities. Recurring narrative templates, such as plotlines of downfall and return, and settings, such as the coffin ship, play a crucial role as textual devices that structure the experiences of loss and exile that were often bound up with Famine migration. As early Famine fiction, however, also demonstrates, blindly identifying the Famine exodus with exile fails to do justice to the more variegated and complex responses to the past that these narratives express.

Conclusion

In Father Hugh Quigley's novel *Profit and Loss* (1873), the Irish immigrant Haley, who was involved in the Fenian rising and found a new home near Lake Minnetonka in Minnesota, pens verses about his native country. His poem "An Exile's Farewell to His Native Land" recalls the Famine past, conjuring up images of deserted "villages in ruins left" and the many Famine deaths: "Two million mouths, by famine shut, / Have ceased to cry for bread."[1] Schoolmaster Haley's literary feat illustrates the transferability of Famine memories across boundaries of time and space to which many early works of Famine fiction bear witness. Furthermore, the stock images that appear in Haley's poem are evidence of the existence of a transcultural repertoire of Famine remembrance that the previous chapters of my study have also mapped out in detail.

This transcultural, mnemonic Famine register often becomes visible through recurring tropes that do not only pass on the Famine past, but, moreover, transmit the idea of recollection itself and its fluidity. Thus, the many *lieux de mémoire* that one finds in both Irish and diaspora novels and stories, such as landscapes, monuments made of stone, homes, and ruins, express the rootedness of Famine memories: in Ireland's past and in ethnic identities at home and abroad. Recurring images, such as emigrant ships and specters, by contrast, stand for the transportability of the Famine past, not only across oceans but also across generations. Apart from recurring tropes, Irish and Irish diaspora Famine fiction written between 1846 and 1870 repeatedly adopts the same literary modes, such as the pastoral and the Gothic, thereby suggesting that cultural recollections of an event are also marked by processes of generic remembrance.

The earliest works of Famine fiction not only engage with the same genres, but also adopt similar narrative techniques, such as narrative voice, following patterns and focalization, as the means to give shape to lived or "prosthetic" Famine experiences.[2] These aspects create complex traces of memory that provide access to the Famine past, demonstrating that the uncritical identification of the Great Famine with silence is problematic in many respects and needs to be reassessed. This study can therefore form the impetus for a reconsideration of trauma in relation to the Great Famine as well, as it suggests alternative registers through which a painful past is conveyed and negotiated that move away from the problematic and invalid idea of traumatic silence. Research into the literary memories of other comparable disruptive pasts may broaden the understanding of cultural reconfigurations of a painful recent event that this present study has generated.

In examining the constellations of Famine memory in fiction written in its immediate aftermath, this book has consistently drawn analogies between the rhetoric and tropes of nonfictional Famine writings and those images employed in the works of Famine fiction. This method has demonstrated the ways in which literary texts have reconfigured discourses from nonliterary Famine texts, making clear that fiction is a very adaptable form in which more traditionally novelistic registers alternate with rhetoric conventionally associated with the political pamphlet, the journalistic report, or the economic treatise. As a result, early Famine fiction is often generically unstable, but it is exactly its tendency to switch between registers that enables its exploration of the Famine past on different levels and from various coexisting perspectives. Thus, as we saw, the narrative interventions in, for example, *Frank O'Donnell* that read like a political exposition of arguments in the style of a pamphlet further direct our understanding of representations of land and emigration in the main plot, offering additional layers of Famine recollection. Future research could even more extensively compare the specific features of fiction that serve as vehicles for the expression of Famine memories to those generic aspects employed in other genres, such as drama, poetry, political treatises, journalism, and travel narratives. The analyses in previous chapters have formed the onset to such a comparative approach, and further investigations would be valuable.

In the introduction, one of the main questions was how memories related to the homeland change in and after processes of emigration. As this study has made clear, it is valid to speak of specific diasporic reconfigurations of the Famine in which nostalgia for an imagined homeland that predates the Great Famine is central. Compared to Famine fiction written in Ireland and Britain, North American Famine novels and stories display a stronger consciousness of the fluidity of Famine memories. These texts often employ framework narratives that establish a communication of the Famine past to other generations and transatlantic communities, or they include references to objects and images of Famine memory that are materially or symbolically transplanted to North American shores. Famine fiction written in Ireland and Britain primarily imagines a temporal transmission of memory, often drawing analogies between the Great Famine and other events from colonial history that generate a palimpsestic heterochrony of Irish time. Famine novels and stories written in or for the North American market, on the other hand, tend to imagine the relocation of Famine memories primarily across space—as legacies that can travel with emigrants to their new homelands, for example—but also as painful pasts that can be pushed back to the safe boundaries of homeland territories, thereby creating the possibilities to reimagine utopian New Irelands in the new settlements in the American West.

The intersections between myths of the frontier and cultural memories of the Irish landscape that emerge in North American Famine fiction from the mid-1860s suggest that cultural encounters between emigrant communities and those people in the host countries lead to the development of "multidirectional" memories.[3] This multidirectionality between transatlantic memory regimes and the Famine past is also illustrated by the many (intertextual) references to especially Harriet Beecher Stowe's *Uncle Tom's Cabin* and the analogies that are drawn between Famine suffering and slavery as well as emigration and the Middle Passage. Interestingly, Famine fiction from subsequent decades that has been examined by me and two colleagues within the larger ERC-funded project[4] suggests a continuing line in this multidirectionality of Famine memories, and even an increase of intersections and overlaps with the cultural legacies of other cultural communities—both old and new—in the United States and Canada. For example, W. C. Upton's *Uncle Pat's Cabin* (1882) clearly refers to Stowe's hero, suggesting that the fate of farmer Pat M'Mahon and his class is reminiscent of the harsh realities faced by plantation slaves. M'Mahon loses his wife and child during the Great Famine and himself perishes with hunger during the Famine of 1879, collapsing during the roadwork in which he is involved. The employers at the public work are likened to "slavedrivers" who treat their starving workers as if they were "a gang of stubborn slaves."[5]

Overall, it is difficult to see any definite developments in Famine memory over time within the centrally examined corpus, and that is why in all the chapters some excursions were made into subsequent decades, as a way to trace longer-term temporal developments in Famine memory, such as the move from an emotional disengagement with Famine miseries to an increasing confrontation with loss and grief. Tendencies to confront as well as displace the acutest aspects of the Famine can be witnessed in writings across the period under examination. One thing that stands out, however, is a stronger engagement with nationalist rhetoric in Famine fiction from the 1860s onward, a trend that, as we have seen, could be attributed to the impulse that Fenianism gave to anticolonial sentiments on both sides of the Atlantic.

Furthermore, there is a clear shift in North American Famine fiction from the mid-1860s onward, from an idealization of the homeland from which the trauma of Famine has to be dispelled to a stronger focus on New Irelands that can be established in North America. This transition can be explained by the recurrence of serious landlord-tenant problems in Ireland as well as the Irish's rise in social status in Canada and the United States. The pattern that emerges is that present developments strongly color perceptions of the past and, additionally, that processes of social integration also result in significant reconfigurations of a past that is related to the country of origin. In these processes, memory may become more multidirectional, connecting to other cultural legacies, as well as employed in different sociopolitical and cultural settings.

This trend becomes even more clear when we move beyond the time confines of this study: a Famine novel like Brennan's *Erin Mór* (1892), for example, consciously situates the Famine in the context of present American politics,[6] for in the preface the author admonishes Irish Americans to vote for the Republican Party because of their awareness of the damaging effects that free trade had on Ireland during the Famine: "The writer of the following pages candidly believes that while foreign rule has been the crowning and all-comprehending curse of Ireland, and while landlordism has been among its most potent ills, yet *British free-trade*, identical with the *tariff reform* which the Democratic party now seeks to inflict upon the United States, was the underlying, if not the immediate, cause of the terrible famine of 1846–47."[7]

As this study has also made clear, fictional recollections of the Great Famine are fluid in that the texts that transmitted and relocated these memories were often published and (re)printed on both sides of the Atlantic. The transnational exchange of Famine fiction through various publication channels would take even more of a flight as the periodical markets further expanded toward the end of the nineteenth century. This area of study is one in which future research would be needed: Which texts were republished for which (ethnically specific or ethnically diverse) audiences, when, and why? Can we discern a development in the markets to which fiction that explicitly or implicitly remembered the Famine past was directed? An engagement with these issues will undoubtedly unveil even more resources as well as significantly contribute to our understanding of literary networks, memory, and identity formation.

Notes

Bibliography

Index

Notes

Introduction

1. William Gorman Wills, *The Love That Kills: A Novel*, 2:98.

2. See Ann Rigney, "Portable Monuments: Literature, Cultural Memory, and the Case of Jeanie Deans."

3. Astrid Erll, "Regional Integration and (Trans)cultural Memory," 306.

4. Ann Rigney speaks of "changing patterns of relevance and shifting social frameworks." Rigney, "Divided Pasts: A Premature Memorial and the Dynamics of Collective Remembrance," 93.

5. According to Marianne Hirsch, "Postmemory . . . characterizes the experience of those who grow up dominated by narratives that preceded their birth." Hirsch, *Family Frames: Photography, Narrative and Postmemory*, 22. For a further discussion of her concept, see Marianne Hirsch and Leo Spitzer, "'We Would Not Have Come without You': Generations of Nostalgia." Alison Landsberg defines "prosthetic memory" as a more extensive concept, namely, as "deeply felt memory of a past event" that has not been experienced directly, even by cultural groups belonging to the same generations. Landsberg, *Prosthetic Memory: The Transformation of American Remembrance in the Age of Mass Culture*, 2.

6. Thomas Faist, *The Volume and Dynamics of International Migration and Transnational Social Spaces*, 240.

7. Aleida Assmann and Sebastian Conrad, introduction to *Memory in a Global Age: Discourses, Practices and Trajectories*, 2.

8. Lucy Bond and Jessica Rapson, introduction to *The Transcultural Turn: Interrogating Memory between and beyond Borders*, 19; Astrid Erll, "Travelling Memory," in *Transcultural Memory*; Astrid Erll and Ann Rigney, "Literature and the Production of Cultural Memory: Introduction," 113.

9. Kendall R. Phillips and G. Mitchell Reyes, "Introduction: Surveying Global Memoryscapes"; Daniel Levy and Natan Sznaider, "Memory Unbound: The Holocaust and the Formation of Cosmopolitan Memory."

10. Emily Lawless, *Ireland*, x; Emilie Pine, *The Politics of Irish Memory: Performing Remembrance in Contemporary Irish Culture*, 16.

11. Jan Assmann, "Collective Memory and Cultural Identity," 129; D. J. Corrigan, *On Famine and Fever as Cause and Effect in Ireland*, 5; A. M. Sullivan, *New Ireland: Political Sketches and Personal Reminiscences of Thirty Years of Irish Public Life*, 67; Emily Lawless, *The Story of the Nations: Ireland*, 402.

12. Emily Mark-FitzGerald, "The 'Irish Holocaust': Historical Trauma and the Commemoration of the Famine," 60.

13. For a further description of these monuments and their development as commemorative spaces, see Emily Mark-FitzGerald, *Commemorating the Famine: Memory and the Monument* and "Famine Memory and the Gathering of Stones: Genealogies of Belonging."

14. "Ireland Prepares to Exit Bailout after 'Biggest Crisis since the Famine'—as It Happened," *Guardian*, Dec. 13, 2013.

15. See, for example, several contributions in Cormac Ó Gráda, Richard Paping, and Eric Vanhaute, eds., *When the Potato Failed: Causes and Effects.*

16. See Charles Fanning, *Exiles of Erin: Nineteenth-Century Irish-American Fiction*, 6. See also Kerby Miller, *Emigrants and Exiles: Ireland and the Irish Exodus to North America*, 104.

17. Landsberg, *Prosthetic Memory*, 2.

18. Terry Eagleton, *Heathcliff and the Great Hunger: Studies in Irish Culture*, 13.

19. For early criticism on this strand in Famine studies, see Niall Ó Ciosáin, "Was There 'Silence' about the Famine?"

20. Miss Mason's text was serialized in the *Rambler* from February to October 1852. The novel was later published in its entirety as *Kate Gearey; or, Irish Life in London: A Tale of 1849* (London: Charles Dolman, 1853). Alice Nolan's Famine novel appeared in the widely read nationalist *Irish Citizen*, between February 22 and September 5, 1868.

21. This goal is in line with Peter Gray's claim that we should speak of multiple heterogeneous Famine memories rather than one homogeneous legacy. Gray, "Memory and the Commemoration of the Great Irish Famine," 47.

22. Jeffrey C. Alexander, "Toward a Theory of Cultural Trauma," 1; Kevin Whelan, "Reading the Ruins: The Presence of Absence in the Irish Landscape," 299.

23. Mark-FitzGerald, "Irish Holocaust," 60; Joseph Lennon, "The Starvation of a Man: Terence MacSwiney and Famine Memory," 65; Joseph Valente, "Ethnostalgia: Irish Hunger and Traumatic Memory," 174–78. For similar views, see Cormac Ó Gráda, "Famine, Trauma, and Memory."

24. Margaret Kelleher, *The Feminization of Famine: Expressions of the Inexpressible*, 52; Oona Frawley, "Cruxes in Irish Cultural Memory: The Famine and the Troubles," 10–11.

25. Kevin Whelan states that "Ireland was culturally traumatised in the immediate post-Famine period." Whelan, "Reading the Ruins," 299.

26. Sullivan, *New Ireland*, 58.

27. Charles Fanning, *The Irish Voice in America: 250 Years of Irish American Fiction*, 150.

28. Elizabeth Hely Walshe, *Golden Hills: A Tale of the Irish Famine*, v–vi.

29. Kevin Whelan, "The Cultural Effects of the Famine," 137.

30. John O'Rourke, *The History of the Great Irish Famine of 1847, with Notices of Earlier Irish Famines*, ix. O'Rourke's history represents an early attempt to combine traditional historiographical research of official papers and reports with collected oral testimonies, thereby accommodating multiple memories of the Famine past. For further reading, see Peter Gray, "The Great Famine in Irish and British Historiographies, c. 1860–1914."

31. See Cormac Ó Gráda, *Ireland before and after the Famine: Explorations in Economic History*, 138–44. See also Christine Kinealy, *A Death-Dealing Famine: The Great Hunger in Ireland*, 2; and Ciarán Ó Murchadha, *The Great Famine: Ireland's Agony, 1845–1852*, 179–80.

32. Mary E. Daly, *Social and Economic History of Ireland since 1800*, 89.

33. Luke Gibbons, *Transformations in Irish Culture*, 60.

34. See, for instance, Diarmuid Ó Giolláin, *Locating Irish Folklore: Tradition, Modernity, Identity*, 16.

35. Kevin Whelan speaks of "the associated decline of vernacular religion and popular culture and the erosion of the Irish language" as major consequences of the Famine. Whelan, "Cultural Effects of the Famine," 139.

36. Stuart McLean, *The Event and Its Terrors: Ireland, Famine, Modernity*, 6.

37. W. H. Smith, *A Twelve Months' Residence in Ireland during the Famine and the Public Works, 1846 and 1847*, 41. See also Michael Turner, *After the Famine: Irish Agriculture, 1850–1914*, 14.

38. Turner, *After the Famine*, 273.

39. Sullivan, *New Ireland*, 67; Lawless, *Ireland*, 401–2.

40. Susanna Radstone, *The Sexual Politics of Time: Confession, Nostalgia, Memory*, 115.

41. Patrick Steward and Bryan McGovern, *The Fenians: Irish Rebellion in the North Atlantic World, 1858–1876*, 2–4.

42. John Mitchel, *The Last Conquest of Ireland (Perhaps)*, 219.

43. See David Sim, *A Union Forever: The Irish Question and U.S. Foreign Relations in the Victorian Age*, chap. 4; and Owen McGee, *The IRB: The Irish Republican Brotherhood, from the Land League to Sinn Féin*.

44. Steward and McGovern, *Fenians*, 188–89.

45. *Irish Pictures: Eighty Sketches Taken on the Spot by F. Dadd, M. Fitzgerald, Harry Furiss, Wallis Mackay and Procter and R. C. Woodville, Republished from the "Illustrated London News,"* 1, 21; "The Famine in Ireland."

46. Breda Gray, "Global Modernities and the Gendered Epic of the 'Irish Empire,'" 157.

47. Kevin Kenny observes that the Irish emigration to America "actually began in the seventeenth century and assumed the character of mass movement as early as 1720." Kenny, *The American Irish: A History*, 7.

48. See Roger Swift, *Irish Migrants in Britain, 1815–1914: A Documentary History*, 6–7; and Donald MacRaild, *The Irish Diaspora in Britain, 1750–1939*, 48–54.

49. See Swift, *Irish Migrants in Britain*, 31. For the demographic effects of Famine-related mortality and emigration, see also Christine Kinealy, *This Great Calamity: The Irish Famine, 1845–52*, 251, 298–300; and James S. Donnelly Jr., *The Great Irish Potato Famine*, 169–86.

50. Fanning, *Exiles of Erin*, 6. As Kevin Kenny observes, the United States formed a host nation whose Irish immigrant population rose to 45.6 percent in the 1840s. Kenny, *American Irish*, 105. *Catholic World*, a New York–based periodical, stated in 1869: "The misgovernment of Ireland, which culminated in the terrible famine of 1846–7–8, and the natural affinity of the people of that country for the advantages afforded by free governments, will easily account for the immensity of their numbers who have sought political and social independence in this republic." See "The Philosophy of Immigration."

51. See K. Miller, *Emigrants and Exiles*, 104. See also Kerby Miller, *Ireland and Irish America: Culture, Class, and Transatlantic Migration*, 75.

52. Donald MacKay, *Flight from Famine: The Coming of the Irish to Canada*, 245.

53. Nicholas Flood Davin, *The Irishman in Canada*, 62, 114.

54. See Swift, *Irish Migrants in Britain*, 122. An example of a newspaper report on these brutal sectarian agitations is "The Murphy Riots of Wolverhampton," *Wolverhampton Chronicle*, Feb. 27, 1867. It describes how an Irish mob smashed the windows of a Protestant school, while Orangeists destroyed a Catholic chapel by carrying out "the furniture and pews, pictures, chalices, surplices and vestments" and subsequently attacked a priest's house.

55. Kenny, *American Irish*, 115–16. John Francis Maguire describes how in Manchester, New Hampshire, in the early 1860s, a mob of Know-Nothings destroyed the Irish Catholic parish church: "They had succeeded in destroying its windows of stained glass, when a party of Irish Catholics gallantly encountered and dispersed the mob, and saved from further injury the church which had cost them so much sacrifice." Maguire, *The Irish in America*, 530. Timothy Sarbaugh writes that Lewis Levin, one of the nativist leaders of the American Republican Party, introduced a bill that "would prohibit immigrants from becoming American citizens by extending the

requirement of naturalization from several days to 21 years." Sarbaugh, "The Spirit of Manifest Destiny: The American Government and Famine Ireland, 1845–1849," 50–51. See also a leading article from the *New York Tribune*, "Native Americanism," Nov. 11, 1844, which states that the "chief remaining principle" of the new American Republican Party "is the extension of the term of probation required of immigrants from five to twenty-one years."

56. *American Citizens! We Appeal to You in All Calmness. Is It Not Time to Pause?*

57. See Bruce S. Elliott, *Irish Migrants in the Canadas: A New Approach*, 6.

58. Robert McLaughlin, *Irish Canadian Conflict and the Struggle for Irish Independence, 1912–1925*, 10.

59. See MacKay, *Flight from Famine*, 328, 335. See also Scott W. See, "'An Unprecedented Influx': Nativism and Irish Famine Immigration to Canada."

60. Mark G. McGowan, *The Waning of the Green: Catholics, the Irish, and Identity in Toronto, 1887–1922*, 346.

61. David A. Wilson, *Thomas D'Arcy McGee: The Extreme Moderate, 1857–1868*, 33.

62. In Henry Mayhew's seminal work on the lower classes in London, one can read that the lodging houses populated by Irish often "found ten human beings living together in a small room" in deprived circumstances. Moreover, as Mayhew pointed out, these tenement districts in London often contained segregated "nests of Irish . . . rarely visiting or mingling with the English costers." Mayhew, *London Labour and the London Poor: The London Street-Folk*, 111, 109. Similarly, in Toronto, Irish immigrants were concentrated in an area of squalor labeled "Cabbagetown," and in American cities the Irish inhabited crowded, dirty tenement houses in districts such as New York's Lower East Side. See, for example, Lawrence J. McCaffrey, *The Irish Catholic Diaspora in America*, 72.

63. For instance, in "Comparative Anthropology of England and Wales," 15, D. Mackintosh portrayed the Irishman as a negroid species, arguing that "Gaelic man" was characterized by "retreating chin and forehead, large mouth and thick lips." In the United States, as David Roediger points out, the Irish were considered "low-browed, savage, groveling, bestial, lazy, wild, simian, and sensual," terms almost identical to the ones used to describe blacks. In fact, immigrants from Ireland were ranked lower than Afro-Americans because of their willingness to undertake undesirable work for very low wages. Roediger, *The Wages of Whiteness: Race and the Making of the American Working Class*, 133.

64. William Halley, *Speech Delivered at the Dinner of St. Patrick's Society, Toronto, on the 17th of March, 1860, in Response to the Sentiment of "the Irish Race at Home and Abroad,"* 1.

65. Benedict Anderson, *Imagined Communities: Reflections on the Origin and Spread of Nationalism*, 15. As Nicholas Flood Davin argues, under the influence of the

archbishop of Halifax, "schools, convents and academies rose around." Davin, *The Irishman in Canada*, 638. In the United States, Archbishop John Hughes of New York played a prominent role in the establishment of Catholic schools and institutions, such as St. Vincent's Hospital. See, for instance, Matthew Jacobson, *Special Sorrows: The Diasporic Imagination of Irish, Polish, and Jewish Immigrants in the United States*, 97.

66. Father Hugh Quigley, *The Cross and the Shamrock*, 3.

67. Andreas Huyssen, "Diaspora and Nation: Migration into Other Pasts," 149. This question also seems relevant in light of Robin Cohen's allegation that "diasporas often *mobilize a collective identity*, not only a place of settlement or only in respect of an imagined, putative, or real homeland, but also *in solidarity with co-ethnic members in other countries*." Cohen, *Global Diasporas: An Introduction*, 7.

68. Stuart Hall, "Cultural Identity and Diaspora," 225.

69. Michael Rothberg, *Multidirectional Memory: Remembering the Holocaust in the Age of Decolonization*, 5, 11.

70. In fact, Anna Hanson Dorsey (1815–96), who was born in Georgetown, Washington, DC, wrote several works of fiction that were set in Ireland for the Irish American weekly the *Pilot*, such as *The Old Landlord's Daughter* (1854) and her Famine novel *Nora Brady's Vow* (1857).

71. Michel Foucault, "Of Other Spaces," 24.

72. K. Miller, *Emigrants and Exiles*, 292. See also William A. Spray's illuminating article "Irish Famine Emigrants and the Passage Trade to North America."

73. Irene Gilsenan Nordin and Elin Holmsten, "Introduction: Borders and States of In-betweenness in Irish Literature and Culture," 7.

74. Bjorn Thomassen, *Liminality and the Modern: Living through the In-between*, 1.

75. Hein Viljoen and C. N. van der Merwe, "Introduction: A Poetics of Liminality and Hybridity," 2.

1. Displacing the Famine

1. James Mahoney, "Sketches in the West of Ireland," Feb. 13, 1847.

2. Niamh O'Sullivan, *The Tombs of a Departed Race: Illustrations of Ireland's Great Hunger*, 40; Mahoney, "Sketches in the West of Ireland," Feb. 20, 1847.

3. Astrid Erll, "Re-writing as Re-visioning: Modes of Representing the 'Indian Mutiny' in British Novels, 1857 to 2000," 165.

4. See Cathy Caruth, *Unclaimed Experience: Trauma, Narrative, and History*, 4; and Bessel A. van der Kolk and Onno van de Hart, "The Intrusive Past: The Flexibility of Memory and the Engraving of Trauma," 160.

5. See James V. Wertsch, *Voices of Collective Remembering*, 47.

6. Ireland [pseud.], *A Tale of the Irish Famine in 1846 and 1847: Founded on Fact*, 18, 35, 18.

7. Monika Fludernik, *Towards a "Natural" Narratology*, 27; Rick Altman, *A Theory of Narrative*, 15; Ireland [pseud.], *Tale of the Irish Famine*, 18.

8. Tina O'Toole, *Dictionary of Munster Women Writers*, 97.

9. Mrs. Hoare, preface to *Shamrock Leaves; or, Tales and Sketches from Ireland*, vi; Mrs. Hoare, "The Black Potatoes," 43, 46.

10. Mrs. Hoare, "A Sketch of Famine," 211.

11. For a further discussion of aspects of the short story that play a role in mediating Famine memory, see Marguérite Corporaal, "'Let Any One Try to Picture What It Is': The Dynamics of the Irish Short Story and the Mediation of Famine Trauma, 1850–1865."

12. Cathy Hartley and Susan Leckey, eds., *A Historical Dictionary of British Women*, 315; M. A. Lloyd, *Susanna Meredith: A Record of a Vigorous Life*, 14.

13. Mrs. Meredith, "Ellen Harrington," 56.

14. Dominic LaCapra, *Writing History, Writing Trauma*, 70.

15. Hoare, "The Black Potatoes," 43, 46.

16. William Carleton, "Owen M'Carthy; or, The Landlord and Tenant," 137, 140, 159.

17. See David Lloyd, *Irish Times: Temporalities of Modernity*, 50; and Christopher Morash, *Writing the Irish Famine*, 187.

18. Mahoney, "Sketches in the West of Ireland," Feb. 13, 1822.

19. Little is known about the anonymous male author, apart from the fact that he wrote *The Irish Widow; or, A Picture from Life of Erin and Her Children* (1855) after the success of *Poor Paddy's Cabin; or, Slavery in Ireland* with the "aim to direct his censures against systems, not against persons; and so to expose what is wrong." See An Irishman [pseud.], *Irish Widow*, iv.

20. An Irishman [pseud.], *Poor Paddy's Cabin*, 13.

21. See W. J. Fitzpatrick, *The Life of Charles Lever*, 312.

22. Charles Lever, *The Martins of Cro' Martin*, 2:42.

23. Ibid., 133.

24. Fanning, *Irish Voice in America*, 56.

25. Charles Cannon, *Bickerton; or, The Immigrant's Daughter*, 8, 5.

26. "Most scenes were witnessed by the Authoress herself." See Miss Mason, preface to *Kate Gearey*, n.p.

27. Ibid., 9.

28. Mrs. J. Sadlier, *The Blakes and Flanagans: A Tale Illustrative of Irish Life in the United States*, 17; Canada West [pseud.], *Tim Doolan; or, The Irish Emigrant*, iv.

29. Canada West [pseud.], *Tim Doolan*, 19, 21.

30. Ibid., 127.

31. See Marjorie Howes, *Colonial Crossings: Figures in Irish Literary History*, 36.

32. Mrs. J. Sadlier, *Elinor Preston: or, Scenes at Home and Abroad*, 191, 76.

33. I have argued something similar in "'The Recollection of Sorrow and Misery Past': Memories of the Great Famine in Irish North-American Fiction, 1855–1870." The argument is repeated here by kind permission of Quinnipiac Univ. Press.

34. Hoare, "The Black Potatoes," 49; Ireland [pseud.], *Tale of the Irish Famine*, 34–35.

35. Ireland [pseud.], *Tale of the Irish Famine*, 129.

36. Mrs. J. Sadlier, *Bessy Conway; or, The Irish Girl in America*, 259, 278.

37. See also Corporaal, "Recollection of Sorrow and Misery Past," 86–88.

38. The novel was later republished in the *Dublin Saturday Magazine* in 1865.

39. Huyssen, "Diaspora and Nation," 149.

40. Cormac Ó Gráda, *Ireland before and after the Famine*, 152.

41. William Ernest Montgomery, *The History of Land Tenure in Ireland*, 127.

42. In the preface the author expresses his conviction that "those who have crossed the Atlantic in a ship with Irish emigrants will not, he flatters himself, charge him with being too imaginative in his description of the passage." Canada West [pseud.], *Tim Doolan*, iv.

43. See Nadje al-Ali and Khalid Koser, "Transnationalism, International Migration and Home," 7. This view is in line with Stuart Hall's notion that people living in diasporas form an imagined concept of the land of ethnic origin, because they "share an *idea* of the nation and what it stands for." Hall, "Cultural Identity and Diaspora," 224.

44. Huyssen, "Diaspora and Nation," 149–50. See also Andreas Huyssen, *Twilight Memories: Marking Time in a Culture of Amnesia*, 88.

45. Kerwin Lee Klein, "On the Emergence of Memory in Historical Discourse," 142–43.

46. Radstone, *Sexual Politics of Time*, 115.

47. See Lawrence J. McCaffrey, *Textures of Irish America*, xiii. See also Joseph J. Lee, "Introduction: Interpreting Irish America," 41.

48. See John Crowley, "Constructing Famine Memory: The Role of Monuments," 65.

49. See Donnelly, *Great Irish Potato Famine*, 186.

50. In British Canada and the United States, there was concern about the plight of the Famine-afflicted Irish in their motherland, and many charity initiatives were launched. For example, The *New Brunswick Reporter* of Feb. 12, 1847, discusses the "liberality" that the inhabitants of St. John "displayed on the behalf of the famishing thousands of their species. And we trust that the free spirit of charity will extend itself also to Fredericton." While there was great sympathy with the suffering of the Irish in their blight-stricken country, it did not extend to the individuals who fled those circumstances and looked for shelter in transatlantic societies.

51. George Brown, "Editorial," *Globe*, Feb. 1, 1858.

52. Thomas D'Arcy McGee, "The Social Duties of Irishmen in America."

53. Mary C. Kelly has recently argued that the Famine was openly confronted in the American diaspora only after the integration of the Irish of the Famine generation. As the prominent presence of Famine memory in early North American fiction suggests, this statement requires nuance. It appears to be more valid to believe that Catholic Irish immigrants at times pushed the legacies of the Famine to the background, because, as Kelly asserts, "to be perceived as productive American citizens, they had to overcome negative associations with starvation and disease." Kelly, *Ireland's Great Famine in Irish American History*, xv.

54. Paul Ricoeur, "Narrative Time," 175.

55. See MacKay, *Flight from Famine*, 28.

56. As John O'Rourke points out, this wide-scale failure of crops was the result of "rain falling to a very unusual extent." O'Rourke, *History of the Great Irish Famine*, 30. See also Cormac Ó Gráda, *Black '47 and Beyond: the Great Irish Famine in History, Economy and Memory*, 14.

57. John Mitchel, *The History of Ireland, from the Treaty of Limerick to the Present Time*, 153.

58. See Ó Gráda, *Black '47 and Beyond*, 14.

59. Carleton, "Owen M'Carthy," 135; William Carleton, *The Black Prophet: A Tale Of Irish Famine*, 248.

60. See Fanning, *Irish Voice in America*, 104.

61. Paul Peppergrass [John Boyce], *Shandy M'Guire; or, Tricks upon Travelers, Being a Story of the North of Ireland*, 99.

62. Hardly anything is known about the author Margaret Percival. *The Irish Dove* suggests that the author had previously written *Rosa, the Work-Girl*, a novel published anonymously in 1847. Moreover, a novel published in 1852, *The Fisherman's Daughter*, also proves to be written by Percival, for it is attributed to "the Author of 'Rosa the Work Girl.'"

63. Percival, *The Irish Dove*, 144.

64. Lever, *Martins of Cro' Martin*, 2:131, 1:1.

65. Carleton, "Owen M'Carthy," 138, 136. For example, this idea of infectious decay figures in a report, published in the *Illustrated London News*, Oct. 18, 1845, that describes the potato plants as follows: "Three-fourths of them are so diseased and rotten that pigs decline to eat them."

66. C. A. Rawlins, *The Famine in Ireland: A Poem*, 9.

67. Hugh McNeile, *The Famine a Rod of God: Its Provoking Cause—Its Merciful Design*, 8; John Travers Robinson, *A Sermon Preached in St. Leonard's Chapel, Newton Abbott, Devonshire*, 10; Carleton, *Black Prophet*, 20.

68. Percival, *The Irish Dove*, 195; Peppergrass, *Shandy M'Guire*, 100–101, 221.

69. See Gordon Bigelow, *Fiction, Famine, and the Rise of Economics in Victorian Britain and Ireland*, 119.

70. See Kinealy, *Death-Dealing Famine*, 68.

71. See Charles Trevelyan, *The Irish Crisis*, 6. Trevelyan felt that the potato, a cheap and base crop, should be brought back to "its original use and intention as an adjunct, and not as a principal article of national food." He also voiced the opinion that the people of Ireland should be compelled "to recur to other more nutritious means of aliment, to restore the energy and the vast industrial capabilities of that country" (8–9).

72. Lever, *Martins of Cro' Martin*, 2:357.

73. Ibid., 421; Daniel Levy, "Changing Temporalities and the Internationalization of Memory Cultures," 26–27.

74. Margaret Dixon McDougall, *The Days of a Life*, 178, 418. For a further discussion of McDougall's Famine novel, see Lindsay Janssen, "Famine Traces: Memory, Landscape, History and Identity in Irish and Irish-Diasporic Famine Fiction, 1871–1891."

75. See Angelika Bammer, introduction to *Displacements: Cultural Identities in Question*, xi–xxi.

76. Faist, *Volume and Dynamics*, 46.

77. Esther Peeren, "Through the Lens of the Chronotope: Suggestions for a Spatio-temporal Perspective on Diaspora," 68.

78. Michael Holquist, *Dialogism: Bakhtin and His World*, 110.

79. Sadlier, *Elinor Preston*, 191.

80. Canada West [pseud.], *Tim Doolan*, 186.

81. See C. E. Dailey Jr., "Dillon O'Brien, Novelist," 527.

82. Dillon O'Brien, *The Dalys of Dalystown*, 498, 502.

83. See Kenny, *American Irish*, 124. As Noel Ignatiev points out, the Irish were often perceived as "niggers turned inside out." Ignatiev, *How the Irish Became White*, 141. This point is illustrated by Thomas Nast's cartoon *The Ignorant Vote—Honors Are Easy*, published in *Harper's Weekly*, Dec. 9, 1876, which, accusing the Irish electorate in the North and African American voters in the reconstructed South of corruption, depicts apelike Irish Democrats in the North balancing out the Republican-voting blacks of the South.

84. "At a late hour on Tuesday night the mob made an attack upon the tenement houses, occupied by colored people, in Sullivan and Thompson-streets. For three hours, and up to two o'clock yesterday morning there was what may be truly said to be a 'reign of terror' throughout all that portion of the City. Several buildings were fired, and a large number of colored persons were beaten so badly that they lay insensible in the street for hours after." Interestingly, in his appeal to the city's Irish American population to refrain from violence, Archbishop John Hughes referred to the Great Famine as a way to evoke consciousness of the opportunities Irish immigrants were given in the United States: "When I cast my thoughts back to the land of my forefathers, and when I think of its desolation, when I see the fertile west and south of

Ireland depopulated and cattle browsing on the ruins of the cottages of the noble race that once lived there, I thank God that I was permitted to be among those who had an opportunity of coming to this country, where at least no such wretched tyranny is practiced." See "The Archbishop and His Flock," *New York Times*, July 18, 1863.

85. See Kenny, *American Irish*, 123. See also Joseph G. Bilby, *The Irish Brigade in the Civil War: The 69th New York and Other Irish Regiments of the Army of the Potomac*; and Daniel M. Callaghan, *Thomas Francis Meagher and the Irish Brigade in the Civil War*. "The Irish Soldier in America," an article published in the *Emerald* on July 17, 1869, emphasized how largely the Americans were "indebted to Irishmen for the battles we have won."

86. See Jay P. Dolan, *The Irish Americans: A History*, 87.

87. See Fanning, *Exiles of Erin*, 18. See also Colleen McDannell, *The Christian Home in Victorian America, 1840–1900*, 73.

88. See McCaffrey, *Textures of Irish America*, 31.

89. For further reading on this topic, see, among others, James Byrne, Philip Coleman, and Jason King, eds., *Ireland and the Americas: Culture, Politics and History, a Multidisciplinary Encyclopaedia*, 384, 881; Thomas Hachey and Lawrence McCaffrey, *The Irish Experience since 1800: A Concise History*, 74; and Michel Snay, *Fenians, Freedmen and Southern Whites: Race and Nationality in the Era of Reconstruction*, 52.

90. Wilbert Sikes, "In the Five Points," 224–25.

91. Sadlier, *Blakes and Flanagans*, 216; Mrs. J. Sadlier, *Con O'Regan; or, Emigrant Life in the New World*, 11; Charles Joseph Kickham, *Sally Cavanagh; or, The Untenanted Graves of Tipperary*, 152.

92. A review at the time stated that the author expressed her concern "with . . . vivacity, and . . . deep interest." See "Notices of Books," *Dublin Review* 35 (1853): 522.

93. Mason, *Kate Gearey*, 20.

94. O'Brien, *The Dalys of Dalystown*, 502, 485; Canada West [pseud.], *Tim Doolan*, 322, 350, 322.

95. Stephan Feuchtwang, "Loss: Transmissions, Recognitions, Authorisations," 78; Rothberg, *Multidirectional Memory*, 13.

96. Very little biographical information concerning Julia and Edmund O'Ryan, author siblings, is known. Edmund O'Ryan, a doctor, was born in 1824 or 1825 and died in Youghal in 1903, at the age of seventy-eight. Edmund wrote for the *Tablet*, the *Nation*, and the *Lamp*, among other journals. Julia also contributed her (short) stories and poetry to literary periodicals such as the *Irish Monthly*, New York's *Catholic World*, and *Chamber's Journal*. See S. Brown, *Ireland in Fiction*, 249.

97. Julia O'Ryan and Edmund O'Ryan, *In re Garland: A Tale of a Transition Time*, 98, 100–101, 103.

98. Mrs. Hoare, "Little Mary: A Tale of the Black Year," 92.

99. O'Ryan and O'Ryan, *In re Garland*, 213.

100. *Desolation: A Story of the Irish Famine*, 7.

101. Alexander, "Toward a Theory of Cultural Trauma," 15; Hall, "Cultural Identity and Diaspora," 225.

2. Spectacles of Starvation

1. Mrs. J. Sadlier, *New Lights; or, Life in Galway*, 76–78, 81, 166; Alice Nolan, *The Byrnes of Glengoulah: A True Tale*, 217–18.

2. Fludernik, *Towards a "Natural" Narratology*, 27.

3. *Christmas 1846 and the New Year 1847 in Ireland: Letters by a Lady*, 18; Lord Dufferin and G. F. Boyle, *Narrative of a Journey from Oxford to Skibbereen, in the Year of the Famine*, 10.

4. Lisa Blackman, *Immaterial Bodies: Affect, Embodiment, Mediation*, x; Julia Kristeva, *Powers of Horror: An Essay on Abjection*, 1–2.

5. Anthony Trollope, *Castle Richmond*, 330–35. For further reading on the representation of Famine victims in the novel, see, among others, Margaret Kelleher, "Trollope's *Castle Richmond*: Famine Narrative and Horrid Novel."

6. *The Widow O'Leary: A Story of the Present Famine*, 3, 10, 11–12, 13.

7. Meredith, "Ellen Harrington," 63–64.

8. Other early Famine narratives that take issue with the Catholic Church include the previously discussed *Poor Paddy's Cabin; or, Slavery in Ireland* (1854), which suggests, through the character of the converted young farmer's boy Dannel Downey, that "God cursed the food of *the body* when the priest has, I may say, been cursin' the food of *the soul* from the altar" by forbidding his flock to read the Bible (4). *Paddy's Leisure Hours in the Poor House; or, Priests, Parsons, Potatoes and Poor Rates* (1849) depicts an utterly selfish priest who tells his congregation that the Famine was a "curse upon the country for harbouring Protestants, and reading Protestant Bibles, and having children taught to be read, that they might learn to be undutiful to their clergy." Furthermore, Father Shanavan spends only part of the money that he receives to relieve the poor "in meal, or in soup, or clothes, or blankets," reserving a great part to pay his "*dues* out of it" (10, 13).

9. *Widow O'Leary*, 5, 19.

10. Richard Baptist O'Brien, *Ailey Moore: A Tale of the Times*, 262.

11. Clington was the pen name of David Power Conyngham, a cousin of Charles Joseph Kickham, who participated in the Young Ireland rebellion of 1848. See Anne M. Brady and Brian Cleeve, eds., *A Biographical Dictionary of Irish Writers*, 43.

12. Allen H. Clington, *Frank O'Donnell*, 413, 412, 390, 414.

13. Wills, *Love That Kills*, 2:268–69; W. Neilson Hancock, *On the Causes of Distress at Skull and Skibbereen during the Famine in Ireland*, 7; Wills, *Love That Kills*, 1:vi–vii, 124, 174.

14. Christopher Morash, "Famine/Holocaust: Fragmented Bodies," 145; Robert Bennett Forbes, *The* Jamestown *on Her Errand of Mercy*, cxix; O'Rourke, *History of the Great Irish Famine*, 145.

15. Henry J. Monahan, *O'Ruark; or, The Chronicles of the Balliquin Family*, 268; Wills, *Love That Kills*, 2:268–69.

16. Page Dubois, "Sappho's Body in Pieces," 19; Philip Shaw, *The Sublime*, 121; Ross Abbinnett, *Culture and Identity: Critical Theories*, 50–51; Shaw, *The Sublime*, 3; Lawless, *Ireland*, 401–2.

17. See Edmund Burke's famous point that "whatever is fitted in any sort to excite the ideas of pain, and danger, that is to say, whatever is in any sort terrible, or is conversant about terrible objects, or operates in a manner analogous to terror, is a source of the *sublime*; that is, it is productive of the strongest emotion which the mind is capable of feeling." Burke, *A Philosophical Enquiry into the Origin of Our Ideas of the Sublime and Beautiful*, 13–14. See also Shaw, *The Sublime*, 71.

18. R. A. Shafto Adair, *The Winter of 1846–7 in Antrim, with Remarks on Out-door Relief and Colonization*, 16; Monahan, *O'Ruark*, 171.

19. Monahan, *O'Ruark*, 73, 268.

20. See, for example, Arnold D. Harvey, *Body Politic: Political Metaphor and Political Violence.*

21. Margaret E. Owens, *Stages of Dismemberment: The Fragmented Body in Late Medieval and Early Modern Drama*, 252; Monahan, *O'Ruark*, 268.

22. The term is interpreted here as those people who, through "state formation and the law" or social relations, such as those individuals operating in colonial contexts, are denied any agency as well as the authority to define themselves through language. See Gayatri Chakravorty Spivak, "Can the Subaltern Speak?," 26.

23. Monahan, *O'Ruark*, 267–68.

24. William Carleton, *The Squanders of Castle Squander*, 2:138–39.

25. Arthuro J. Aldama, "Violence, Bodies, and the Color of Fear: An Introduction," 5; Thomas Carlyle, *Reminiscences of My Irish Journey in 1849*, 16, 24.

26. Christopher Morash, "Literature, Memory, Atrocity," 114.

27. Monahan, *O'Ruark*, 267, 271.

28. Ibid., 222.

29. Kinealy, *Death-Dealing Famine*, 123; Ó Gráda, *Ireland before and after the Famine*, 124.

30. Monahan, *O'Ruark*, 227, 226.

31. Ibid., 226, 227, 222.

32. Ibid., 73.

33. Carleton, *Squanders of Castle Squander*, 2:268, 272.

34. Many writings about the Great Famine identify the period with keening. For instance, *The Famine in Ireland: A Poem* speaks of the shrill "cry of Death" that

"re-echoes through the land." Rawlins, *Famine in Ireland*, 8. At the same time, the Famine was seen as a disruption of traditional Irish mourning practices, as the rural population was eliminated by hunger and disease and as those individuals who survived were too weakened to perform mourning rituals. A sermon, read by John Travers Robinson in 1847, speaks of "corpses being carried to their last home by mourners scarcely able to crawl along the roads to perform the melancholy duty." J. Robinson, *Sermon, Preached in St. Leonard's Chapel*, 11.

35. David Lloyd, *Irish Culture and Colonial Modernity, 1800–2000: The Transformation of Oral Space*, 53; Carleton, *Squanders of Castle Squander*, 1:47, 133, 2:85.

36. See Roger Travis, *Allegory and the Tragic Chorus in Sophocles' "Oedipus at Colonus,"* 2–3; Sarah Dewar-Watson, *Tragedy*, 26–28.

37. See, among others, Sarah Kember, *Virtual Anxiety: Photography, New Technologies and Subjectivity*, 6; and Jean Petrucelli, *Longing: Psychoanalytical Musings on Desire*, 115.

38. Daniel Miller, *The Comfort of Things*, 26; Bill Brown, *A Sense of Things: The Object Matter of American Literature*, 184.

39. Anthony Synnott, "Shame and Glory: A Sociology of Hair," 381, 404; Elaine Freedgood, *The Ideas in Things: Fugitive Meaning in the Victorian Novel*, 8; Galia Ofrek, *Representations of Hair in Victorian Literature and Culture*, 21, 23.

40. Ofrek, *Representations of Hair*, 26 (quote); Marcia Pointon, "Wearing Memory: Mourning, Jewellery and the Body," 66.

41. Deborah Lutz, "The Dead Still among Us: Victorian Secular Relics, Hair and Death Culture," 135.

42. Ofrek, *Representations of Hair*, 26; Lutz, "Dead Still among Us," 128.

43. Ofrek, *Representations of Hair*, 26.

44. Trollope, *Castle Richmond*, 169.

45. Carleton, "Owen M'Carthy," 138, 140.

46. As Stuart McLean illustrates, accounts of the Irish Famine would often describe how hair on the victims' heads "in many cases fell out," while, disturbingly, facial hair would grow and cover the entire countenance. McLean, *Event and Its Terrors*, 125.

47. Fludernik, *Towards a "Natural" Narratology*, 27.

48. Ireland [pseud.], *Tale of the Irish Famine*, 25, 18, 33.

49. By contrast, in Charles Joseph Kickham's novel *Sally Cavanagh* (1869), hair is a painful reminder of Famine-related loss. The eponymous heroine's daughter, Norah, is known for her "long yellow hair shining like gold in the setting sun." When Sally's family has to look for shelter in the workhouse and her little daughter dies, Sally is deluded by the "yellow hair" of one of the pauper girls, thinking she sees her dead daughter, Norah. Kickham, *Sally Cavanagh*, 122, 168.

50. Wills, *Love That Kills*, 2:275–76.

51. Margaret Brew, *The Chronicles of Castle Cloyne*, 2:280.

52. Rosa Mulholland, "The Hungry Death," 391.

53. Canon Patrick Sheehan, *Glenanaar: A Story of Irish Life*, 203.

54. Charles Trevelyan, "Letter of Charles Edward Trevelyan to Thomas Spring-Rice, Lord Mounteagle"; William Pulteney Allison, *Observations on the Famine of 1846–7, in the Highlands of Scotland and in Ireland*, 6; Mrs. Maberly, *The Present State of Ireland and Its Remedy*, 3, 6. For further reading on abjection and colonization, see, among others, Robert Miles, "Abjection, Nationalism and the Gothic."

55. Brendan Kane, *The Politics and Culture of Honour in Britain and Ireland, 1541–1641*, 23.

56. See Elisabeth Gitter, "The Power of Women's Hair in the Victorian Imagination," 939.

57. Sydney Owenson, Lady Morgan, *The Wild Irish Girl: A National Tale*, 48, 111.

58. See William Williams, *Tourism, Landscape and the Irish Character: British Travel Writers in Pre-Famine Ireland*, 105.

59. J. E. Bicheno, *Ireland and Its Economy*, 38–39.

60. Carleton, *Black Prophet*, 385–86, 35, 357–58.

61. Mulholland, "The Hungry Death," 395; Sheehan, *Glenanaar*, 205.

62. Keith Oatley, "Emotion and the Story Worlds of Fiction," 64.

63. Ron Eyerman, "Cultural Trauma: Slavery and the Formation of African American Identity," 68; Werner Bohleber, *Destructiveness, Intersubjectivity and Trauma: The Identity Crisis of Modern Psychoanalysis*, 962.

3. Beyond Boundaries

1. O'Sullivan, *Tombs of a Departed Race*, 40.

2. Glenn Hooper, ed., *The Tourist's Gaze: Travellers to Ireland, 1800–2000*, 102.

3. Asenath Nicholson, *Annals of the Famine in Ireland in 1847, 1848 and 1849*, vi. For a recent biography of Nicholson, see Maureen Murphy, *Compassionate Stranger: Asenath Nicholson and the Great Irish Famine.*

4. *Ireland and Her Famine: A Discourse, Preached in Paradise Street Chapel, Liverpool, on Sunday, January 31, 1847 by James Martineau*, 23.

5. Jim Shanahan, "Suffering Rebellion: Irish Gothic Fiction, 1799–1830," 75.

6. Robinson, *Sermon Preached in St. Leonard's Chapel*, 10; Burke, *Philosophical Enquiry*, 202, 181, 93, 104, 109, 234. Burke argues that the notion of being at a safe distance from sublime phenomena also generates feelings of pleasure, but this aspect of the sublime is not explored in Famine fiction.

7. Carleton, *Black Prophet*, 204; Carleton, *Squanders of Castle Squander*, 2:212, 110–12.

8. Carleton, *Black Prophet*, 24, 211. Interestingly, Carleton's novel here seems to echo contemporary representations of afflicted Ireland as one vast burial pit. See, for

instance, John Travers Robinson's apocalyptic portrayal of Famine Ireland as "a huge sepulchre, steaming with corruption up to heaven." J. Robinson, *Sermon Preached in St. Leonard's Chapel*, 10.

9. Clington, *Frank O'Donnell*, 412.

10. Monahan, *O'Ruark*, 24; Ireland [pseud.], "Narrative of Malcolm McGregor," Oct. 17, 24, 1846; Monahan, *O'Ruark*, 171.

11. Carleton, *Squanders of Castle Squander*, 2:212; A Barrister [pseud.], *What Have the Whigs Done for Ireland? or, The English Whigs and the Irish Famine*, 10.

12. John Forbes, *Memorandums Made in Ireland in the Autumn of 1852*, 39; Rigby Watson, Esq., *Letter to the Right Honourable Lord John Russell, M.P.*, 6; Carleton, *Squanders of Castle Squander*, 2:105, 87–88.

13. David Lloyd, "The Indigent Sublime: Specters of Irish Hunger," 152, 160, 162.

14. Dufferin and Boyle, *Narrative of a Journey*, 13.

15. For an overview of Jones's involvement with the Reform League, see Aldon D. Bell, "Administration and Finance of the Reform League, 1865–1867."

16. T. Mason Jones, *Old Trinity*, 2:86, 87.

17. Mrs. Lorenzo Nunn, *Heirs of the Soil: A Tale*, 20.

18. William Bennett, *Narrative of a Recent Journey of Six Weeks in Ireland*, 27; Mrs. Meredith, "Ellen Harrington," 63.

19. Trollope, *Castle Richmond*, 330–32.

20. Ibid., 333.

21. Burke, *Philosophical Enquiry*, 233–35; *Widow O'Leary*, 10–12; Burke, *Philosophical Enquiry*, 214.

22. Ann Radcliffe, *The Mysteries of Udolpho: A Romance*, 324, 121; Charles Maturin, *Melmoth the Wanderer: A Tale*, 30–31, 29; David Punter, *The Literature of Terror*, 17, 59; Eugenia DeLamotte, *Perils of the Night: A Feminist Study of Nineteenth-Century Gothic*.

23. T. Jones, *Old Trinity*, 86.

24. For an extensive historiographical study on the position of middlemen, see Ciarán Reilly, *The Irish Land Agent, 1830–60: The Case of King's County*.

25. Trollope, *Castle Richmond*, 170–71.

26. Meredith, "Ellen Harrington," 56–57.

27. Janssen, "Famine Traces," 214–15; Brew, *The Chronicles of Castle Cloyne*, 2:279–80, 283, 287.

28. Janssen, "Famine Traces," 213; Brew, *Chronicles of Castle Cloyne*, 2:258–59; Mulholland, "The Hungry Death," 392.

29. David Punter and Glennis Byron, *The Gothic*, 37.

30. Christina Morin and Niall Gillespie, introduction to *Irish Gothics: Genres, Forms, Modes, and Traditions, 1760–1890*, 1. See also Jarlath Killeen, *The Emergence of Irish Gothic Fiction: History, Origins, Theories*, 48.

31. Morin and Gillespie, introduction to *Irish Gothics*, 2. Claire Connolly makes a similar point in *A Cultural History of the Irish Novel, 1790–1829*, 167. Jarlath Killeen explains that Gothic conventions were adopted by writers in Ireland from various backgrounds, including Irish Protestant middle classes who looked upon themselves as a "liminal community trapped in a liminal space," as well as by Catholic authors who rewrote the traditionally anti-Catholic Gothic in order to write back to religious and ethnic prejudice. See Killeen, *Emergence of Irish Gothic Fiction*, 47, 54.

32. Scott Brewster, "Seeing Things: Gothic and the Madness of Interpretation," 483.

33. J. Robinson, *Sermon Preached in St. Leonard's Chapel*, 11; Bennett, *Narrative of a Recent Journey*, 28; *Widow O'Leary*, 7; D. O'C Townley, "The Tale of a Tombstone," 800–801.

34. Carleton, *Black Prophet*, 249, 155, 156–57.

35. Shoshana Felman, "Women and Madness: The Critical Phallacy," 8; Robert Goode Hogan et al., eds., *Dictionary of Irish Literature*, 664.

36. Kickham, *Sally Cavanagh*, 153.

37. Ibid., 164.

38. See Ciarán Reilly, *Strokestown and the Great Irish Famine.*

39. Kickham, *Sally Cavanagh*, 195–96, 16.

40. Bryan P. McGovern, *John Mitchel: Irish Nationalist, Southern Secessionist*, 150. See also Christine Kinealy, *Daniel O'Connell and the Anti-slavery Movement: "The Saddest People the Sun Sees,"* chap. 3.

41. See John Mitchel, *Jail Journal; or, Five Years in British Prisons*, 170

42. Thomas Doolan, *Practical Suggestions on the Improvement of the Present Condition of the Peasantry of Ireland*, 9–10.

43. Rothberg, *Multidirectional Memory*, 13; W. C. Upton, *Uncle Pat's Cabin; or, Life among the Agricultural Labourers of Ireland*, 157–58; F. H. Clayton [An Irishman, pseud.], *Scenes and Incidents in Irish Life*, 81. See also Janssen, *Famine Traces*, 137–47.

44. Nolan, *Byrnes of Glengoulah*, 326, 329, 330.

45. Trollope, *Castle Richmond*, 176; O'Brien, *Ailey Moore*, 260–61.

46. Jane Chaplin Dunbar, *Gems of the Bog: A Tale of the Irish Peasantry*, 107, 117, 120, 110.

47. John Curwen, *Observations on the State of Ireland*, 184. Extracts from this text can also be found in Hooper, *Tourist's Gaze.*

48. See, for example, "The State of Ireland"; and *Irish Improvidence Encouraged by English Bounty.*

49. Maberly, *Present State of Ireland*, 27; Harriet Vaughan Cheney, "Sketches on a Journey," 378.

50. Carleton, *Black Prophet*, 249–50; Ireland [pseud.], "Narrative of Malcolm McGregor," Oct. 24, 1846; Kickham, *Sally Cavanagh*, 4, 155.

51. Wills, *Love That Kills*, 2:266–68.

52. Ireland [pseud.], *Tale of the Irish Famine*, 12; Hoare, "Little Mary," 87.

53. See M. Kelleher, *Feminization of Famine*, 7–8, 23. See also Claudia Nelson, *Family Ties in Victorian England*, 107.

54. Rawlins, *Famine in Ireland*, 14.

55. Carleton, *Squanders of Castle Squander*, 2:267–68, 1:277, 265; F. B. Ryan, *The Spirit's Lament; or, The Wrongs of Ireland*, 33.

56. Julian Wolfreys, *Victorian Hauntings: Spectrality, Gothic, the Uncanny and Literature*, 34–35; D. Lloyd, "The Indigent Sublime," 156.

57. Colin Davis, "Hauntology, Spectres and Phantoms," 373; Jacques Derrida, *Spectres de Marx*, 25, 23; Nicholson, *Annals of the Famine in Ireland*, 184; Monahan, *O'Ruark*, 73; Clington, *Frank O'Donnell*, 200.

58. Corrigan, *On Famine and Fever*, 5; Nicholson, *Annals of the Famine in Ireland*, 38–39; Monahan, *O'Ruark*, 73; Carleton, *Black Prophet*, 154–55.

59. Mrs. E. M. Field, *Denis: A Study in Black and White*, 175–76.

60. Ibid., 77; Sheehan, *Glenanaar*, 98–99.

61. Ross Poole, "Memory, History and the Claims of the Past," 152; Avery Gordon, *Ghostly Matters: Haunting and the Sociological Imagination*, 8.

62. *The Feast of Famine: An Irish Banquet, with Other Poems*, 10, 13.

63. Clington, *Frank O'Donnell*, 84–85; Nolan, *Byrnes of Glengoulah*, 215, 217–18, 223.

64. Nolan, *Byrnes of Glengoulah*, 324–25.

65. Dylan Trigg, "The Place of Trauma: Memory, Hauntings, and the Temporality of Ruins," 99; Caruth, *Unclaimed Experience*, 181.

66. Nolan, *Byrnes of Glengoulah*, 229; Townley, "Tale of a Tombstone," 804, 801.

67. Emily Lawless, "After the Famine," 180, 170, 196; Marguérite Corporaal, "Haunted by Hunger: Images of Spectrality in Literary Recollections of the Great Irish Famine, 1850–1900," 101; Katharine Tynan, "A Village Priest," 240–41.

68. Nicholson, *Annals of the Famine in Ireland*, 128; O'Rourke, *History of the Great Irish Famine*, 409; Carleton, *Squanders of Castle Squander*, 2:138; Clington, *Frank O'Donnell*, 353.

4. From Wasteland to Paradise Regained

1. James Clarence Mangan, "The Warning Voice," 437; James Clarence Mangan, "A Voice of Encouragement: A New Year's Lay," 100; Mahoney, "Sketches in the West of Ireland," Feb. 20, 1847.

2. See Oona Frawley, *Irish Pastoral: Nostalgia and Twentieth-Century Irish Literature*, 45, 51.

3. John Wylie, *Landscape*, 14.

4. Barbara Bender, *Landscape, Politics and Perspectives*, 3.

5. Morash, *Writing the Irish Famine*, 54; Carleton, *Black Prophet*, 21; J. Robinson, *Sermon Preached in St. Leonard's Chapel*, 10.

6. For instance, "The Potato Disease," published in the *Illustrated London News*, Oct. 18, 1845, cites landlord John Chester, of Kilscorne House in Magshole, who states that his field of twenty acres of potatoes "had been perfectly dry and sound, when they were attacked by the blight, and three-fourths of them are so diseased and rotten that pigs decline to eat them."

7. Carleton, *Black Prophet*, 20, 23.

8. Ibid., 62; O'Brien, *Ailey Moore*, 260, 264, 260.

9. Rothberg, *Multidirectional Memory*, 13.

10. Wertsch, *Voices of Collective Remembering*, 47.

11. Thomas J. Scanlan, *Colonial Writing and the New World, 1583–1671: Allegories of Desire*, 83.

12. Matthew Potteiger and Jamie Purinton, *Landscape Narratives: Design Practices for Telling Stories*, 216.

13. J. Robinson, *Sermon Preached in St. Leonard's Chapel*, 10; Ireland [pseud.], *Tale of the Irish Famine*, 10–11.

14. "Russell, T[homas] O'Neill (1828–1908)," in *The Oxford Companion to Irish Literature*, edited by Robert Welch and Bruce Stewart, 504.

15. Reginald Tierney [Thomas O'Neill Russell], *The Struggles of Dick Massey; or, The Battles of a Boy*, 1, 400.

16. Walshe, *Golden Hills*, 29–30; *The Farmer of Inniscreen: A Tale of the Irish Famine, in Verse*, 7; Walshe, *Golden Hills*, 191.

17. See, for example, John Agnew, "Landscape and National Identity in Europe: England versus Italy in the Role of Landscape in Identity Formation," 38. See also Rachel Platonov, "Remapping Arcadia: 'Pastoral Space' in Nineteenth-Century Russian Prose."

18. *Mount Leinster, a Poem, Descriptive of Irish Scenery*, 8, 22.

19. Clington, *Frank O'Donnell*, 85.

20. Fanning, *Irish Voice in America*, 79.

21. McCorry, *The Lost Rosary*, 9–10, 12.

22. For a discussion of this concept of pastoral *otium*, see, among others, Juan Christian Pelicer, "Pastoral and Georgic"; and Paul Alpers, *What Is Pastoral?*, 22–25.

23. McCorry, *The Lost Rosary*, 109.

24. See John Chalker, *The English Georgic: A Study in the Development of a Form*, 211.

25. Bruce Graver defines the Georgic as a mode that "celebrates the toil of farming" rather than *otium*, which is identified with the pastoral. See Bruce Graver, "Pastoral and Georgic," 986, 989.

26. Laurence Buell, *The Future of Environmental Criticism: Environmental Crisis and Literary Imagination*, 145; Carleton, "Owen M'Carthy," 164, 115, 136.

27. Neil Smelser, "Psychological Trauma and Cultural Trauma," 39; Rothberg, *Multidirectional Memory*, 13; Carleton, "Owen M'Carthy," 159.

28. Clington, *Frank O'Donnell*, 72, 433–34; Curtis, "McCormack's Grudge," Sept. 20, 1862; Emily Bowles, *Irish Diamonds; or, The Chronicles of Peterstown*, 160, 164.

29. McCorry, *The Lost Rosary*, 109; Sadlier, *Bessy Conway*, 10, 263–64.

30. Nicholas Royle, *The Uncanny: An Introduction*, 1.

31. Potteiger and Purinton, *Landscape Narratives*, 214.

32. O'Brien, *The Dalys of Dalystown*, 514.

33. Hoare, "The Black Potatoes," 32–33.

34. Through its interaction with the discourses of tourism, Mrs. Hoare's story exemplifies the intricate interrelations between travel writing and fiction in the nineteenth century, in particular in the form of the national tale. See Ina Ferris, *The Romantic National Tale and the Question of Ireland*.

35. Thomas Kitson Cromwell, *The Irish Tourist; or, Excursions through Ireland*, 240; Henrietta Chatterton, *Rambles in the South of Ireland during the Year 1838*, 16; William Williams, *Creating Irish Tourism: The First Century, 1750–1850*, 183, 184; Spencer T. Hall, *Life and Death in Ireland, as Witnessed in 1849*, 47; Bennett, *Narrative of a Recent Journey*, 128, 131; Raymond Williams, *The Country and the City*, 22.

36. In this respect, the story fits into the mid-nineteenth-century regionalist tradition, which, as Marjorie Pryse and Judith Fetterley state, countered the traditional "touristic images and allow[ed] regional persons to insert articulations of their own understanding of region," thereby disrupting popular conceptions and critiquing its commodification. See Pryse and Fetterley, *Writing Out of Place: Regionalism, Women and American Literary Culture*, 5.

37. Hester Sigerson, *A Ruined Race; or, The Last Macmanus of Dumroosk*, 58, 230–31; Annie Keary, *Castle Daly: The Story of an Irish Home Thirty Years Ago*, 3:332. See also Janssen, *Famine Traces*, 54, 76–77.

38. Denis Cosgrove, "Introduction to Social Formation and Symbolical Landscape," 20; Hoare, "Little Mary," 84–85.

39. Isaac Butt, *Land Tenure in Ireland: A Plea for the Celtic Race*, 8; Lord Dufferin, *Irish Emigration and the Tenure of Land in Ireland*, 2; Jonathan Pym, *Observations on the Evils Resulting to Ireland*, 10, 7.

40. G. Poulett Scrope, *Letters to Lord John Russell, M.P.: On the Further Measures Required for the Social Amelioration of Ireland*, 28, 25–26; Lawrence Rawsterne, Esq., *The Cause of the Potato Disease: Ascertained by Proofs*, 29. See also W. W. Robinson, *The Dawn of Ireland's Prosperity: General Employment; Blight of the Potato Crop; A Visitation*, 10.

41. Ó Murchadha, *Great Famine*, 50.

42. David S. Jones, "The Transfer of Land and the Emergence of the Graziers during the Famine Period," 93.

43. See Ó Gráda, *Ireland before and after the Famine*, 110, 124. See also Nick Pelling, *Anglo-Irish Relations, 1789–1922*, 47.

44. D. Jones, "Transfer of Land," 93.

45. Kickham, *Sally Cavanagh*, 151.

46. See Scanlan, *Colonial Writing and the New World*, 83; and Susan Egenolf, *The Art of Political Fiction in Hamilton, Edgeworth and Owenson*, 111. See also Matthew Potteiger and Jamie Purinton who argue that wastelands suggest "entropic narratives" that express a "critique of progress." Potteiger and Purinton, *Landscape Narratives*, 221.

47. Clington, *Frank O'Donnell*, 187; Nunn, *Heirs of the Soil*, 25.

48. Tierney, *Struggles of Dick Massey*, 135, 131; Smith, *Twelve Months' Residence*, 101; Scrope, *Letters to Lord John Russell*, 26.

49. Egenolf, *Art of Political Fiction*, 111; William Gilpin, *Three Essays: On Picturesque Beauty, on Picturesque Travel, and on Sketching Landscape*, iii.

50. See Pellicer, "Pastoral and Georgic," 295.

51. Monahan, *O'Ruark*, 41; Sidney Godolphin Osborne, *Gleanings in the West of Ireland*, 68.

52. Wills, *Love That Kills*, 1:1–2; Nolan, *Byrnes of Glengoulah*, 176, 170.

53. Pierre Nora, "Between Memory and History: *Les lieux de mémoire*," 7.

54. Nolan, *Byrnes of Glengoulah*, 176–77.

55. As such the novel illustrates Oona Frawley's statement that emerging postcolonialism involves "processes by which cultures must imaginatively repossess land." Frawley, "Toward a Theory of Cultural Memory in an Irish Postcolonial Context," 31.

56. Ireland [pseud.], *Tale of the Irish Famine*, 10–11; Hoare, "The Black Potatoes," 32–33; Carleton, "Owen M'Carthy," 164.

57. Tierney, *Struggles of Dick Massey*, 400.

58. For a further discussion of this pastoral concept of a place of happiness, see Alpers, *What Is Pastoral?*, 6.

59. Terry Gifford, *Pastoral*, 11; Donna Potts, *Contemporary Irish Poetry and the Pastoral Tradition*, 107; Tierney, *Struggles of Dick Massey*, 401, 192.

60. Tierney, *Struggles of Dick Massey*, 192, 430; Greg Gerrard, *Ecocriticism*, 108.

61. Curtis, "McCormack's Grudge," Sept. 27, 1862.

62. See Carolyn Conley, *Melancholy Accidents: The Meaning of Violence in Post-Famine Ireland*, 5; and Peter Gray, "Famine and Land, 1845–80," 555.

63. Nolan, *Byrnes of Glengoulah*, 332, 347.

64. Ibid., 347, 354, 1, 346.

65. Walshe, *Golden Hills*, 266.

66. See Alpers, *What Is Pastoral?*, 81.

67. Walshe, *Golden Hills*, 271. I have argued something similar in "From Golden Hills to Sycamore Trees: Pastoral Homelands and Ethnic Identity in Irish Immigrant Fiction, 1860–1875," 340–41.

68. Walshe, *Golden Hills*, 139, 224, 249, 64, 224.

69. Sadlier, *Bessy Conway*, 263–64, 298. See also Marguérite Corporaal, "Black Patches and Rotting Weeds: The Great Famine as a Transcultural Figure of Memory in Irish (Diaspora) Fiction, 1860–1880," 256.

70. McGee, "Social Duties of Irishmen in America"; "The Irish Americans"; Alpers, *What Is Pastoral?*, 28; Julia M. Wright, *Representing the National Landscape in Irish Romanticism*, xi; Frawley, *Irish Pastoral*, 51.

71. It must be noted that a similar contrast between a pastoral Ireland and the urban climate of the host country can be found in Miss Mason's Irish British novel *Kate Gearey; or, Irish Life in London: A Tale of 1849*. Here Kate's childhood in a mud cabin "on the fair banks of the Awbeg, amidst the fertile valleys of Castletown Roche," while "the blue sky of Ireland was above her, its soft green turf beneath her feet, its pure air around her," forms a stark contrast with Kate's habitation in a London tenement house: "a square hole looking into a damp filthy passage" (9, 3). This passage not only shows that the living conditions of Irish Famine immigrants in Britain and America were similarly bleak, but also illustrates Andreas Huyssen's earlier quoted point about the idealization of the homeland in diaspora cultures.

72. John Boyle O'Reilly, "Our Own Green Island Home"; David O'Callohan, "Will He Return."

73. Oona Frawley, introduction to *Memory Ireland*, 5; Joep Leerssen, *National Thought in Europe: A Cultural History*, 16; Sadlier, *Elinor Preston*, 146, 181, 177, 214. Sadlier's novel thus underscores Julia M. Wright's point that "diasporic nationalism understands the land as absent origin." Wright, *Representing the National Landscape*, xvii.

74. Sadlier, *Bessy Conway*, 10, 3; McCorry, *The Lost Rosary*, 102–3, 13.

75. Sadlier, *Bessy Conway*, 106.

76. See also Corporaal, "Black Patches and Rotting Weeds," 260.

77. The term "ethnoscape," which means the "landscapes of group identity," is derived from Arjun Appadurai, "Global Ethnoscapes: Notes and Queries for a Transnational Anthropology," 191.

78. Astrid Erll, "Travelling Memory," *Parallax*, 8.

79. See Terre Ryan, *The Ecstatic Nation: The American Landscape and the Aesthetics of Patriotism*, 123. See also Steven Jacobs, "Landscape," 821.

80. McCorry, *The Lost Rosary*, 181; William B. Dewees, *Letters from an Early Settler of Texas*, 218; Henry T. Newton, *Canada in 1864: A Hand-Book for Settlers*, 11.

81. See Richard Panchyk, *The Keys to American History: Understanding Our Most Important Historic Documents*, 107.

82. "Canada and Ireland," 346.

83. I have argued something similar in "Recollection of Sorrow and Misery Past." The argument is repeated here by kind permission of Quinnipiac Univ. Press.

84. McCorry, *The Lost Rosary*, 9–10, 180.

85. As Luke Gibbons has recently noted, it is interesting that the term "Manifest Destiny" was first coined by Irish American journalist John L. O'Sullivan, to describe the expansion westward, in an article that appeared in the *Morning Star*, Dec. 27, 1845. See Luke Gibbons, "'The Old Far West and the New': Bram Stoker, Race, and Manifest Destiny."

86. Major Strickland, *Twenty-Seven Years in Canada West; or, The Experience of an Early Settler*, 134; Dewees, *Letters from an Early Settler of Texas*, 145; Mrs. C. P. Traill, *The Canadian Emigrant Housekeeper's Guide*, 3. Frederick Jackson Turner's *The Frontier in American History* (1893) later gave expression to these traditions of the American West that identified pioneering with opportunity, stating that with "natural gifts" such as "the best bottom lands, the finest timber tracts, the best salt-springs, the richest ore beds," the West offered "varied chances for advancement" and prosperity to those individuals "who knew how to seize the opportunity." Jackson, *Frontier in American History*, 270.

87. Sadlier, *Con O'Regan*, 353, 371, 373.

88. O'Brien, *The Dalys of Dalystown*, 484, 466, 468.

89. Homi Bhabha, *The Location of Culture*, 53.

90. Faist, *Volume and Dynamics*, 240.

91. Rothberg, *Multidirectional Memory*, 5, 11.

92. David Emmons, *Beyond the American Pale: The Irish in the West, 1845–1910*, 212, 214; McGee, "Social Duties of Irishmen in America," 1. See also Patricia Kelleher, "Young Irish Workers: Class Implications of Men's and Women's Experiences in Gilded Age Chicago," 191. See also Timothy J. Meagher, *Inventing Irish America: Generation, Class, and Ethnic Identity in a New England City, 1880–1920*, 134. Kerby Miller has argued that this process of an emerging Irish American middle class was completed by 1895. Miller, *Ireland and Irish America*, 299.

93. Lindsay Janssen, "The Impossibility of Transporting Identity: The Representation of Diasporic Irishness in Transatlantic Irish Fiction, 1860–1900"; McDougall, *The Days of a Life*, 208–9; John Brennan, *Erin Mór: The Story of Irish Republicanism*, 126.

94. Rudy Koshar, *From Monuments to Traces: Artifacts of German Memory, 1870–1990*, 18; Jacobson, *Special Sorrows*, 97.

95. Christopher Daase, "Addressing Painful Memories: Apologies as a New Practice in International Relations," 19; Poole, "Memory, History and the Claims of the Past," 160.

5. Ruins of the Past

1. Nora, "Between Memory and History," 7, 19; Anderson, *Imagined Communities*, 15. For seminal scholarship on the role of monuments as sites of memory, see,

for example, Joep Leerssen, "Monuments and Trauma: Varieties of Remembrance"; and Roy Foster, "Remembering 1798." For studies on Ireland's landscape as a *lieu de mémoire*, see, among others, Paul Claval, "Changing Conceptions of Heritage and Landscape."

2. Niamh Ann Kelly has published on workhouses and cottages as physical and symbolical sites of Famine memory. See Kelly, "Narrative Sites of Memory: Workhouses and Famine Memory" and "Remembering Homelessness in the Great Irish Famine." Kevin Whelan's work on the cultural effects of the Famine on the Irish landscape, as well as John Crowley, William J. Smyth, and Mike Murphy's recently issued *Atlas of the Great Irish Famine, 1845–52* (2012), has further mapped the constellations of space in relation to Ireland's past. See Whelan, "Reading the Ruins" and "Cultural Effects of the Famine"; and Crowley, Smyth, and Murphy, eds., *Atlas of the Great Irish Famine.* A very comprehensive study of Famine memorials is Mark-FitzGerald, *Commemorating the Famine.*

3. Several reports of such clearances exist. For example, "Expulsion of Tenantry," published in the *Cork Examiner*, Sept. 20, 1847, states that in Tonnymageera, County Cavan, "ninety nine houses were pulled down, and the unfortunate occupants set adrift upon the world." "Condition of Ireland: Illustrations of the New Poor Law," appearing in the *Illustrated London News*, Dec. 15, 1849, describes "a destroyed village," once the abode of many of the Famine-stricken "wretched beings," where "the ruthless spoiler has been at work and swept away the shelter that honest industry had prepared for suffering and toiling humanity."

4. As Scott Brewster and Virginia Crossman have argued, depopulation left "the family homes as gaunt ruins." Brewster and Crossman, "Re-writing the Famine: Witnessing in Crisis," 42.

5. Monahan, *O'Ruark*, 441.

6. Carleton, *Squanders of Castle Squander*, 2:235.

7. Gilpin, *Three Essays*, 7–8. For a discussion of the role of ruins in Ruskin's work, see John Dixon Hunt, *Gardens and the Picturesque: Studies in the History of Landscape Architecture*, 196.

8. See Gibbons, *Transformations in Irish Culture*; Ferris, *Romantic National Tale*; Claire Connolly, *Cultural History of the Irish Novel*; and Wright, *Representing the National Landscape.*

9. Owenson, *Wild Irish Girl*, 56, 79; Coílín Parsons, "The Archive in Ruins: James Clarence Mangan and Colonial Cartography," 474.

10. McLean, *Event and Its Terrors*, 6.

11. Máirín Ní Cheallaigh, "Women and the Survival of Archeological Monuments in Nineteenth-Century Ireland," 85, 83.

12. Trigg, "Place of Trauma," 95; Dylan Trigg, *The Aesthetics of Decay: Nothingness, Nostalgia and the Absence of Reason*, 131; McLean, *Event and Its Terrors*, 28; Whelan,

"Reading the Ruins," 319. In a similar vein, Claire Connolly states that "ruins operate as an index of cultural value, encoding a future appeal to some future appreciation of a once-great civilization." Connolly, *Cultural History of the Irish Novel*, 41.

13. Nicholson, *Annals of the Famine in Ireland*, 136; Mitchel, *History of Ireland*, 244; Lawless, *Ireland*, 403; John, Earl of Shrewesbury, *Thoughts on the Poor Relief Bill for Ireland, Together with Reflections on Their Miseries, Their Causes, and Their Remedies*, 13. See also David S. Jones, "The Great Famine, Land and the Making of the Graziers." Before the Famine, many of the landed families were already heavily indebted, having upheld a lavish lifestyle in times of economic depression, and, as James Donnelly has observed, "defective laws . . . permitted their accumulation of debts far beyond the value of security." Donnelly, *Great Irish Potato Famine*, 26. The financial prospects of the gentry received a further blow by the outbreak of the blight: as Thomas Benningham remarked in 1847, "When the payment of rents has been (and is likely still to be) so difficult" owing to the failure of the potato crops, "the total ruin of many proprietors and occupiers of land must ensue." Benningham, *The Thames, the Shannon and the St. Lawrence; or, The Good of Great Britain*, iv. Furthermore, abandoned to the care of the famishing by the London government, many landlords found themselves "at the verge of ruin," Andrew J. Maley stated in 1849. Maley, *Observations upon the Inability of Exterminating the Resident Landlord of Ireland*, 30. For further details on how the burden of Famine relief affected the incomes of the landed class, see Peter Gray, *Famine, Land and Politics: British Government and Irish Society, 1843–50*, 197.

14. Sadlier, *New Lights*, 284, 6–7.

15. Ibid., 245, 247. The proselytizing movement was notorious for striving to convert Famine victims, as Donal Kerr illuminates in *The Catholic Church and the Famine*, 86. William Henry Smith championed the British evangelicals who, "well becoming their holy vocation, labour in the universal cause of charity." Smith, *Twelve Months' Residence*, 42. However, the representation of the selfish Souperist whose mission was to win souls among the famishing for the Protestant cause prevails in Catholic fiction. For example, Emily Bowles's *Irish Diamonds* shows how Bible reader Israel Brooker "took a tithe of souls" among the "cast down and destitute parents" who succumbed to conversion because they could not endure their children's impending starvation. Bowles, *Irish Diamonds*, 173. For a further discussion of proselytism in Sadlier's novel, see Marguérite Corporaal, "Memories of the Great Famine and Ethnic Identity in Novels by Victorian Irish Women Writers."

16. See, for example, Denis Murphy, *Cromwell in Ireland: Cromwell's Irish Campaign*; or James Scott Wheeler, *Cromwell in Ireland*.

17. At the same time, Sadlier's narrative underscores Susan Egenolf's observation that ruins were often interpreted as signs of imperial superiority and native impotence. Egenolf, *Art of Political Fiction*, 105.

18. During the later years of the Famine in particular, the fortunes of once prosperous families, such as the landed classes, were alike affected by the dire consequences of the blight, and many became debt ridden by governmental measures such as the Encumbered Estates Act of 1848–49. The *Spectator*, Aug. 5, 1848, wrote that Parliament had passed a bill that made it possible to "sell encumbered lands without the concurrence of all persons interested," thus facilitating the transference of heavily indebted property from impoverished upper-class families to new owners.

19. Sadlier, *Elinor Preston*, 76, 94, 23.

20. Ibid., 140–41, 266, 187.

21. Ibid., 133–34.

22. Philip Ethington, "Placing the Past: 'Groundwork' for a Spatial Theory of History," 465–66.

23. Foucault, "Of Other Spaces," 26.

24. Sadlier, *Elinor Preston*, 141, 68.

25. Sadlier, *Bessy Conway*, 10.

26. See, for instance, Maurice Lenihan, *Limerick: Its History and Antiquities, Ecclesiastical, Civil, and Military*, 130. See also Robert Southey, *Life of Oliver Cromwell*, 142.

27. Sadlier, *Bessy Conway*, 263.

28. Peppergrass, *Shandy M'Guire*, 263, 99.

29. Kickham, *Sally Cavanagh*, 188.

30. "Anna Hanson Dorsey."

31. Dorsey, *Nora Brady's Vow and Mona the Vestal*, 77.

32. Ibid., 115.

33. Ibid.; Kickham, *Sally Cavanagh*, 188.

34. Lloyd, *Irish Times*, 25.

35. Sadlier, *New Lights*, 284, 147–48.

36. Ibid., 285, 118; Foucault, "Of Other Spaces," 25.

37. See Emmett Larkin, "The Devotional Revolution in Ireland, 1850–75." See also David W. Miller, "Irish Catholicism and the Great Famine."

38. Paul Cullen, *The Making of the Roman Catholic Church in Ireland, 1850–1860*, 22.

39. Archbishop John Hughes, "The Importance of Being in Communion with Christ's One Holy, Catholic and Apostolic Church," 589.

40. Sadlier, *New Lights*, 325.

41. Ibid., 287.

42. This notion of savagery is, for instance, forwarded in Mrs. Maberly's Famine treatise *The Present State of Ireland and Its Remedy*, which compares the Famine-stricken Irish peasants to "brawling, idle, dirty creatures" who "are too indolent to go out of their way for improvement" (27, 16).

43. Sadlier, *Elinor Preston*, 141–43.

44. Dorsey, *Nora Brady's Vow*, 77–78; Dufferin and Boyle, *Narrative of a Journey*, 14–15. From the late eighteenth well into the mid-nineteenth centuries, throughout the British Isles, ruins of castles, convents, and abbeys were conventionally designated as examples of the picturesque. Thus, Samuel Lewis, *A Topographical Dictionary of Wales* (1833), speaks of the castle ruins in Lewhaden as having "a most beautiful and picturesque appearance from every point of view" (C1). In his "Essay on Architecture and Buildings" (1810), Sir Uvedale Price argues that a site of construction "never displays a marked picturesque character, till in ruin" (2:261). And John Leighton in *History of the County of Fife, from the Earliest Period to the Present Time* (1840) describes the abbey ruins in Balmerino as "picturesque and interesting" (2:75).

45. Sadlier, *Bessy Conway*, 312.

46. O'Brien, *Ailey Moore*, 23, 31; Foucault, "Of Other Spaces," 24–25.

47. O'Brien, *Ailey Moore*, 262, 23; Trigg, *Aesthetics of Decay*, 133.

48. Burke, *Philosophical Enquiry*, 107.

49. Kickham, *Sally Cavanagh*, 193–94.

50. "For the further illustration of this subject, it is proper to remark, that all ideas of the solemn and awful kind, and even bordering on the terrible, tend greatly to assist the sublime." Robert Chambers, *Cyclopaedia of English Literature*, 219.

51. Dylan Trigg, *The Memory of Place: A Phenomenology of the Uncanny*, 37. See also Royle, *The Uncanny: An Introduction*: "The uncanny is not simply an experience of strangeness or alienation. More specifically, it is a peculiar commingling of the familiar and unfamiliar" (1).

52. David Sim, "Filibusters, Fenians, and a Contested Neutrality: The Irish Question and U.S. Diplomacy, 1848–1871," 266.

53. See Jonathan Gantt, *Irish Terrorism in the Atlantic Community, 1865–1922*, 31.

54. See Brian Jenkins, *The Fenian Problem: Insurgency and Terrorism in a Liberal State, 1858–1874*; and Steward and McGovern, *Fenians.*

55. Whelan, "Reading the Ruins," 307.

56. Dorsey, *Nora Brady's Vow*, 149.

57. Kickham, *Sally Cavanagh*, 208–9.

58. Dorsey, *Nora Brady's Vow*, 157.

59. Svetlana Boym, "Ruins of the Avant-Garde: From Tatlin's Tower to Paper Architecture," 58.

60. Ann Rigney, "Portable Monuments," introduced this term in relation to literary texts.

6. Recollections of (Re)migration

1. Halley, *Speech Delivered at the Dinner of St. Patrick's Society*, 3–4.

2. Kinealy, *This Great Calamity*, 304.

3. Edward E. Hale mentioned that "the large proportion of the emigrants have been sent for by their friends" in North America. Hale, *Letters on Irish Emigration*, 32.

4. David Fitzpatrick, "Flight from Famine," 179.

5. See, for example, Mark McGowan, *Death or Canada: The Irish Famine Emigration to Toronto, 1847* and "Contemporary Links between Irish and Canadian Famine Commemoration."

6. Cohen, *Global Diasporas: An Introduction*, 161, 4. Cohen's definition bears strong similarities to Jana Evan Braziel and Anita Mannur's description of diaspora as "an exilic or nostalgic dislocation from homeland." Braziel and Mannur, introduction to *Theorizing Diaspora*, 4.

7. As James S. Donnelly asserts, 1847 can be seen as an important watershed as from that year the Irish exodus to America came particularly to be viewed as "forced exile." Donnelly, *Great Irish Potato Famine*, 186.

8. Thomas D'Arcy McGee, "The Exile's Meditation," 105.

9. "The Emigrant Ship," 508; Wills, *Love That Kills*, 3:95–96, 99.

10. Cohen, *Global Diasporas: An Introduction*, 1.

11. James Stephens fled Ireland to escape imprisonment, after his involvement in the failed 1848 rebellion. Kerby Miller claims that "the Young Irelanders' personal experiences" of deportation or flight "gave them special authority" to "interpret all emigration as exile." Many of these Young Irelanders who looked upon themselves as exiles came to play a prominent role in nationalist movements on both sides of the Atlantic. See Miller, *Emigrants and Exiles*, 310.

12. Clington, *Frank O'Donnell*, 297.

13. Tierney, *Struggles of Dick Massey*, 66, 160. In this respect the novel raises the same points as Robert Whyte's *The Ocean Plague; or, A Voyage to Quebec in an Irish Emigrant Vessel.* This text, which is often regarded as a fictional autobiography, states that landlords would ship off their tenants to Canada and pay for their fares, because "the expense of transporting each individual was less than the cost of the year's support in a workhouse" (12). For further reading on the reception of Whyte's narrative, see Jason King, "The Genealogy of Famine Diary in Ireland and Quebec: Ireland's Famine Migration in Historical Fiction, Historiography and Memory."

14. Tierney, *Struggles of Dick Massey*, 373; John Mitchel, *Ireland since '98: Daniel O'Connell; The Repeal Agitation; The Miseries of the Famine; The Young Ireland Party, Etc.*, 132.

15. See Fanning, *Irish Voice in America*, 56.

16. Cannon, *Bickerton*, 5.

17. "The Emigrant," 801, 803, 801.

18. Mason, *Kate Gearey*, 151, 146, 151; Meredith, "Ellen Harrington," 80–81.

19. Sadlier, *Elinor Preston*, 258–60.

20. Ibid., 239–40.

21. There were frequent reports on the arrival of ships full of disease-ridden passengers who had to be taken to quarantine stations, such as Grosse Isle, Partridge Island, Shippegan, and Miramichi (Sheldrake Island) in the Canadian press. For example, "Deaths on Partridge Island since July 31, 1847" enumerates: "The passengers by the Magnes from Galway were all landed before the vessel went on shore. The Ship British Merchant from Cork, 338 passengers, arrived at Quarantine on Thursday. Thirty-three deaths occurred on board this vessel during the voyage, and five more since her arrival at Quarantine. Fifty of the passengers are very ill with fever." *New Brunswick Courier*, Aug. 7, 1847.

22. "The Stranger's Grave," *New Brunswick Courier*, Sept. 25, 1847.

23. Tierney, *Struggles of Dick Massey*, 373–74. Before and during the Famine years, several members of the Repeal movement, and especially Daniel O'Connell, supported the abolitionist movement. O'Donnell was known for his passionate antislavery speeches. See Kinealy, *Daniel O'Connell and the Anti-slavery Movement*, 15. See also Angela Murphy, *American Slavery: Abolition, Immigrant Citizenship, and the Transatlantic Movement for Irish Identity*, 3. Conversely, some abolitionists in the United States expressed a strong interest in the plight of Famine-stricken Ireland. A letter by William Lloyd Garrison to Elizabeth Pease, dating from Apr. 1, 1847, speaks of the "distress in Ireland" and American initiatives to supply aid to "save from suffering and death, those who reside across the wide Atlantic." See William Lloyd Garrison Papers, 1835–1875, Library of Congress, MSS 1498.

24. Tierney, *Struggles of Dick Massey*, 374–75.

25. Christopher Cusack and Lindsay Janssen have explored the ways in which Famine fiction from subsequent decades reconfigures traditional representations of the Irish family. Cusack and Janssen, "Death in the Family: Reimagining the Irish Family in Famine Fiction, 1871–1912."

26. *Paddy's Leisure Hours in the Poor House*, 54–55.

27. T. L. N., "Captain Patrick Malony; or, The Irishman in Alabama," June 2, 9, 16, 1860.

28. M. B., "Rose McCarthy's Sorrow," 464, 465.

29. "Cusack, Margaret Anna," in *A Guide to Irish Fiction, 1650–1900*, edited by Rolf Loeber and Magda Loeber, with Anne Mullin Burnham. Electronic version, created by An Foras Feasa in 2012: see http://www.lgif.ie.

30. Margaret Anna Cusack ("Sister Mary Frances Clare"), "From Killarney to New York; or, How Thade Became a Banker," 182–83, 347.

31. Mary Synon, "My Grandmother and Myself," 227, 224, 231.

32. Tierney, *Struggles of Dick Massey*, 374; *Grosse-Isle Emigrant Station: A Letter Addressed to the Inspectors of Hospitals, Prisons and Asylums*, 5.

33. Donnelly, *Great Irish Potato Famine*, 179. As William A. Spray explains, moreover, from 1846 many Irish emigrants were entirely unprepared for their crossing

and left "with little or no money and no stock of foodstuffs for the voyage." Spray, "Irish Famine Emigrants," 5.

34. Maguire, *The Irish in America*, 181.

35. K. Miller, *Emigrants and Exiles*, 292.

36. See Michael Quigley, "Grosse Île: Canada's Famine Memorial," 136; Susan Campbell Bartoletti, *Black Potatoes: The Story of the Great Irish Famine, 1845–1850*, 128; and Ó Murchadha, *Great Famine*, 147.

37. Whyte, *Ocean's Plague*, 15, 17. Whyte here appears to quote a leading article from the *Times*, Sept. 17, 1847, that mentions exactly the same figures.

38. For further reading on these fever sheds, see Maguire, *The Irish in America*, 145. See also Jason King, "Remembering Famine Orphans: The Transmission of Famine Memory between Ireland and Quebec"; and MacKay, *Flight from Famine*, 270, 274, 277. The Annals of the Sisters of Charity (Grey Nuns) (1847), which were edited by Jason King and translated by Jean-François Bernard and were recently published by NUI Galway, further testify to the wide-scale misery within these sheds at Grosse Isle. For the full texts of the annals, see http://faminearchive.nuigalway.ie/eyewitness-accounts/grey-nuns.

39. For an elaborate discussion of this painting, see Jason King, "The Remembrance of Irish Famine Migrants in the Fever Sheds of Montreal."

40. "The Emigrant Ship," 509. Intriguingly, in February of the same year the *Literary Garland* published a story by American Canadian writer Harriet Vaughan Cheney, entitled "The Emigrants." This sketch narrates how "a strict quarantine was enforced on every vessel" arriving at Grosse Isle. Although set in 1832, the year in which an outbreak of cholera indeed led to the placement in isolation of many incoming immigrants, the story also reminds one of the exodus of the Famine generation: especially in the years 1847 and 1848, the quarantine station accommodated many Irish emigrants who had contracted typhoid fever. Like "The Emigrant Ship," Cheney's story also casts the deprivations undergone by Irish emigrants in terms that remind one of conventional representations of Famine victims, even if the story is actually set a decade earlier. The "pale emaciated countenances" of the children on board are marked by "hungry looks . . . traces of early care and sorrow," because the captain hardly "chose to furnish them" with food "from his own stores" (276).

41. Tierney, *Struggles of Dick Massey*, 168, 162.

42. Marguérite Corporaal and Christopher Cusack, "Rites of Passage: The Coffin Ship as Site of Immigrants' Identity Formation in Irish and Irish-American Fiction, 1855–1885." The argument is reproduced here with kind permission of Taylor and Francis publishers.

43. For the terminology, see Rothberg, *Multidirectional Memory*, 13.

44. Whyte, *Ocean's Plague*, 15; Tierney, *Struggles of Dick Massey*, 376.

45. Bhabha, *The Location of Culture*, 64; Bammer, introduction to *Displacements*, xii.

46. Caroline Brettell, *Anthropology and Migration: Essays on Transnationalism, Ethnicity, and Identity*, 18.

47. See Corporaal and Cusack, "Rites of Passage," 347–48.

48. Kickham, *Sally Cavanagh*, 86, 89.

49. Quigley, *Cross and the Shamrock*, 55, 57.

50. Ibid., 14, 20–21.

51. Portrayals of Irish emigrants who, upon coming to the United States, would fall victim to abuse would also feature in fiction written by authors without Irish roots or without a specific Irish audience in mind. Thus, Lydia Maria Child's collection *Fact and Fiction* includes the story "The Irish Heart," which shows how a young emigrant is swindled out of his Sunday suit and watch by a stranger who presents him with a false note of twenty dollars. Child's collection was originally published during the Famine, in 1846, by C. S. Francis from New York. Perhaps because of the inclusion of this story on Irish emigration, the collection was reprinted in Dublin by James M'Glashan in 1849.

52. Cannon, *Bickerton*, 37, 65, 16, 181–82.

53. See Edward Wakin, *Enter the Irish American*, 82; and Andrew Henry Stern, *Southern Crucifix, Southern Cross: Catholic-Protestant Relations in the Old South*, 173.

54. Journals directed at Irish North American readerships would often report on the skirmishes between nativists and the Irish. "Protestant Violence in Canada," an article published in the *Pilot*, Apr. 3, 1858, provides an account of a "riotous attack upon the St. Lawrence hotel" in Toronto "while the St. Patrick's Society was dining there" with Thomas D'Arcy McGee in their midst, who fortunately "escaped bodily injury at their hands" (4). Many novels that were serialized in Irish North American periodicals would also comment upon the violence used by nativists against Irish newcomers. The novel "Us Here; or, A Glimpse behind Know-Nothingness, by an Irish Collegian," printed in the *Irish-American* in the winter of 1857, contrasts the "frenzy" and relentless aggression of nativists with the conciliatory approach of the Catholic Irish community, personified by Father Eustace, who pleads for "confidence" in and support of the Democratic Party, "the only party that has steadily befriended the foreigner and been consistent in it advocacy of *equal rights for equal men*." See *Irish-American*, Feb. 21, 1857.

55. Quigley, *Cross and the Shamrock*, 117–18, 81, 80, 81.

56. Ibid., 173, 176; Percival, *The Irish Dove*, 244, 245.

57. "The Emigrant Ship," 509; Dorsey, *Nora Brady's Vow*, 86, 84, 86.

58. Sadlier, *Elinor Preston*, 226–27. Lower Canada contained the largest Catholic population, as opposed to Upper Canada, where at the time very "few of the English

population . . . are Catholics," apart from "a considerable number of Scotch Catholics." The number of French Canadians in Upper Canada was "supposed to be about 26,000; they are in general located at Ottawa City and on the banks of the Ottawa river." *A Brief View of the State of the Catholic Church in Upper Canada: By an Association of Irish Gentlemen*, 16.

59. For an explanation of these movements within Irish American Catholicism, see Kenny, *American Irish*, 164–65.

60. McCorry, *The Lost Rosary*, 61–63; Sadlier, *New Lights*, 407.

61. Sadlier, *Bessy Conway*, 22–23; McCaffrey, *Irish Catholic Diaspora in America*, 83–84, 45, 206, 211, 212, 3.

62. Mason, *Kate Gearey*, 146; O'Brien, *Ailey Moore*, 199–200.

63. Sadlier, *Bessy Conway*, 296. The fact that Sadlier appeals to the Irish immigrant girl to uphold their religious and moral duties is not surprising, since many Irish immigrants were young single women, 81 percent of whom came to make a living as domestic servants. See Donna Gabaccia, *From the Other Side: Women, Gender and Immigrant Life*, 47.

64. Sadlier, *Bessy Conway*, 205.

65. McCorry, *The Lost Rosary*, 62–64, 137.

66. Halley, *Speech Delivered at the Dinner of St. Patrick's Society*, 1.

67. Cohen, *Global Diasporas: An Introduction*, 7.

68. See Sudesh Mishra, *Diaspora Criticism*, 133.

69. Anderson, *Imagined Communities*, 16.

70. McCorry, *The Lost Rosary*, 54; Clington, *Frank O'Donnell*, 345.

71. Dorsey, *Nora Brady's Vow*, 84, 87.

72. Sadlier, *Bessy Conway*, 56, 57, 62; Corporaal and Cusack, "Rites of Passage," 355; Sadlier, *Bessy Conway*, 65; Corporaal and Cusack, "Rites of Passage," 355–57.

73. Sadlier, *Bessy Conway*, 207–8, 312.

74. Tierney, *Struggles of Dick Massey*, 226.

75. See Marjorie Howes, "Discipline, Sentiment and the Irish-American Public: Mary Ann Sadlier's Popular Fiction," 144. See also McCaffrey, *Textures of Irish America*, 1.

76. Tierney, *Struggles of Dick Massey*, 161; Ignatiev, *How the Irish Became White*, 5, 96, 137. The novel appears to exemplify that the assumption that "the Irish should have identified with another people who were undergoing dispossession, exploitation or racism—or, indeed, shown solidarity with oppressed people in general" is oversimplified. See Peter O'Neill and David Lloyd, introduction to *The Black and Green Atlantic: Cross-Currents in the African and Irish Diasporas*, xvii. For similar viewpoints, see David Lloyd, "Black Irish, Irish Whiteness and Atlantic State Formation."

77. Dorsey, *Nora Brady's Vow*, 96. Intriguingly, in the Famine novel *Poor Paddy's Cabin*, which was written in Ireland and informed by evangelical ideology, racial

mixing, also with Afro-Americans, is viewed as an essential good, for it helps convert the superstitious Irish from their enslavement by popery. In this novel, the storm at sea from which the Sheehans and their fellow travelers eventually emerge unscathed brings them into contact with a Protestant poor black woman on board who consoles the frightened Irish passengers by telling them to "Look to Jesus," who is the rock on which they will not *shiprach*." This encounter forms the onset to the Sheehans' adoption of the Protestant creed later in the novel. See "An Irishman," *Poor Paddy's Cabin*, 172.

78. Clington, *Frank O'Donnell*, 344.

79. Parts of this section were previously published in "Remigration in Irish and Irish Diaspora Famine Fiction, 1860–1870." These parts are reproduced here with kind permission of Notre Dame University Press.

80. *Desolation*, 7–8.

81. See James Fisher, *Communion of Immigrants: A History of Catholics in America*, 47. See also Kenny, *The American Irish*, 14.

82. As such, these works of fiction partially confirm Aidan Arrowmith's recent observation that "exile and return became central motifs around which nineteenth-century emigrants constructed Irish identities." Arrowsmith, "Imaginary Connections? Postmemory and Irish Diaspora Writing," 14.

83. See, for instance, Faist, *Volume and Dynamics*; and Huyssen, "Diaspora and Nation."

84. Tierney, *Struggles of Dick Massey*, 71, 192, 180.

85. Brettell, *Anthropology and Migration*, 18.

86. Potts, *Contemporary Irish Poetry*, 2.

87. Sadlier, *Bessy Conway*, 284.

88. Claudia Kinmonth, *Irish Rural Interiors in Art*, 7, 2.

89. E. Estyn Evans, *Irish Folk Ways*, 59.

90. Kinmonth, *Irish Rural Interiors in Art*, 12.

91. Adair, *Winter of 1846–7 in Antrim*, 16; Trollope, *Castle Richmond*, 330; *Widow O'Leary*, 10.

92. Clington, *Frank O'Donnell*, 492, 433, 496.

93. See Bammer, introduction to *Displacements*, xii.

94. Faist, *Volume and Dynamics*, 46.

95. See, for instance, Radstone, *Sexual Politics of Time*, 115.

96. Caruth, *Unclaimed Experience*, 7; Lloyd, *Irish Times*, 27.

97. Clington, *Frank O'Donnell*, 489; Tierney, *Struggles of Dick Massey*, 167, 196.

98. Frawley, "Toward a Theory of Cultural Memory," 31; Clington, *Frank O'Donnell*, 424.

99. Clington, *Frank O'Donnell*, 433; Maberly, *Present State of Ireland*, 29, 27.

100. Trigg, *Aesthetics of Decay*, 55–56.

101. Trigg, "Place of Trauma," 98.

102. O'Brien, *The Dalys of Dalystown*, 474, 526, 524, 521, 514.

103. Ibid., 515; Royle, *The Uncanny: An Introduction*, 1.

104. Connolly, *Cultural History of the Irish Novel*, 172.

105. See Julia M. Wright, *Ireland, India and Nationalism in Nineteenth-Century Literature*; and Christina Morin, "Recognisably Irish? The Diasporic Fiction of Regina Maria Roche."

106. Kickham, *Sally Cavanagh*, 198, 202.

107. Ibid., 209.

108. See McCaffrey, *Textures of Irish America*, 141–51. See also Timothy J. Meagher, *The Columbia Guide to Irish American History*, 240–50.

109. LaCapra, *Writing History, Writing Trauma*, 70.

Conclusion

1. Father Hugh Quigley, *Profit and Loss*, 284–85.

2. Landsberg, *Prosthetic Memory*, 3.

3. Rothberg, *Multidirectional Memory*, 13.

4. Relocated Remembrance: The Great Famine in Irish (Diaspora) Fiction, 1847–1921, grant agreement no. 262898–Famine.

5. Upton, *Uncle Pat's Cabin*, 133.

6. See also Christopher Cusack, "Famine Memory and Diasporic Identity in US Periodical Fiction, 1891–1918."

7. Brennan, *Erin Mór*, v.

Bibliography

Primary Texts

Famine Fiction

Bowles, Emily. *Irish Diamonds; or, The Chronicles of Peterstown.* London: Thomas Richardson and Son, 1864.

Brennan, John. *Erin Mór: The Story of Irish Republicanism.* San Francisco: P. M. Diers, 1892.

Brew, Margaret. *The Chronicles of Castle Cloyne.* London: Chapman and Hall, 1885.

Canada West [pseud.] *Tim Doolan; or, The Irish Emigrant.* London: Partridge, 1869.

Cannon, Charles. *Bickerton; or, The Immigrant's Daughter.* New York: P. O'Shea, 1855.

Carleton, William. *The Black Prophet: A Tale of Irish Famine.* London and Belfast: Simms and M'Intyre, 1847.

———. "Owen M'Carthy; or, The Landlord and Tenant." In *Alley Sheridan, and Other Stories,* 113–66. Dublin: P. Dixon Hardy and Sons, 1857.

———. *The Squanders of Castle Squander.* London: Office of the Illustrated London Library, 1852.

Cheney, Harriet Vaughan. "The Emigrants." *Literary Garland* 8, no. 2 (1850): 275–81.

Clayton, F. H. [An Irishman, pseud.]. *Scenes and Incidents in Irish Life.* Montreal: John Lovell, 1884.

Clington, Allen H. *Frank O'Donnell.* Dublin and London: James Duffy, 1861.

Curtis, Robert. "McCormack's Grudge." *Irish-American,* Sept. 20–27, 1862.

Cusack, Margaret Anna [Sister Mary Frances Clare, pseud.]. "From Killarney to New York; or, How Thade Became a Banker." *McGee's Illustrated Weekly* 2 (May–Nov. 1877).

Dorsey, Anna. *Nora Brady's Vow and Mona the Vestal*. Boston: Patrick Donahoe, 1869.

Dunbar, Jane Chaplin. *Gems of the Bog: A Tale of the Irish Peasantry*. Boston: American Tract Society, 1869.

"The Emigrant." *Catholic World* 11, no. 66 (1870): 800–806.

"The Emigrant Ship." *Literary Garland* 8, no. 11 (1850): 507–10.

Field, Mrs. E. M. *Denis: A Study in Black and White*. London and New York: Macmillan, 1896.

Hoare, Mrs. "The Black Potatoes." In *Shamrock Leaves; or, Tales and Sketches from Ireland*, 32–50. Dublin and London: J. M'Glashan, Patrick, and Oakey, 1851.

———. "Little Mary: A Tale of the Black Year." In *Shamrock Leaves; or, Tales and Sketches from Ireland*, 80–94. Dublin and London: J. M'Glashan, Patrick, and Oakey, 1851.

———. Preface to *Shamrock Leaves; or, Tales and Sketches from Ireland*, v–vi. Dublin and London: J. M'Glashan, Patrick, and Oakey, 1851.

———. "A Sketch of Famine." In *Shamrock Leaves; or, Tales and Sketches from Ireland*, 205–14. Dublin and London: J. M'Glashan, Patrick, and Oakey, 1851.

Ireland [pseud.]. "Narrative of Malcolm McGregor." *Northern Star*, Oct. 17–Dec. 16, 1846.

———. *A Tale of the Irish Famine in 1846 and 1847: Founded on Fact*. Reigate: William Allingham, 1847.

An Irishman [pseud.]. *The Irish Widow; or, A Picture from Life of Erin and Her Children*. London: Wertheim and Macintosh, 1855.

———. *Poor Paddy's Cabin; or, Slavery in Ireland*. London: Wertheim and MacIntosh, 1854.

Jones, T. Mason. *Old Trinity*. London: Richard Bentley, 1867.

Keary, Annie. *Castle Daly: The Story of an Irish Home Thirty Years Ago*. London: Macmillan, 1875.

Kickham, Charles Joseph. *Sally Cavanagh; or, The Untenanted Graves of Tipperary*. Dublin: J. J. Lalor, 1869.

Lawless, Emily. "After the Famine." In *Traits and Confidences*, 163–218. London: Methuen, 1898.

———. "Famine Roads and Memories " In *Traits and Confidences*, 142–63. London: Methuen, 1898.

Lever, Charles. *The Martins of Cro' Martin*. London: Chapman and Hall, 1856.

M. B. "Rose McCarthy's Sorrow." *Literary Garland* 8, no. 10 (1850): 463–65.

Mason, Miss. *Kate Gearey; or, Irish Life in London: A Tale of 1849*. London: Charles Dolman, 1853.

McCorry, Peter. *The Lost Rosary*. Boston: Patrick Donahoe, 1870.

McDougall, Margaret Dixon. *The Days of a Life*. Almonte: W. Templeman, 1883.

Meredith, Mrs. "Ellen Harrington." In *The Lacemakers*, 56–113. London: Jackson, Walford, and Hodder, 1865.

Monahan, Henry J. *O'Ruark; or, The Chronicles of the Balliquin Family*. Dublin: James Duffy, 1852.

Mulholland, Rosa. "The Hungry Death." In *Representative Irish Tales*, edited by W. B. Yeats, 367–96. London and New York: Putnam, 1891.

Nolan, Alice. *The Byrnes of Glengoulah: A True Tale*. New York: P. O'Shea, 1868.

Nunn, Mrs. Lorenzo. *Heirs of the Soil: A Tale*. Dublin and London: Moffat, 1870.

O'Brien, Dillon. *The Dalys of Dalystown*. St. Paul, MN: Pioneer, 1866.

O'Brien, Richard Baptist. *Ailey Moore: A Tale of the Times*. London: Charles Dolman, 1856.

O'Ryan, Julia, and Edmund O'Ryan. *In re Garland: A Tale of a Transition Time*. London: Thomas Richardson and Son, 1870.

Paddy's Leisure Hours in the Poor House; or, Priests, Parsons, Potatoes and Poor Rates. Dublin: Hodges and Smith, 1849.

Peppergrass, Paul [John Boyce]. *Shandy M'Guire; or, Tricks upon Travelers, Being a Story of the North of Ireland*. Boston: Patrick Donahoe, 1853.

Percival, Margaret. *The Irish Dove*. Dublin: John Robertson, 1849.

Quigley, Father Hugh. *The Cross and the Shamrock*. Boston: Patrick Donahoe, 1853.

———. *Profit and Loss*. New York: T. O'Kane, 1873.

Sadlier, Mrs. J. *Bessy Conway; or, The Irish Girl in America*. New York: D. and J. Sadlier, 1862.

———. *The Blakes and Flanagans: A Tale Illustrative of Irish Life in the United States*. New York and Boston: D. and J. Sadlier, 1858.

———. *Con O'Regan; or, Emigrant Life in the New World*. New York: D. and J. Sadlier, 1864.

———. *Elinor Preston: or, Scenes at Home and Abroad*. New York: D. and J. Sadlier, 1861.

———. *New Lights; or, Life in Galway.* New York: D. and J. Sadlier, 1853.

Sheehan, Canon Patrick. *Glenanaar: A Story of Irish Life.* London: Longmans, Green, 1905.

Sigerson, Hester. *A Ruined Race; or, The Last Macmanus of Dumroosk.* London: Ward and Downey, 1889.

Synon, Mary. "My Grandmother and Myself." *Scribner's Magazine* (Aug. 1916): 224–33.

T. L. N. "Captain Patrick Malony; or, The Irishman in Alabama." *Pilot,* June 2–23, 1860.

Tierney, Reginald [Thomas O'Neill Russell]. *The Struggles of Dick Massey; or, The Battles of a Boy.* Dublin: James Duffy, 1860.

Townley, D. O'C. "The Tale of a Tombstone." *Catholic World* 24, no. 4 (1867): 792–804.

Trollope, Anthony. *Castle Richmond.* London: Chapman and Hall, 1860.

Tynan, Katharine. "A Village Priest." In *A Cluster of Nuts: Being Sketches among My Own People,* 231–42. London: Lawrence and Bullen, 1894.

Upton, W. C. *Uncle Pat's Cabin; or, Life among the Agricultural Labourers of Ireland.* Dublin: M. H. Gill, 1882.

Walshe, Elizabeth Hely. *Golden Hills: A Tale of the Irish Famine.* London: Religious Tracts Society, 1865.

The Widow O'Leary: A Story of the Present Famine. Cork: G. Nash, 1847.

Wills, William Gorman. *The Love That Kills: A Novel.* London: John Milner, 1867.

Other Texts

Adair, R. A. Shafto. *The Winter of 1846–7 in Antrim, with Remarks on Outdoor Relief and Colonization.* London: James Ridgway, 1847.

Allison, William Pulteney. *Observations on the Famine of 1846–7, in the Highlands of Scotland and in Ireland.* Edinburgh and London: William Blackwood and Sons, 1847.

American Citizens! We Appeal to You in All Calmness. Is it Not Time to Pause? Boston: J. E. Farwell, 1852.

"The American Irish." *Irish People,* Nov. 12, 1864.

"Another Potato Famine: Emigration to New Brunswick Should Be Encouraged." *Morning Freeman,* Oct. 19, 1861.

A Barrister [pseud.]. *What Have the Whigs Done for Ireland? or, The English Whigs and the Irish Famine*. Dublin: Edward J. Millihen, 1851.

Bennett, William. *Narrative of a Recent Journey of Six Weeks in Ireland*. London: Gilpin, 1847.

Benningham, Thomas. *The Thames, the Shannon and the St. Lawrence; or, The Good of Great Britain*. London: Messrs. Fores, 1847.

Bicheno, J. E. *Ireland and Its Economy*. London: Murray, 1830.

A Brief View of the State of the Catholic Church in Upper Canada: By an Association of Irish Gentlemen. Toronto: n.p., 1858.

Burke, Edmund. *A Philosophical Enquiry into the Origin of Our Ideas of the Sublime and Beautiful*. London: R. and J. Dodsley, 1757.

Butt, Isaac. *Land Tenure in Ireland: A Plea for the Celtic Race*. Dublin: John Falconer, 1866.

"Canada and Ireland." *Duffy's Hibernian Sixpenny Magazine*, Apr. 4, 1862.

Carlyle, Thomas. *Reminiscences of My Irish Journey in 1849*. New York: Harper and Sons, 1882.

"Castle Richmond." *Spectator* 33 (1860): 477.

Chambers, Robert. *Cyclopaedia of English Literature*. Vol. 2. London and Edinburgh: William and Robert Chambers, 1857.

Chatterton, Henrietta. *Rambles in the South of Ireland during the Year 1838*. Vol. 2. London: Saunders and Otley, 1839.

Cheney, Harriet Vaughan. "Sketches on a Journey." *Literary Garland* 7, no. 8 (1849): 376–79.

Child, Lydia Maria. "The Irish Heart." In *Fact and Fiction*, 77–91. Boston: Munroe and Francis, 1846.

Christmas 1846 and the New Year 1847 in Ireland: Letters by a Lady. Durham: G. Andrews, 1847.

"Condition of Ireland: Illustrations of the New Poor Law." *Illustrated London News*, Dec. 15, 1849.

Corrigan, D. J. *On Famine and Fever as Cause and Effect in Ireland*. Dublin: J. Fannin, 1846.

Cromwell, Thomas Kitson. *The Irish Tourist; or, Excursions through Ireland*. London: Darton and Harvey, 1837.

Cullen, Paul. *The Making of the Roman Catholic Church in Ireland, 1850–1860*. Edited by Emmett Larkin. Chapel Hill: Univ. of North Carolina Press, 1980.

Cummins, J. J. *On! On! Erin! On!* New York: H. de Marsan, 1859.
Curwen, John. *Observations on the State of Ireland.* London: Baldwin, 1818.
Davin, Nicholas Flood. *The Irishman in Canada.* London: Sampson Low, Marston, 1877.
Desolation: A Story of the Irish Famine. London: Nisbet, 1869.
Dewees, William B. *Letters from an Early Settler of Texas.* Louisville, KY: Hull and Brother, 1854.
Doolan, Thomas. *Practical Suggestions on the Improvement of the Present Condition of the Peasantry of Ireland.* London: George Barclay, 1847.
Dufferin, Helen Selina. "The Emigrant Ship." In *Songs, Poems and Verses,* 189. Dublin: Murray, 1894.
Dufferin, Lord. *Irish Emigration and the Tenure of Land in Ireland.* London: Willis, Sotheran, 1867.
Dufferin, Lord, and G. F. Boyle. *Narrative of a Journey from Oxford to Skibbereen, in the Year of the Famine.* Oxford: John Henry Parker, 1847.
"The Emigrant's Mother." *Literary Garland* 8, no. 6 (1850): 274.
"The Famine in Ireland." *Pilot,* Jan. 25, 1862.
The Farmer of Inniscreen: A Tale of the Irish Famine, in Verse. London: Jarrold and Sons, 1863.
The Feast of Famine: An Irish Banquet, with Other Poems. London: Chapman and Hall, 1870.
Fitzpatrick, W. J. *The Life of Charles Lever.* London and New York: Ward, Lock, 1884.
Forbes, John. *Memorandums Made in Ireland in the Autumn of 1852.* London: Smith and Elder, 1853.
Forbes, Robert Bennett. *The* Jamestown *on Her Errand of Mercy.* Boston: Eastburn's Press, 1847.
Gilpin, William. *Three Essays: On Picturesque Beauty, on Picturesque Travel, and on Sketching Landscape.* London: T. Balmire, 1794.
Grosse-Isle Emigrant Station: A Letter Addressed to the Inspectors of Hospitals, Prisons and Asylums. Quebec: J. T. Brousseau, 1861.
Hale, Edward E. *Letters on Irish Emigration.* Boston: Philips, Sampson, 1852.
Hall, Spencer T. *Life and Death in Ireland, as Witnessed in 1849.* Manchester: Parkes, 1850.
Halley, William. *Speech Delivered at the Dinner of St. Patrick's Society, Toronto, on the 17th of March, 1860, in Response to the Sentiment of "the Irish Race at Home and Abroad."* Toronto: n.p., 1860.

Hancock, W. Neilson. *On the Causes of Distress at Skull and Skibbereen during the Famine in Ireland.* Dublin: Hodges and Smith, 1850.

Hughes, John. "The Importance of Being in Communion with Christ's One Holy, Catholic and Apostolic Church." In *Complete Works of the Most Rev. Archbishop John Hughes,* 1:583–90. New York: Lawrence Kehoe, 1866.

Ireland and Her Famine: A Discourse, Preached in Paradise Street Chapel, Liverpool, on Sunday, January 31, 1847 by James Martineau. London: John Chapman, 1847.

"The Irish Emigrant's Lament." *Pilot,* Jan. 23, 1858.

Irish Improvidence Encouraged by English Bounty. London: James Ridgway, 1847.

Irish Pictures: Eighty Sketches Taken on the Spot by F. Dadd, M. Fitzgerald, Harry Furiss, Wallis Mackay and Procter and R. C. Woodville, Republished from the "Illustrated London News." London: Vizetelly, 1870.

"The Irish Soldier in America." *Emerald,* July 17, 1869.

John, Earl of Shrewesbury. *Thoughts on the Poor Relief Bill for Ireland, Together with Reflections on Their Miseries, Their Causes, and Their Remedies.* London: Charles Dolman, 1847.

Lawless, Emily. *Ireland.* London: T. Fisher Unwin, 1891.

———. *The Story of the Nations: Ireland.* London: T. Fisher Unwin, 1887.

Leighton, John M. *History of the County of Fife, from the Earliest Period to the Present Time.* Vol. 2. Glasgow: Joseph Swan, 1840.

Lenihan, Maurice. *Limerick: Its History and Antiquities, Ecclesiastical, Civil, and Military.* Dublin: Hodges, Smith, 1866.

Lewis, Samuel. *A Topographical Dictionary of Wales.* London: S. Lewis, 1833.

Lloyd, M. A. *Susanna Meredith: A Record of a Vigorous Life.* London: Hodder and Stoughton, 1903.

Maberly, Mrs. *The Present State of Ireland and Its Remedy.* London: James Ridgway, 1847.

Mackintosh, D. "Comparative Anthropology of England and Wales." *Anthropological Review* 12 (1866): 1–22.

Maguire, John Francis. *The Irish in America.* New York: D. and J. Sadlier, 1868.

Mahoney, James. "Sketches in the West of Ireland." *Illustrated London News,* Feb. 13, 1847.

———. "Sketches in the West of Ireland." *Illustrated London News,* Feb. 20, 1847.

Maley, Andrew John. *Observations upon the Inability of Exterminating the Resident Landlord of Ireland.* Dublin: Hodges and Smith, 1849.

Mangan, James Clarence. "A Voice of Encouragement: A New Year's Lay." In *Poems of James Clarence Mangan, Many Hitherto Uncollected,* 100–103. Dublin: M. H. Gill, 1922.

———. "The Warning Voice." In *Poems by James Clarence Mangan, with Biographical Introduction by John Mitchel,* 437–41. New York: P. M. Haverty, 1859.

Martineau, Harriet. "The Famine Time." *Household Words* 6, no. 138 (1852): 315.

Maturin, Charles. *Melmoth the Wanderer: A Tale.* Edinburgh: Archibald Constable, 1820.

Mayhew, Henry. *London Labour and the London Poor: The London Street-Folk.* London: Griffin, Bohn, 1861.

McGee, Thomas D'Arcy. "Dream Journeys." In *The Poems of Thomas D'Arcy McGee, with Copious Notes: With an Introduction and Biographical Sketch of the Author by Mrs. J. Sadlier,* 141. New York: D. and J. Sadlier, 1869.

———. "The Exile's Meditation." In *The Poems of Thomas D'Arcy McGee, with Copious Notes,* 105–6. New York: D. and J. Sadlier, 1869.

———. "The Irish Wife." In *The Ballads of Ireland,* edited by Edward Hayes, 1–2. London and Dublin: A. Fullerton, 1855.

———. "The Social Duties of Irishmen in America." *American Celt,* July 23, 1853.

McNeile, Hugh. *The Famine a Rod of God: Its Provoking Cause—Its Merciful Design.* London: Burnside and Seeley, 1847.

Mitchel, John. *The History of Ireland, from the Treaty of Limerick to the Present Time.* Glasgow: Cameron and Ferguson, 1859.

———. *Ireland since '98: Daniel O'Connell; The Repeal Agitation; The Miseries of the Famine; The Young Ireland Party, Etc.* Glasgow: Cameron and Ferguson, 1871.

———. *Jail Journal; or, Five Years in British Prisons.* New York: Office of the "Citizen," 1854.

———. *The Last Conquest of Ireland (Perhaps).* Dublin: Irishman Office, 1861.

Montgomery, William Ernest. *The History of Land Tenure in Ireland.* Cambridge: Cambridge Univ. Press, 1889.

Mount Leinster, a Poem, Descriptive of Irish Scenery. London: Longman, Hurst, Ree, Orme, and Browne, 1819.

Nast, Thomas. "The Ignorant Vote—Honors Are Easy." *Harper's Weekly*, Dec. 9, 1876.

Newton, Henry T. *Canada in 1864: A Hand-Book for Settlers*. London: Sampson Low, 1864.

"The New Year for Ireland." *Irish Pictorial*, Jan. 26, 1861.

Nicholson, Asenath. *Annals of the Famine in Ireland in 1847, 1848 and 1849*. New York: E. French, 1851.

O'Callohan, David. "Will He Return." *Emerald*, Oct. 2, 1869.

"The Old Homestead." *Emerald*, Feb. 26, 1870.

O'Reilly, John Boyle. "Our Own Green Island Home." *Emerald*, Feb. 19, 1870.

O'Rourke, John. *The History of the Great Irish Famine of 1847, with Notices of Earlier Irish Famines*. Dublin: M'Glashan and Gill, 1875.

Osborne, Sidney Godolphin. *Gleanings in the West of Ireland*. London: T. and W. Boone, 1850.

Owenson, Sidney, Lady Morgan. *The Wild Irish Girl: A National Tale*. London: Richard Philips, 1806.

"The Philosophy of Immigration." *Catholic World* 9, no. 53 (1869): 2.

"The Potato Disease." *Illustrated London News*, Oct. 18, 1845.

Price, Sir Uvedale. "Essay on Architecture and Buildings." In *Essays on the Picturesque, as Compared with the Sublime and the Beautiful*, 2:171–370. London: J. Mawman, 1810.

"The Protestant Propaganda." *Pilot*, Mar. 13, 1858.

"Protestant Violence in Canada." *Pilot*, Apr. 3, 1858.

Pym, Jonathan. *Observations on the Evils Resulting to Ireland*. Dublin: Hodges and Smith, 1847.

Radcliffe, Ann. *The Mysteries of Udolpho: A Romance*. London: J. Limbird, 1824.

Rawlins, C. A. *The Famine in Ireland: A Poem*. London: Joseph Masters, 1847.

Rawsterne, Lawrence, Esq. *The Cause of the Potato Disease: Ascertained by Proofs*. London: Simpkin, Marshall, 1847.

Robinson, John Travers. *A Sermon Preached in St. Leonard's Chapel, Newton Abbott, Devonshire*. Feignmouth: E. and G. H. Croydon, 1847.

Robinson, W. W. *The Dawn of Ireland's Prosperity: General Employment; Blight of the Potato Crop; A Visitation*. Dublin: John Robertson, 1847.

Ryan, F. B. *The Spirit's Lament; or, The Wrongs of Ireland*. Montreal: J. Starke, 1847.

Scrope, G. Poulett. *Letters to Lord John Russell, M.P.: On the Further Measures Required for the Social Amelioration of Ireland.* London: James Ridgway, 1847.

Sikes, Wilbert. "In the Five Points." *Harper's New Monthly* 26 (1868): 223–26.

Smith, William Henry. *A Twelve Months' Residence in Ireland during the Famine and the Public Works, 1846 and 1847.* London: Longman, 1848.

"The Social Duties of Irishmen in America." *American Celt*, July 23, 1853.

"Society for Land Traffic in Ireland." *Spectator*, Aug. 5, 1848.

Southey, Robert. *Life of Oliver Cromwell.* New York: D. Appleton, 1845.

"The State of Ireland." *Blackwood's Edinburgh Magazine* 33 (1831): 467–84.

Strickland, Major. *Twenty-Seven Years in Canada West; or, The Experience of an Early Settler.* Edmonton: M. G. Hurtig, 1853.

Sullivan, A. M. *New Ireland: Political Sketches and Personal Reminiscences of Thirty Years of Irish Public Life.* Glasgow and London: Cameron and Ferguson, 1877.

Traill, Mrs. C. P. *The Canadian Emigrant Housekeeper's Guide.* Montreal: James Lovell, 1861.

Trevelyan, Charles. *The Irish Crisis.* London: Longman, Brown, Green, and Longmans, 1848.

———. "Letter of Charles Edward Trevelyan to Thomas Spring-Rice, Lord Mounteagle." Treasury, Oct. 9, 1846.

Turner, Frederick Jackson. *The Frontier in American History.* 1893. Reprint, Mineola, NY: Dover, 1996.

"Two Sides to a Question." *O'Neill's Irish Pictorial*, Mar. 5, 1859.

"Us Here; or, A Glimpse behind Know-Nothingness, by an Irish Collegian." *Irish-American*, Feb. 21, 1857.

Varian, Elizabeth Willoughby. "Proselytizing." In *Poems by "Finola,"* 41. Belfast: John Henderson, 1851.

Watson, Rigby, Esq. *Letter to the Right Honourable Lord John Russell, M.P.* Edinburgh: W. F. Watson, 1847.

What Irish Boys Can Do: An Answer to "No Irish Need Apply." New York: James Wrigley, 1864.

Whyte, Robert. *The Ocean's Plague; or, A Voyage to Quebec in an Irish Emigrant Vessel.* Boston: Coolidge and Wiley, 1848.

Wills, Freeman. *Life of W. G. Wills.* London: Longmans, Green, 1898.

Wordsworth, William. "Lines Composed a Few Miles above Tintern Abbey." In *Lyrical Ballads, with a Few Other Poems*, edited by William

Wordsworth and Samuel Taylor Coleridge, 201–2. London: J. and A. Arch, 1798.

Secondary Literature

Abbinnett, Ross. *Culture and Identity: Critical Theories*. London: Sage, 2003.

Agnew, John. "Landscape and National Identity in Europe: England versus Italy in the Role of Landscape in Identity Formation." In *Landscapes, Identities and Development*, edited by Zoran Roca et al., 37–51. Farnham: Ashgate, 2011.

Aguirre, Manuel. "Liminal Terror: The Poetics of Gothic Space." In *The Dynamics of the Threshold: Essays on Liminal Negotiations*, edited by Jesús Benito and Ana M. Manzanas, 13–38. Madrid: Gateway Press, 2007.

Aldama, Arthuro J. "Violence, Bodies, and the Color of Fear: An Introduction." In *Violence and the Body: Race, Gender, and the State*, edited by Arthuro J. Aldama, 1–39. Bloomington: Indiana Univ. Press, 2003.

Alexander, Jeffrey C. "Toward a Theory of Cultural Trauma." In *Cultural Trauma and Collective Identity*, edited by Jeffrey C. Alexander et al., 1–22. Berkeley: Univ. of California Press, 2004.

al-Ali, Nadje, and Khalid Koser. "Transnationalism, International Migration and Home." In *New Approaches to Migration? Transnational Communities and the Transformation of Home*, edited by Nadje al-Ali and Khalid Koser, 1–15. London and New York: Routledge, 2002.

Alpers, Paul. *What Is Pastoral?* Chicago: Univ. of Chicago Press, 1996.

Alphen, Ernst van. "Symptoms of Discursivity: Experience, Memory and Trauma." In *Acts of Memory: Cultural Recall in the Present*, edited by Mieke Bal et al., 24–39. Hanover, NH: Univ. Press of New England, 1999.

Altman, Rick. *A Theory of Narrative*. New York: Columbia Univ. Press, 2008.

Anderson, Benedict. *Imagined Communities: Reflections on the Origin and Spread of Nationalism*. London and New York: Verso, 1987.

"Anna Hanson Dorsey." In *Catholic Encyclopedia*, edited by Charles Herbermann, 5:116. New York: Robert Appleton, 1913.

Appadurai, Arjun. "Global Ethnoscapes: Notes and Queries for a Transnational Anthropology." In *Recapturing Anthropology: Working in the Present*, edited by Richard G. Fox, 191–211. Santa Fe, NM: School of American Research Press, 1991.

Arrowsmith, Aidan. "Imaginary Connections? Postmemory and Irish Diaspora Writing." In *Memory Ireland*. Vol. 2, *Diaspora and Memory Practices*, edited by Oona Frawley, 12–24. Syracuse, NY: Syracuse Univ. Press, 2012.

Assmann, Aleida, and Sebastian Conrad. Introduction to *Memory in a Global Age: Discourses, Practices and Trajectories*, edited by Aleida Assmann and Sebastian Conrad, 1–17. Basingstoke: Palgrave Macmillan, 2010.

Assmann, Jan. "Collective Memory and Cultural Identity." *New German Critique* 65 (1995): 125–33.

Bammer, Angelika. Introduction to *Displacements: Cultural Identities in Question*, edited by Angelika Bammer, xi–xxi. Bloomington: Indiana Univ. Press, 1994.

Bartoletti, Susan Campbell. *Black Potatoes: The Story of the Great Irish Famine, 1845–1850*. New York: Houghton Mifflin, 2001.

Beiner, Guy. *Remembering the Year of the French: Irish Folk History and Social Memory*. Madison: Univ. of Wisconsin Press, 2007.

Bell, Aldon D. "Administration and Finance of the Reform League, 1865–1867." *International Review of Social History* 10 (1965): 385–409.

Bender, Barbara. *Landscape, Politics and Perspectives*. Oxford: Berg, 1993.

Bhabha, Homi. *The Location of Culture*. London: Routledge, 2004.

Bigelow, Gordon. *Fiction, Famine, and the Rise of Economics in Victorian Britain and Ireland*. Cambridge: Cambridge Univ. Press, 2003.

———. "Trollope and Ireland." In *The Cambridge Companion to Anthony Trollope*, edited by Carolyn Dever and Lisa Niles, 196–210. Cambridge: Cambridge Univ. Press, 2011.

Bilby, Joseph G. *The Irish Brigade in the Civil War: The 69th New York and Other Irish Regiments of the Army of the Potomac*. Cambridge, MA: Da Capo, 1997.

Blackman, Lisa. *Immaterial Bodies: Affect, Embodiment, Mediation*. London: Sage, 2012.

Bohleber, Werner. *Destructiveness, Intersubjectivity and Trauma: The Identity Crisis of Modern Psychoanalysis*. London: Karnac Books, 2010.

Bond, Lucy, and Jessica Rapson. Introduction to *The Transcultural Turn: Interrogating Memory between and beyond Borders*, edited by Lucy Bond and Jessica Rapson, 1–26. Berlin: de Gruyter, 2014.

Boym, Svetlana. "Ruins of the Avant-Garde: From Tatlin's Tower to Paper Architecture." In *Ruins of Modernity*, edited by Julia Hell and Andreas Schönle, 58–87. Durham, NC: Duke Univ. Press, 2010.

Brady, Anne M., and Brian Cleeve, eds. *A Biographical Dictionary of Irish Writers*. Gigginstown: Lilliput Press, 1985.

Braziel, Jana Evans, and Anita Mannur. Introduction to *Theorizing Diaspora*, edited by Jana Evans Braziel and Anita Mannur, 1–22. Malden, MA: Blackwell, 2003.

Brettell, Caroline. *Anthropology and Migration: Essays on Transnationalism, Ethnicity, and Identity*. Walnut Creek, CA: Alta Mira Press, 2003.

Brewster, Scott. "Seeing Things: Gothic and the Madness of Interpretation." In *A New Companion to the Gothic*, edited by David Punter, 481–95. Malden, MA: Blackwell, 2012.

Brewster, Scott, and Virginia Crossman. "Re-writing the Famine: Witnessing in Crisis." In *Ireland in Proximity: History, Gender, Space*, edited by Scott Brewster et al., 42–59. London: Routledge, 1999.

Brown, Bill. *A Sense of Things: The Object Matter of American Literature*. Chicago: Univ. of Chicago Press, 2003.

Brown, S. J. M. *Ireland in Fiction*. Dublin and London: Maunsel, 1919.

Buell, Lawrence. *The Future of Environmental Criticism: Environmental Crisis and Literary Imagination*. London: Blackwell, 2005.

Byrne, James, Philip Coleman, and Jason King, eds. *Ireland and the Americas: Culture, Politics and History, a Multidisciplinary Encyclopaedia*. Vol. 1. Santa Barbara, CA: ABC-CLIO, 2008.

Callaghan, Daniel M. *Thomas Francis Meagher and the Irish Brigade in the Civil War*. Jefferson, NC: McFarland, 2006.

Callon, D. J. *Converting Catholicism: Orestes A. Brownson, Anna H. Dorsey, and Irish America, 1840–1896*. St. Louis: Washington Univ., 2008.

Caruth, Cathy. "Recapturing the Past: Introduction." In *Trauma: Explorations in Memory*, edited by Cathy Caruth, 151–57. Baltimore: Johns Hopkins Univ. Press, 1995.

———. *Unclaimed Experience: Trauma, Narrative, and History*. Baltimore: Johns Hopkins Univ. Press, 1996.

Chalker, John. *The English Georgic: A Study in the Development of a Form*. Baltimore: Johns Hopkins Univ. Press, 1969.

Claval, Paul. "Changing Conceptions of Heritage and Landscape." In *Heritage, Memory and the Politics of Identity: New Perspectives on the Cultural Landscape*, edited by Niamh Moore and Yvonne Whelan, 85–95. Aldershot: Ashgate, 2007.

Cohen, Robin. *Global Diasporas: An Introduction*. London: Routledge, 2008.

Conley, Carolyn. *Melancholy Accidents: The Meaning of Violence in Post-Famine Ireland*. Oxford: Lexington Books, 1999.

Connolly, Claire. *A Cultural History of the Irish Novel, 1790–1829*. Cambridge: Cambridge Univ. Press, 2012.

Corporaal, Marguérite. "Black Patches and Rotting Weeds: The Great Famine as a Transcultural Figure of Memory in Irish (Diaspora) Fiction, 1860–1880." In *The Transcultural Turn: Interrogating Memory between and beyond Borders*, edited by Jessica Rapson and Lucy Bond, 247–66. Berlin: de Gruyter, 2014.

———. "From Golden Hills to Sycamore Trees: Pastoral Homelands and Ethnic Identity in Irish Immigrant Fiction, 1860–1875." *Irish Studies Review* 18, no. 3 (2010): 331–46.

———. "Haunted by Hunger: Images of Spectrality in Literary Recollections of the Great Irish Famine, 1850–1900." In *Performances of Memory in the Arts*, edited by Anneke Smelik and Liedeke Plate, 92–104. London: Routledge, 2013.

———. "'Let Any One Try to Picture What It Is': The Dynamics of the Irish Short Story and the Mediation of Famine Trauma, 1850–1865." In *The Irish Short Story: Traditions and Trends*, edited by Elke D'Hoker and Stephanie Eggermont, 21–43. Oxford: Peter Lang, 2015.

———. "Memories of the Great Famine and Ethnic Identity in Novels by Victorian Irish Women Writers." *English Studies* 90, no. 2 (2009): 1–15.

———. "'The Recollection of Sorrow and Misery Past': Memories of the Great Famine in Irish North-American Fiction, 1855–1870." In *Irish Hunger and Emigration: Myth, Memory and Memorialization*, edited by Christine Kinealy, Patrick Fitzgerald, and Gerard Moran, 83–95. Hamden, CT: Quinnipiac Univ. Press, 2015.

———. "Remigration in Irish and Irish Diaspora Famine Fiction, 1860–1870." *Breac: A Digital Journal of Irish Studies* 1, no. 1 (2013). http://breac.nd.edu/articles/36996-remigration-in-irish-and-irish-diaspora-famine-fiction-1860-1870/.

Corporaal, Marguérite, and Christopher Cusack. "Rites of Passage: The Coffin Ship as Site of Immigrants' Identity Formation in Irish and Irish-American Fiction, 1855–1885." *Atlantic Studies* 8, no. 3 (2011): 343–59.

Cosgrove, Denis. "Introduction to Social Formation and Symbolical Landscape." In *Landscape Theory*, edited by James Elkins and Rachel DeLue, 17–43. London: Routledge, 2008.

Crowley, John. "Constructing Famine Memory: The Role of Monuments." In *Heritage, Memory and the Politics of Identity: New Perspectives on the Cultural Landscape*, edited by Niamh Moore and Yvonne Whelan, 55–69. Aldershot: Ashgate, 2007.

Crowley, John, William J. Smyth, and Mike Murphy, eds. *Atlas of the Great Irish Famine, 1845–52*. Cork: Cork Univ. Press, 2012.

Cusack, Christopher. "Famine Memory and Diasporic Identity in US Periodical Fiction, 1891–1918." *Symbiosis: A Journal of Transatlantic Literary and Cultural Relations* 19, no. 2 (2015): 153–69.

Cusack, Christopher, and Lindsay Janssen. "Death in the Family: Reimagining the Irish Family in Famine Fiction, 1871–1912." In *New Voices, Inherited Lines: Literary and Cultural Representations of the Irish Family*, edited by Yvonne O'Keeffe and Claudia Reese, 7–34. Oxford: Peter Lang, 2013.

Daase, Christopher. "Addressing Painful Memories: Apologies as a New Practice in International Relations." In *Memory in a Global Age: Discourses, Practices and Trajectories*, edited by Aleida Assmann and Sebastian Conrad, 19–31. Basingstoke: Palgrave Macmillan, 2010.

Dailey, C. E., Jr. "Dillon O'Brien, Novelist." In *The Dalys of Dalystown*, edited by C. E. Dailey, 527–39. St. Paul, MN: Pioneer, 2004.

Daly, Mary E. *Social and Economic History of Ireland since 1800*. Dublin: Educational Company of Ireland, 1981.

Davis, Colin. "Hauntology, Spectres and Phantoms." *French Studies* 59, no. 3 (2005): 373–79.

Dawson, Graham. *Making Peace with the Past? Memory, Trauma and the Irish Troubles*. Manchester: Manchester Univ. Press, 2008.

DeLamotte, Eugenia. *Perils of the Night: A Feminist Study of Nineteenth-Century Gothic*. Oxford: Oxford Univ. Press, 1990.

Derrida, Jacques. *Spectres de Marx*. Paris: Édition Galilée, 1993.

Dewar-Watson, Sarah. *Tragedy*. Basingstoke: Palgrave, 2014.

Dolan, Jay P. *The Irish Americans: A History*. New York: Bloomsbury Press, 2008.

Donnelly, James S., Jr. *The Great Irish Potato Famine*. Stroud: Sutton, 2003.

Dubois, Page. "Sappho's Body in Pieces." In *Textual Bodies: Changing Boundaries of Literary Representation*, edited by Lori Hope Lefkovitz, 19–33. Albany: State Univ. of New York, 1997.

Eagleton, Terry. *Heathcliff and the Great Hunger: Studies in Irish Culture*. London: Verso, 1995.

Egenolf, Susan. *The Art of Political Fiction in Hamilton, Edgeworth and Owenson*. Farnham: Ashgate, 2009.

Elliott, Bruce S. *Irish Migrants in the Canadas: A New Approach*. Montreal: McGill-Queen's Univ. Press, 2004.

Emmons, David. *Beyond the American Pale: The Irish in the West, 1845–1910*. Norman: Univ. of Oklahoma Press, 2010.

Erll, Astrid. "Narratology and Cultural Memory Studies." In *Narratology in the Age of Cross-Disciplinary Narrative Research*, edited by Sandra Heinen and Roy Sommer, 212–28. Berlin: de Gruyter, 2009.

———. "Regional Integration and (Trans)cultural Memory." *Asia Europe Journal* 8 (2010): 305–15.

———. "Re-writing as Re-visioning: Modes of Representing the 'Indian Mutiny' in British Novels, 1857 to 2000." *European Journal of English Studies* 10, no. 2 (2006): 163–85.

———. "Travelling Memory." In *Transcultural Memory*, edited by Rick Crownshaw, 20–24. London: Routledge, 2014.

———. "Travelling Memory." *Parallax* 17, no. 4 (2011): 4–18.

Erll, Astrid, and Ann Rigney. "Literature and the Production of Cultural Memory: Introduction." *European Journal of English Studies* 10, no. 2 (2006): 111–15.

Ethington, Philip. "Placing the Past: 'Groundwork' for a Spatial Theory of History." *Rethinking History* 11 (2007): 465–95.

Evans, E. Estyn. *Irish Folk Ways*. London: Routledge and Paul, 1957.

Eyerman, Ron. "Cultural Trauma: Slavery and the Formation of African American Identity." In *Cultural Trauma and Collective Identity*, edited by Jeffrey Alexander et al., 60–112. Berkeley: Univ. of California Press, 2004.

Faist, Thomas. *The Volume and Dynamics of International Migration and Transnational Social Spaces*. Oxford: Oxford Univ. Press, 2000.

Fanning, Charles. *Exiles of Erin: Nineteenth-Century Irish-American Fiction*. Notre Dame, IN: Univ. of Notre Dame Press, 1987.

———. *The Irish Voice in America: 250 Years of Irish American Fiction*. Lexington: Univ. Press of Kentucky, 2000.

Fegan, Melissa. *Literature and the Irish Famine, 1845–1919*. Oxford: Oxford Univ. Press, 2002.

Felman, Shoshana. "Women and Madness: The Critical Phallacy." In *Feminisms: An Anthology of Literary Theory and Criticism*, edited by Robyn

Warhol and Diane Price Herndl, 7–21. New Brunswick, NJ: Rutgers Univ. Press, 1997.

Ferris, Ina. *The Romantic National Tale and the Question of Ireland.* Cambridge: Cambridge Univ. Press, 2002.

Feuchtwang, Stephan. "Loss: Transmissions, Recognitions, Authorisations." In *Regimes of Memory*, edited by Susannah Radstone and Katharine Hodgkin, 76–89. London: Routledge, 2003.

Fisher, James. *Communion of Immigrants: A History of Catholics in America.* Oxford: Oxford Univ. Press, 2002.

Fitzpatrick, David. "Flight from Famine." In *The Great Irish Famine*, edited by Cathal Póirtéir, 174–85. Cork and Dublin: Mercier Press, 1995.

Fludernik, Monika. *Towards a "Natural" Narratology.* London: Routledge, 1996.

Foster, Roy. "Remembering 1798." In *History and Memory in Modern Ireland*, edited by Ian MacBride, 67–95. Cambridge: Cambridge Univ. Press, 2001.

Foucault, Michel. "Of Other Spaces." *Diacritics* 16 (1986): 22–27.

Frawley, Oona. "Cruxes in Irish Cultural Memory: The Famine and the Troubles." In *Memory Ireland.* Introduction to vol. 3, *The Famine and the Troubles*, edited by Oona Frawley, 1–17. Syracuse, NY: Syracuse Univ. Press, 2014.

———. Introduction to *Memory Ireland.* Vol. 2, *Diaspora and Memory Practices*, edited by Oona Frawley, 1–11. Syracuse, NY: Syracuse Univ. Press, 2012.

———. *Irish Pastoral: Nostalgia and Twentieth-Century Irish Literature.* Dublin: Irish Academic Press, 2005.

———, ed. *Memory Ireland.* 4 vols. Syracuse, NY: Syracuse Univ. Press, 2010–14.

———. "Toward a Theory of Cultural Memory in an Irish Postcolonial Context." In *Memory Ireland.* Vol. 1, *History and Modernity*, edited by Oona Frawley, 18–34. Syracuse, NY: Syracuse Univ. Press, 2010.

Freedgood, Elaine. *The Ideas in Things: Fugitive Meaning in the Victorian Novel.* Chicago: Chicago Univ. Press, 2006.

Gabaccia, Donna. *From the Other Side: Women, Gender and Immigrant Life.* Bloomington: Indiana Univ. Press, 1994.

Gantt, Jonathan. *Irish Terrorism in the Atlantic Community, 1865–1922.* Basingstoke: Palgrave Macmillan, 2010.

Gerrard, Greg. *Ecocriticism*. London: Routledge, 2011.

Gibbons, Luke. "'The Old Far West and the New': Bram Stoker, Race, and Manifest Destiny." In *Irish Gothics: Genres, Forms, Modes, and Traditions, 1760–1890*, edited by Christina Morin and Niall Gillespie, 188–206. Basingstoke: Palgrave Macmillan, 2014.

———. *Transformations in Irish Culture*. Cork: Cork Univ. Press, 1996.

Gifford, Terr. *Pastoral*. London: Routledge, 1999.

Gitter, Elisabeth. "The Power of Women's Hair in the Victorian Imagination." *PMLA* 99 (1984): 936–54.

Glendinning, Victoria. *Trollope*. London: Hutchinson, 1992.

Gordon, Avery. *Ghostly Matters: Haunting and the Sociological Imagination*. Minneapolis: Univ. of Minnesota Press, 2008.

Graver, Bruce. "Pastoral and Georgic." In *The Encyclopedia of Romantic Literature: H–Re*, edited by Frederick Burwick, 2:986–90. Chichester: Blackwell, 2012.

Gray, Breda. "Global Modernities and the Gendered Epic of the 'Irish Empire.'" In *Uprootings/Regroundings: Questions of Home and Migration*, edited by Sara Ahmed et al., 157–78. Oxford: Berg, 2003.

Gray, Peter. *Famine, Land and Politics: British Government and Irish Society, 1843–50*. Dublin: Irish Academic Press, 1999.

———. "Famine and Land, 1845–80." In *The Oxford Handbook of Modern Irish History*, edited by Alvin Jackson, 544–62. Oxford: Oxford Univ. Press, 2014.

———. "The Great Famine in Irish and British Historiographies, c. 1860–1914." In *Global Legacies of the Great Irish Famine: Transnational and Interdisciplinary Perspectives*, edited by Marguérite Corporaal et al., 39–61. Bern and New York: Peter Lang, 2014.

———. "Memory and the Commemoration of the Great Irish Famine." In *The Memory of Catastrophe*, edited by Peter Gray and Oliver Kendrick, 46–65. Manchester: Manchester Univ. Press, 2004.

Hachey, Thomas, and Lawrence McCaffrey. *The Irish Experience since 1800: A Concise History*. New York: M. E. Sharpe, 2010.

Hall, Stuart. "Cultural Identity and Diaspora." In *Identity: Community, Culture, Difference*, edited by Jonathan Rutherford, 222–37. London: Lawrence and Wishart, 1990.

Hartely, Cathy, and Susan Leckey, eds. *A Historical Dictionary of British Women*. London: Routledge, 2003.

Harvey, Arnold D. *Body Politic: Political Metaphor and Political Violence*. Cambridge: Cambridge Scholars, 2007.

Hirsch, Marianne. *Family Frames: Photography, Narrative and Postmemory*. Cambridge, MA: Harvard Univ. Press, 1997.

Hirsch, Marianne, and Leo Spitzer. "'We Would Not Have Come without You': Generations of Nostalgia." In *Memory, History, Nation: Contested Pasts*, edited by Katharine Hodgkin and Susannah Radstone, 79–97. New Brunswick, NJ: Transaction, 2006.

Hodgkin, Katherine, and Susannah Radstone. "Introduction: Contested Pasts." In *Memory, History, Nation: Contested Pasts*, edited by Katharine Hodgkin and Susannah Radstone, 1–23. New Brunswick, NJ: Transaction, 2006.

Hogan, Robert Goode, et al., eds. *Dictionary of Irish Literature*. Vol. 2. 2nd ed. London: Aldwych, 1996.

Holquist, Michael. *Dialogism: Bakhtin and His World*. London: Routledge, 1990.

Hooper, Glenn, ed. *The Tourist's Gaze: Travellers to Ireland, 1800–2000*. Cork: Cork Univ. Press, 2001.

Howes, Marjorie. *Colonial Crossings: Figures in Irish Literary History*. Dublin: Field Day, 2006.

———. "Discipline, Sentiment and the Irish-American Public: Mary Ann Sadlier's Popular Fiction." *Éire-Ireland* 40, nos. 1–2 (2005): 140–69.

Hunt, John Dixon. *Gardens and the Picturesque: Studies in the History of Landscape Architecture*. Boston: Massachusetts Institute of Technology, 1997.

Huyssen, Andreas. "Diaspora and Nation: Migration into Other Pasts." *New German Critique* 88 (2003): 147–64.

———. *Twilight Memories: Marking Time in a Culture of Amnesia*. London: Routledge, 1995.

Ignatiev, Noel. *How the Irish Became White*. New York: Routledge, 1996.

Jacobs, Steven. "Landscape." In *Encyclopedia of Nineteenth-Century Photography*, edited by John Hannavy. New York: Routledge, 2013.

Jacobson, Matthew. *Special Sorrows: The Diasporic Imagination of Irish, Polish, and Jewish Immigrants in the United States*. Berkeley: Univ. of California Press, 2002.

Janssen, Lindsay. "Famine Traces: Memory, Landscape, History and Identity in Irish and Irish-Diasporic Famine Fiction, 1871–1891." PhD diss., Radboud Univ. Nijmegen, 2015.

———. "The Impossibility of Transporting Identity: The Representation of Diasporic Irishness in Transatlantic Irish Fiction, 1860–1900." In *Mobile Narratives: Travel, Migration, and Transculturation*, edited by Eleftheria Arapoglou, Mónika Fodor, and Jopi Nyman, 162–73. New York: Routledge, 2014.

Jenkins, Brian. *The Fenian Problem: Insurgency and Terrorism in a Liberal State, 1858–1874*. Montreal: McGill-Queen's Univ. Univ. Press, 2008.

Jones, David S. "The Great Famine, Land and the Making of the Graziers." In *Ireland's Great Famine and Popular Politics*, edited by Enda Delaney and Breandán Mac Suibhne, 142–72. London: Routledge, 2015.

———. "The Transfer of Land and the Emergence of the Graziers during the Famine Period." In *The Great Famine and the Irish Diaspora in America*, edited by Arthur Gribben, 85–104. Amherst: Univ. of Massachusetts Press, 1999.

Kane, Brendan. *The Politics and Culture of Honour in Britain and Ireland, 1541–1641*. Cambridge: Cambridge Univ. Press, 2010.

Kelleher, Margaret. *The Feminization of Famine: Expressions of the Inexpressible*. Cork: Cork Univ. Press, 1997.

———. "Trollope's *Castle Richmond*: Famine Narrative and Horrid Novel." *Irish University Review* 25, no. 2 (1995): 242–62.

Kelleher, Patricia. "Young Irish Workers: Class Implications of Men's and Women's Experiences in Gilded Age Chicago." In *New Directions in Irish American History*, edited by Kevin Kenny, 185–209. Madison: Univ. of Wisconsin Press, 2003.

Kelly, Mary C. *Ireland's Great Famine in Irish American History*. Lanham, MD: Rowman and Littlefield, 2014.

Kelly, Niamh Ann. "Narrative Sites of Memory: Workhouses and Famine Memory." In *Memory Ireland*. Vol. 3, *The Famine and the Troubles*, edited by Oona Frawley, 152–74. Syracuse, NY: Syracuse Univ. Press, 2014.

———. "Remembering Homelessness in the Great Irish Famine." In *Ireland's Great Hunger*. Vol. 2, *Relief, Representations and Remembrance*, edited by David A. Valone, 140–60. Lanham, MD: Univ. Press of America, 2010.

Kember, Sarah. *Virtual Anxiety: Photography, New Technologies and Subjectivity*. Manchester: Manchester Univ. Press, 1998.

Kenny, Kevin. *The American Irish: A History*. London: Longman, 2000.

Kerr, Donal. *The Catholic Church and the Famine*. Blackrock, NY: Columbia Press, 1996.

Killeen, Jarlath. *The Emergence of Irish Gothic Fiction: History, Origins, Theories*. Edinburgh: Edinburgh Univ. Press, 2014.

Kinealy, Christine. *Daniel O'Connell and the Anti-slavery Movement: "The Saddest People the Sun Sees."* London and New York: Routledge, 2015.

———. *A Death-Dealing Famine: The Great Hunger in Ireland*. London: Pluto Press, 1997.

———. *This Great Calamity: The Irish Famine, 1845–52*. Dublin: Gill and Macmillan, 1994.

King, Jason. "The Genealogy of Famine Diary in Ireland and Quebec: Ireland's Famine Migration in Historical Fiction, Historiography and Memory." *Éire-Ireland* 47, nos. 1–2 (2012): 45–69.

———. Irish Famine Archive. 2015. http://www.faminearchive.nuigalway.ie.

———. "Remembering Famine Orphans: The Transmission of Famine Memory between Ireland and Quebec." In *Holodomor and Gorta Mór: Histories, Memories and Representations of Famine in Ukraine and Ireland*, edited by Christian Noack, Lindsay Janssen, and Vincent Comerford, 115–45. London: Anthem Press, 2012.

———. "The Remembrance of Irish Famine Migrants in the Fever Sheds of Montreal." In *Global Legacies of the Great Irish Famine: Transnational and Interdisciplinary Perspectives*, edited by Marguérite Corporaal et al., 245–67. Bern and New York: Peter Lang, 2014.

Kinmonth, Claudia. *Irish Rural Interiors in Art*. New Haven, CT: Yale Univ. Press, 2006.

Klein, Kerwin Lee. "On the Emergence of *Memory* in Historical Discourse." *Representations* 69 (2000): 127–50.

Kolk, Bessel A. van der, and Onno van de Hart. "The Intrusive Past: The Flexibility of Memory and the Engraving of Trauma." In *Trauma: Explorations in Memory*, edited by Cathy Caruth, 158–76. Baltimore: Johns Hopkins Univ. Press, 1995.

Koshar, Rudy. *From Monuments to Traces: Artifacts of German Memory, 1870–1990*. Berkeley: Univ. of California Press, 2000.

Kristeva, Julia. *Powers of Horror: An Essay on Abjection*. Translated by Leon S. Roudiez. New York: Columbia Univ. Press, 1982.

LaCapra, Dominick. *Writing History, Writing Trauma*. Baltimore: Johns Hopkins Univ. Press, 2001.

Landsberg, Alison. *Prosthetic Memory: The Transformation of American Remembrance in the Age of Mass Culture*. New York: Columbia Univ. Press, 2004.

Larkin, Emmett. "The Devotional Revolution in Ireland, 1850–75." *American Historical Review* 77, no. 3 (1972): 625–52.

Lee, Joseph J. "Introduction: Interpreting Irish America." In *Making the Irish American: History and Heritage of the Irish in the United States*, edited by Joseph J. Lee and Marion Casey, 1–63. New York: New York Univ. Press, 2006.

Leerssen, Joep. "Monuments and Trauma: Varieties of Remembrance." In *History and Memory in Modern Ireland*, edited by Ian MacBride, 204–23. Cambridge: Cambridge Univ. Press, 2001.

———. *National Thought in Europe: A Cultural History*. Amsterdam: Amsterdam Univ. Press, 2006.

Lennon, Joseph. "The Starvation of a Man: Terence MacSwiney and Famine Memory." In *Memory Ireland*. Vol. 3, *The Famine and the Troubles*, edited by Oona Frawley, 59–91. Syracuse, NY: Syracuse Univ. Press, 2014.

Levy, Daniel. "Changing Temporalities and the Internationalization of Memory Cultures." In *Memory and the Future: Transnational Politics, Ethics and Society*, edited by Yifat Gutman et al., 15–31. Basingstoke: Palgrave Macmillan, 2010.

Levy, Daniel, and Natan Sznaider. "Memory Unbound: The Holocaust and the Formation of Cosmopolitan Memory." *European Journal of Social Theory* 5 (2002): 87–106.

Lloyd, David. "Black Irish, Irish Whiteness and Atlantic State Formation." In *The Black and Green Atlantic: Cross-Currents in the African and Irish Diasporas*, edited by Peter O'Neill and David Lloyd, 3–20. Basingstoke: Palgrave Macmillan, 2009.

———. "The Indigent Sublime: Specters of Irish Hunger." *Representations* 92 (2005): 152–85.

———. *Irish Culture and Colonial Modernity, 1800–2000: The Transformation of Oral Space*. Cambridge: Cambridge Univ. Press, 2011.

———. *Irish Times: Temporalities of Modernity*. Dublin: Field Day, 2008.

Loeber, Rolf, and Magda Loeber, with Anne Mullin Burnham. *A Guide to Irish Fiction, 1650–1900*. Dublin: Four Courts Press, 2006.

Lutz, Deborah. "The Dead Still among Us: Victorian Secular Relics, Hair and Death Culture." *Victorian Literature and Culture* 39, no. 1 (2011): 127–42.

MacKay, Donald. *Flight from Famine: The Coming of the Irish to Canada*. Toronto: Natural Heritage Books, 1991.

MacRaild, Donald. *The Irish Diaspora in Britain, 1750–1939*. Basingstoke: Palgrave Macmillan, 2010.

Mark-FitzGerald, Emily. *Commemorating the Famine: Memory and the Monument*. Liverpool: Liverpool Univ. Press, 2013.

———. "Famine Memory and the Gathering of Stones: Genealogies of Belonging." *Atlantic Studies: Global Currents* 11, no. 3 (2014): 419–35.

———. "The 'Irish Holocaust': Historical Trauma and the Commemoration of the Famine." In *The Visual Politics of Psychoanalysis in a Post-traumatic World*, edited by Griselda Pollock, 60–78. London: I. B. Tauris, 2013.

Maume, Patrick. *The Long Gestation: Irish Nationalist Life, 1891–1918*. New York: St. Martin's Press, 1999.

McCaffrey, Lawrence J. *The Irish Catholic Diaspora in America*. Washington, DC: Catholic Univ. of America Press, 1997.

———. *Textures of Irish America*. Syracuse, NY: Syracuse Univ. Press, 1992.

McDannell, Colleen. *The Christian Home in Victorian America, 1840–1900*. New York: First Midland Book, 1994.

McGee, Owen. *The IRB: The Irish Republican Brotherhood, from the Land League to Sinn Féin*. Dublin: Four Courts Press, 2005.

McGovern, Bryan P. *John Mitchel: Irish Nationalist, Southern Secessionist*. Knoxville: Univ. of Tennessee Press, 2009.

McGowan, Mark. "Contemporary Links between Irish and Canadian Famine Commemoration." In *Global Legacies of the Great Irish Famine: Transnational and Interdisciplinary Perspectives*, edited by Marguérite Corporaal et al., 267–85. Bern and New York: Peter Lang, 2014.

———. *Death or Canada: The Irish Famine Emigration to Toronto, 1847*. Toronto: Ireland Park Foundation, 2009.

———. *The Waning of the Green: Catholics, the Irish, and Identity in Toronto, 1887–1922*. Toronto: McGill-Queen's Univ. Press, 1999.

McGrattan, Cillian. *Memory, Politics and Identity: Haunted by History*. Basingstoke: Palgrave Macmillan, 2012.

McLaughlin, Robert. *Irish Canadian Conflict and the Struggle for Irish Independence, 1912–1925*. Toronto: Univ. of Toronto Press, 2013.

McLean, Stuart. *The Event and Its Terrors: Ireland, Famine, Modernity*. Stanford, CA: Stanford Univ. Press, 2004.

Meagher, Timothy J. *The Columbia Guide to Irish American History*. New York: Columbia Univ. Press, 2005.

———. *Inventing Irish America: Generation, Class, and Ethnic Identity in a New England City, 1880–1920*. Notre Dame, IN: Univ. of Notre Dame Press, 2001.

Miles, Robert. "Abjection, Nationalism and the Gothic." In *The Gothic*, edited by Fred Botting, 47–68. Rochester, NY: Boydell and Brewer, 2001.

Miller, Daniel. *The Comfort of Things*. London: Polity Press, 2008.

Miller, David W. "Irish Catholicism and the Great Famine." *Journal of Social History* 9 (1975): 81–98.

Miller, Kerby. *Emigrants and Exiles: Ireland and the Irish Exodus to North America*. Oxford: Oxford Univ. Press, 1985.

———. *Ireland and Irish America: Culture, Class, and Transatlantic Migration*. Dublin: Field Day, 2008.

———. "'Revenge for Skibbereen': Irish Emigration and the Meaning of the Great Famine." In *The Great Famine and the Irish Diaspora in America*, edited by Arthur Gribben, 180–96. Amherst: Univ. of Massachusetts Press, 1999.

Mishra, Sudesh. *Diaspora Criticism*. Edinburgh: Edinburgh Univ. Press, 2005.

Morash, Christopher. "Famine/Holocaust: Fragmented Bodies." *Eire-Ireland* 32, no. 1 (1997): 136–50.

———. *The Hungry Voice: The Poetry of the Irish Famine*. Dublin: Irish Academic Press, 1989.

———. "Literature, Memory, Atrocity." In *Fearful Realities: New Perspectives on the Famine*, edited by Chris Morash and Richard Hayes, 110–18. Dublin: Irish Academic Press, 1996.

———. *Writing the Irish Famine*. Oxford: Clarendon Press, 1996.

Morin, Christina. "Recognisably Irish? The Diasporic Fiction of Regina Maria Roche." *Journal of Irish and Scottish Studies* 5, no. 2 (2012): 155–73.

Morin, Christina, and Niall Gillespie. Introduction to *Irish Gothics: Genres, Forms, Modes, and Traditions, 1760–1890*, edited by Christina Morin and Niall Gillespie, 1–13. Basingstoke: Palgrave, 2014.

Murphy, Angela. *American Slavery: Abolition, Immigrant Citizenship, and the Transatlantic Movement for Irish Identity*. Baton Rouge: Louisiana State Univ. Press, 2010.

Murphy, Denis. *Cromwell in Ireland: Cromwell's Irish Campaign*. Cheltenham: Orchard Press, 2010.

Murphy, James H. *Catholic Fiction and Social Reality in Ireland, 1873–1922*. Westport, CT: Greenwood Press, 1997.

———. *Irish Novelists and the Victorian Age*. Oxford: Oxford Univ. Press, 2011.

Murphy, Maureen. *Compassionate Stranger: Asenath Nicholson and the Great Irish Famine*. Syracuse, NY: Syracuse Univ. Press, 2014.

Nelson, Claudia. *Family Ties in Victorian England*. Westport, CT: Praeger, 2007.

Ní Cheallaigh, Máirín. "Women and the Survival of Archeological Monuments in Nineteenth-Century Ireland." In *Memory Ireland*. Vol. 1, *History and Modernity*, edited by Oona Frawley, 83–98. Syracuse, NY: Syracuse Univ. Press, 2011.

Nora, Pierre. "Between Memory and History: *Les lieux de mémoire*." *Representations* 26 (1989): 7–25.

Nordin, Irene Gilsenan, and Elin Holmsten. "Introduction: Borders and States of In-betweenness in Irish Literature and Culture." In *Liminal Borderlands in Irish Literature and Culture*, edited by Irene Gilsenan Nordin and Elin Holmsten, 7–13. Oxford: Peter Lang, 2009.

Oatley, Keith. "Emotion and the Story Worlds of Fiction." In *Narrative Impact: Social and Cognitive Foundations*, edited by Melanie C. Green et al., 39–71. Mahwah, NJ: Lawrence Erlbaum Associates, 2002.

Ó Ciosáin, Niall. "Was There 'Silence' about the Famine?" *Irish Studies Review* 13 (1996): 7–10.

Ofrek, Galia. *Representations of Hair in Victorian Literature and Culture*. Farnham: Ashgate, 2009.

Ó Giolláin, Diarmuid. *Locating Irish Folklore: Tradition, Modernity, Identity*. Cork: Cork Univ. Press, 2000.

Ó Gráda, Cormac. *Black '47 and Beyond: The Great Irish Famine in History, Economy and Memory*. Princeton, NJ: Princeton Univ. Press, 1999.

———. "Famine, Trauma, and Memory." *Bealoideas* 69 (2001): 121–43.

———. *Ireland before and after the Famine: Explorations in Economic History*. Manchester: Manchester Univ. Press, 1993.

Ó Gráda, Cormac, Richard Paping, and Eric Vanhaute, eds. *When the Potato Failed: Causes and Effects*. Turnhout: Brepols, 2007.

Ó Murchadha, Ciarán. *The Great Famine: Ireland's Agony, 1845–1852*. London: Continuum, 2011.

O'Neill, Peter, and David Lloyd. Introduction to *The Black and Green Atlantic: Cross-Currents in the African and Irish Diasporas*, edited by Peter O'Neill and David Lloyd, xv–xx. Basingstoke: Palgrave Macmillan, 2009.

O'Sullivan, Niamh. *The Tombs of a Departed Race: Illustrations of Ireland's Great Hunger*. Hamden, CT: Quinnipiac Univ. Press, 2014.

O'Toole, Tina. *Dictionary of Munster Women Writers*. Cork: Cork Univ. Press, 2005.

Owens, Margaret E. *Stages of Dismemberment: The Fragmented Body in Late Medieval and Early Modern Drama*. Cranbury, NJ: Associated Univ. Presses, 2005.

Panchyk, Richard. *The Keys to American History: Understanding Our Most Important Historic Documents*. Chicago: Chicago Review Press, 2009.

Parsons, Coílín. "The Archive in Ruins: James Clarence Mangan and Colonial Cartography." *Interventions* 13 (2011): 464–82.

Peeren, Esther. "Through the Lens of the Chronotope: Suggestions for a Spatio-temporal Perspective on Diaspora." In *Diaspora and Memory*, edited by Marie-Aude Baronian, Stephan Besser, and Yolanda Jansen, 67–77. New York and Amsterdam: Rodopi, 2006.

Pellicer, Juan Christian. "Pastoral and Georgic." In *The Oxford History of Classical Reception in English Literature*, edited by David Hopkins and Charles Martindale, 3:287–323. Oxford: Oxford Univ. Press, 2012.

Pelling, Nick. *Anglo-Irish Relations, 1789–1922*. London: Routledge, 2003.

Petrucelli, Jean. *Longing: Psychoanalytical Musings on Desire*. London: Karnac, 2006.

Phillips, Kendall R., and G. Mitchell Reyes. "Introduction: Surveying Global Memoryscapes." In *Global Memoryscapes: Contesting Remembrance in a Transnational Age*, edited by Kendall R. Phillips and G. Mitchell Reyes, 1–27. Tuscaloosa: Univ. of Alabama Press, 2011.

Pine, Emilie. *The Politics of Irish Memory: Performing Remembrance in Contemporary Irish Culture*. Basingstoke: Palgrave Macmillan, 2010.

Platonov, Rachel. "Remapping Arcadia: 'Pastoral Space' in Nineteenth-Century Russian Prose." *Modern Language Review* 102 (2007): 1105–21.

Pointon, Marcia. "Wearing Memory: Mourning, Jewellery and the Body." In *Trauer Trager—Trauer Zeigen: Inszenierungen der Geschlechter*, edited by Gisela Ecker, 65–83. Munich: Fink, 1999.

Poole, Ross. "Memory, History and the Claims of the Past." *Memory Studies* 1 (2008): 149–66.

Potteiger, Matthew, and Jamie Purinton. *Landscape Narratives: Design Practices for Telling Stories*. New York: John Wiley and Sons, 1998.

Potts, Donna. *Contemporary Irish Poetry and the Pastoral Tradition*. Columbia: Univ. of Missouri Press, 2012.

Pryse, Marjorie, and Judith Fetterley. *Writing Out of Place: Regionalism, Women and American Literary Culture*. Urbana: Univ. of Illinois Press, 2003.

Punter, David. *The Literature of Terror*. Vol. 1, *The Gothic Tradition*. London: Routledge, 2013.

Punter, David, and Glennis Byron. *The Gothic*. Malden, MA: Blackwell, 2004.

Quigley, Michael. "Grosse Île: Canada's Famine Memorial." In *The Great Famine and the Irish Diaspora in America*, edited by Arthur Gribben, 133–55. Amherst: Univ. of Massachusetts Press, 1999.

Radstone, Susannah. *The Sexual Politics of Time: Confession, Nostalgia, Memory*. London: Routledge, 2007.

Reilly, Ciarán. *The Irish Land Agent, 1830–60: The Case of King's County*. Dublin: Four Courts Press, 2014.

———. *Strokestown and the Great Irish Famine*. Dublin: Four Courts Press, 2014.

Ricoeur, Paul. "Narrative Time." *Critical Inquiry* 7, no. 1 (1980): 169–90.

Rigney, Ann. "All This Happened, More or Less: What a Novelist Made of the Bombing of Dresden." *History and Theory* 47 (2009): 5–24.

———. "Divided Pasts: A Premature Memorial and the Dynamics of Collective Remembrance." *Memory Studies* 1, no. 1 (2008): 89–98.

———. "Portable Monuments: Literature, Cultural Memory, and the Case of Jeanie Deans." *Poetics Today* 25, no. 2 (2004): 361–96.

Robertson, Iain, and Tim Hall. "Memory, Identity and the Memorialization of Conflict in the Scottish Highlands." In *Heritage, Memory and the Politics of Identity: New Perspectives on the Cultural Landscape*, edited by Niamh Moore and Yvonne Whelan, 19–37. Aldershot: Ashgate, 2007.

Roediger, David. *The Wages of Whiteness: Race and the Making of the American Working Class*. Rev. ed. London and New York: Verso Books, 1999.

Rothberg, Michael. *Multidirectional Memory: Remembering the Holocaust in the Age of Decolonization*. Stanford, CA: Stanford Univ. Press, 2009.

Royle, Nicholas. *The Uncanny: An Introduction*. Manchester: Manchester Univ. Press, 2003.

Ryan, Terre. *The Ecstatic Nation: The American Landscape and the Aesthetics of Patriotism*. Amherst: Univ. of Massachusetts Press, 2011.

Sarbaugh, Timothy. "The Spirit of Manifest Destiny: The American Government and Famine Ireland, 1845–1849." In *Fleeing the Famine: North-America and Irish Refugees, 1845–1851*, edited by Margaret M. Mulrooney, 45–59. Westport, CT: Praeger, 2003.

Scanlan, Thomas J. *Colonial Writing and the New World, 1583–1671: Allegories of Desire*. Cambridge: Cambridge Univ. Press, 1999.

See, Scott W. "'An Unprecedented Influx': Nativism and Irish Famine Immigration to Canada." *American Review of Canadian Studies* 30 (2000): 429–53.

Shanahan, Jim. "Suffering Rebellion: Irish Gothic Fiction, 1799–1830." In *Irish Gothics: Genres, Forms, Modes, and Traditions, 1760–1890*, edited by Christina Morin and Niall Gillespie, 74–92. Basingstoke: Palgrave Macmillan, 2014.

Shaw, Philip. *The Sublime*. London: Routledge, 2006.

Sikes, Wilbert. "In the Five Points." *Harper's New Monthly* 26 (1868): 223–26.

Sim, David. "Filibusters, Fenians, and a Contested Neutrality: The Irish Question and U.S. Diplomacy, 1848–1871." *American Nineteenth-Century History* 12, no. 3 (2011): 265–87.

———. *A Union Forever: The Irish Question and U.S. Foreign Relations in the Victorian Age*. Ithaca, NY: Cornell Univ. Press, 2013.

Smelser, Neill. "Psychological Trauma and Cultural Trauma." In *Cultural Trauma and Collective Identity*, edited by Jeffrey C. Alexander et al., 31–60. Berkeley: Univ. of California Press, 2004.

Snay, Mitchel. *Fenians, Freedmen and Southern Whites: Race and Nationality in the Era of Reconstruction*. Baton Rouge: Louisiana State Univ. Press, 2007.

Spivak, Gayatri Chakravorty. "Can the Subaltern Speak?" In *Can the Subaltern Speak? Reflections on the History of an Idea*, edited by Rosalind C. Morris, 21–78. New York: Columbia Univ. Press, 2010.

Spray, William A. "Irish Famine Emigrants and the Passage Trade to North America." In *Fleeing the Famine: North-America and Irish Refugees, 1845–1851*, edited by Margaret M. Mulrooney, 3–21. Westport, CT: Praeger, 2003.

Stern, Andrew Henry. *Southern Crucifix, Southern Cross: Catholic-Protestant Relations in the Old South*. Tuscaloosa: Univ. of Alabama Press, 2012.

Steward, Patrick, and Bryan McGovern. *The Fenians: Irish Rebellion in the North Atlantic World, 1858–1876*. Knoxville: Univ. of Tennessee Press, 2013.

Sutherland, John. *The Stanford Companion to Victorian Fiction*. Stanford, CA: Stanford Univ. Press, 1989.

Swift, Roger. *Irish Migrants in Britain, 1815–1914: A Documentary History*. Cork: Cork Univ. Press, 2002.

Synnott, Anthony. "Shame and Glory: A Sociology of Hair." *British Journal of Sociology* 38, no. 3 (1987): 381–413.

Thomassen, Bjorn. *Liminality and the Modern: Living through the In-between*. Farnham: Ashgate, 2014.

Travis, Roger. *Allegory and the Tragic Chorus in Sophocles' "Oedipus at Colonus."* New York: Rowman and Littlefield, 1999.

Trigg, Dylan. *The Aesthetics of Decay: Nothingness, Nostalgia and the Absence of Reason*. New York: Peter Lang, 2009.

———. *The Memory of Place: A Phenomenology of the Uncanny*. Athens: Ohio Univ. Press, 2012.

———. "The Place of Trauma: Memory, Hauntings, and the Temporality of Ruins." *Memory Studies* 2 (2009): 87–101.

Turner, Mark W. "Trollope's Literary Life and Times." In *The Cambridge Companion to Anthony Trollope*, edited by Carolyn Dever and Lisa Niles, 6–17. Cambridge: Cambridge Univ. Press, 2011.

Turner, Michael. *After the Famine: Irish Agriculture, 1850–1914*. Cambridge: Cambridge Univ. Press, 1996.

Valente, Joseph. "Ethnostalgia: Irish Hunger and Traumatic Memory." In *Memory Ireland*. Vol. 3, *The Famine and the Troubles*, edited by Oona Frawley, 174–95. Syracuse, NY: Syracuse Univ. Press, 2014.

Vertovec, Steven, and Robin Cohen. Introduction to *Migration, Diasporas and Transnationalism*, edited by Steven Vertovec and Robin Cohen, xiii–xxviii. Cheltenham: Edgar Elgar, 1999.

Viljoen, Hein, and C. N. van der Merwe. "Introduction: A Poetics of Liminality and Hybridity." In *Beyond the Threshold: Explorations of Liminality in Literature*, edited by Hein Viljoen and C. N. van der Merwe, 1–29. Oxford: Peter Lang, 2007.

Wakin, Edward. *Enter the Irish American*. Lincoln, NE: IUniverse, 2002.

Welch, Robert, and Bruce Stewart, eds. *The Oxford Companion to Irish Literature*. Oxford: Oxford Univ. Press, 1996.

Wertsch, James V. *Voices of Collective Remembering*. New York: Cambridge Univ. Press, 2002.

Wheeler, James Scott. *Cromwell in Ireland.* Basingstoke: Gill and Macmillan, 1999.

Whelan, Kevin. "The Cultural Effects of the Famine." In *The Cambridge Companion to Modern Irish Culture*, edited by Joe Cleary and Claire Connolly, 137–54. Cambridge: Cambridge Univ. Press, 2005.

———. "Reading the Ruins: The Presence of Absence in the Irish Landscape." In *Surveying Ireland's Past: Multidisciplinary Essays in Honour of Anngret Simms*, edited by Howard B. Clarke et al., 297–329. Dublin: Geography Publications, 2004.

———. "The Region and the Intellectuals." In *On Intellectuals and Intellectual Life in Ireland: International, Comparative and Historical Contexts*, edited by Liam O'Dowd, 116–31. Belfast: Institute of Irish Studies, 1996.

Williams, Raymond. *The Country and the City.* New York: Oxford Univ. Press, 1975.

Williams, William. *Creating Irish Tourism: The First Century, 1750–1850.* London: Anthem Press, 2010.

———. *Tourism, Landscape and the Irish Character: British Travel Writers in Pre-Famine Ireland.* Madison: Univ. of Wisconsin Press, 2008.

Wilson, David A. *Thomas D'Arcy McGee: The Extreme Moderate, 1857–1868.* Toronto: McGill-Queen's Univ. Press, 2011.

Wolfreys, Julian. *Victorian Hauntings: Spectrality, Gothic, the Uncanny and Literature.* Basingstoke: Palgrave, 2002.

Wright, Julia M. *Ireland, India and Nationalism in Nineteenth-Century Literature.* Cambridge: Cambridge Univ. Press, 2007.

———. *Representing the National Landscape in Irish Romanticism.* Syracuse, NY: Syracuse Univ. Press, 2014.

Wylie, John. *Landscape.* London: Routledge, 2007.

Zerubavel, Eviatar. *Time Maps: Collective Memory and the Social Shape of the Past.* Chicago: Univ. of Chicago Press, 2003.

Index

Marguérite Corporaal is associate professor of English literature at Radboud University Nijmegen, the Netherlands. She was the principal investigator and coordinator of the research project Relocated Remembrance: The Great Famine in Irish (Diaspora) Fiction, 1847–1921, for which she obtained a Starting Grant from the European Research Council (2010–15). Furthermore, she is the director of the International Network of Irish Famine Studies that is funded by the Dutch research council NWO (2014–17). Among her recent and forthcoming international publications are *Recollecting Hunger: An Anthology; Cultural Memories of the Great Famine in Irish Fiction, 1847–1920* (coauthored, 2012), *Global Legacies of the Great Irish Famine: Transnational and Interdisciplinary Perspectives* (coedited, 2014), *Irish Studies and the Dynamics of Memory* (coedited, 2016), and *Travelling Irishness in the Long Nineteenth Century* (coedited, forthcoming).